Globalization and American Popular Culture

GLOBALIZATION

Series Editors
Manfred B. Steger
*Illinois State University, University of Hawai'i—Manoa,
and Royal Melbourne Institute of Technology*
and
Terrell Carver
University of Bristol

"Globalization" has become *the* buzzword of our time. But what does it mean? Rather than forcing a complicated social phenomenon into a single analytical framework, this series seeks to present globalization as a multidimensional process constituted by complex, often contradictory interactions of global, regional, and local aspects of social life. Since conventional disciplinary borders and lines of demarcation are losing their old rationales in a globalizing world, authors in this series apply an interdisciplinary framework to the study of globalization. In short, the main purpose and objective of this series is to support subject-specific inquiries into the dynamics and effects of contemporary globalization and its varying impacts across, between, and within societies.

Globalization and Culture
Jan Nederveen Pieterse
Rethinking Globalism
Edited by
Manfred B. Steger
Globalization and Terrorism
Jamal R. Nassar
Globalism, Second Edition
Manfred B. Steger
Globaloney
Michael Veseth
Globalization and Law
Adam Gearey
Globalization and War
Tarak Barkawi
Globalization and International Political Economy
Mark Rupert and M. Scott Solomon
Globalization and Feminist Activism
Mary E. Hawkesworth
Globalization and American Popular Culture
Lane Crothers

Forthcoming in the Series
Globalization and Militarization
Cynthia Enloe
Globalization and American Empire
Kiichi Fujiwara
Globalization and Labor
Dimitris Stevis and Terry Boswell

 Supported by the Globalization Research Center at the University of Hawai'i, Manoa

GLOBALIZATION AND AMERICAN POPULAR CULTURE

LANE CROTHERS

ROWMAN & LITTLEFIELD PUBLISHERS, INC.
Lanham • Boulder • New York • Toronto • Plymouth, UK

ROWMAN & LITTLEFIELD PUBLISHERS, INC.

Published in the United States of America
by Rowman & Littlefield Publishers, Inc.
A wholly owned subsidiary of The Rowman & Littlefield Publishing Group, Inc.
4501 Forbes Boulevard, Suite 200, Lanham, Maryland 20706
www.rowmanlittlefield.com

Estover Road
Plymouth PL6 7PY
United Kingdom

British Library Cataloguing in Publication Information Available

Library of Congress Cataloging-in-Publication Data

Crothers, Lane.
  Globalization and American popular culture / Lane Crothers.
     p.   cm.—(Globalization)
  Includes bibliographical references and index.
  ISBN-13: 978-0-7425-4138-2 (cloth : alk. paper)
  ISBN-10: 0-7425-4138-X (cloth : alk. paper)
  ISBN-13: 978-0-7425-4139-9 (pbk. : alk. paper)
  ISBN-10: 0-7425-4139-8 (pbk. : alk. paper)
     1. Popular culture—United States.   2. Mass media—Social aspects—
  United States.   3. Globalization—Social aspects—United States.
  4. Civilization, Modern—American influences.   5. United States—
  Foreign economic relations.   6. United States—Foreign public opinion.
  I. Title.   II. Series: Globalization (Lanham, Md.)
  E169.12.C74   2006
  306.0973—dc22

                                                        2006008530

Printed in the United States of America

♾ ™ The paper used in this publication meets the minimum requirements of
American National Standard for Information Sciences—Permanence of Paper
for Printed Library Materials, ANSI/NISO Z39.48-1992.

For Richard Pride
Mentor and teacher, with thanks

CONTENTS

TABLES

ACKNOWLEDGMENTS

No book is ever the product of one person's efforts. It is important to acknowledge the many people who have helped in the creation of this work.

I owe thanks to four different editors who have reviewed, commented on, and otherwise nurtured this book from its earliest imagining: Susan McEachern at Rowman & Littlefield; series editors Manfred Steger and Terrell Carver; and Jennifer Knerr, who originally accepted the book for Rowman & Littlefield. The book is stronger for their work. Manfred Steger is owed particular thanks for the many conversations, discussions, and words of encouragement he shared with me regarding this project and many others. His early insights into the project profoundly shaped its outcome, and he deserves special credit for this.

I also owe thanks to Steve Bragg at Illinois State University, who read an early draft of an early chapter and challenged, argued about, and identified every incomplete thought, weak argument, and evidentiary gap in my thinking. I hope I have answered his concerns.

Tammy Johnson provided invaluable research support for this project, and her ideas and experiences are reflected at several points throughout the book. I also appreciate the opportunity Illinois State University gave me to work on a project that, on its face, seems to fall outside the mainstream of political science academic research—although, as I found, popular culture is a central issue in debates about contemporary globalization. It is, in fact, at the heart of the mainstream.

The plain fact of the matter is that the life of an academic is a privileged one. We are given the freedom to think about things we like to think about, to talk about things we like to talk about, and to write about things we like to write about. This is a rare gift in the modern world, and I appreciate the many teachers, family members, and friends who have supported me over the years as I have worked to fully inhabit life as an academic. It is a rare thing to know one is doing what one is meant to do; I have the privilege of living that knowledge every day.

Thanks to you all. This book would not have been possible without you. Any errors and weaknesses are mine alone.

AMERICAN POPULAR CULTURE AND GLOBALIZATION

At first glance, the idea of writing—or for that matter reading—a book on the relationship between the profound economic, social, political, and cultural changes going on in the modern world that are collectively labeled "globalization" and the movies, music, and television programs (among other features) that compose American popular culture may seem a bit odd. Globalization, after all, seems "heavy": it is the result of numerous powerful forces and is, at least in part, remaking the way the world works. Popular culture, by contrast, seems "light": whether in theme or in impact, it is intuitively hard to see how even a movie megahit like *Titanic* can play a meaningful role in such a profound thing as globalization.

Popular culture has played, and continues to play, an important role in world affairs, however. It was, for example, a central issue in the nearly fifty-year political and military standoff between the United States and the Soviet Union known as the Cold War, 1945–1991. During the Cold War, the United States and the Soviet Union established vast international coalitions that promoted their interests and tried to check the actions of the other. The U.S.-led coalition was centered in the Americas, Western Europe (which came into being only as a result of post–World War II policies), and the Pacific area of Australasia. The Soviet coalition consisted of the Eurasian landmass on which the Soviet Union was located, Eastern Europe, and, at times, China. (China was allied with the Soviet Union after its Communist revolution in 1949; however, it subsequently developed an independent agenda as a Communist nation outside the control of the Soviet Union.) These coalitions promoted dramatically different social, political, and economic philosophies: capitalism and liberal representative democracy in the Western U.S.-led coalition, and communism and state control in the Soviet Eastern bloc. These coalitions occasionally engaged in armed struggle, usually at a distance by allowing third parties with support from one major alliance or the other to clash (as happened in the wars in Korea, 1950–1952; Vietnam, 1964–1975; and Afghanistan, 1979–1989, for example). However, as each side built over twenty thousand nuclear weapons of all shapes, sizes, and levels of destructiveness, more often their fights were at the level of propaganda, as each side insisted its way of life was superior.

Global relationships of trade, immigration, ideas, security, and even entertainment were profoundly shaped by the Cold War. The Western bloc advocated relative freedom in personal choice, economic trade, and immigration, while the Eastern bloc practiced state control, the limitation of personal freedom, and government ownership of factories and other productive enterprises. Each side claimed that its own was the best way to build good lives for its people: The West insisted that personal liberty promoted maximum happiness and growth, thereby benefiting a majority of its people, even though some people might suffer from poverty and lack of opportunities; the East insisted that government control would allow the products of society to be distributed among all people equally, thereby limiting the maximum gain any individual might enjoy in order to ensure that everyone had the basics of life. Notably, the dividing line between these great alliances substantially limited their citizens' options: people living in one camp rarely experienced the ideas, products, entertainment, and values of the other.

At least part of this struggle was linked to popular culture. Soviet leaders and their ideological allies regularly referred to the West as culturally corrupt. By this they meant that Western—often American—movies, music, television, and other cultural artifacts were insubstantial and meaningless or, worst of all, promoted poor moral values. (Why this might be so is addressed in detail in chapter 2.) While Westerners insisted that popular entertainment and performers like the singer-superstar Elvis Presley or television shows like *Leave It to Beaver* provided individuals with opportunities to create, invent, and provide joy and pleasure to others, Soviet leaders argued that the moral values expressed in these acts and programs tended to erode public morals and social order. The Soviets, accordingly, worked hard to keep Western-style music, movies, and television programs away from their people.

Yet in working to exclude Western entertainment from their societies, the leaders of the Soviet-Communist bloc (including the People's Republic of China) managed to stimulate interest among their citizens in American popular music, movies, and television. By making the fruit forbidden, the leadership made it attractive. A vigorous black market developed across the Soviet Union and among its allies as people smuggled or otherwise brought Western popular culture (along with books, magazines, food, clothes, and other products) into their lives. Western popular culture was thus present in the Soviet Union (and China) well before the Soviet Union finally collapsed in 1991.

In addition, Western leaders exploited the lure of their popular culture during the Cold War. They created radio and television stations such as Radio Free Europe/Radio Liberty to broadcast as much popular culture material into the Soviet bloc as could be programmed. This programming was done to achieve the very purpose the Soviets accused it of having in the West: to corrupt the values of those who watched or listened to it. Thus while they denied such programming was corruptive in the West, Western leaders relied on the apparently corrupting power of American popular culture to help win the hearts and minds of people inside the Communist bloc.

It would be too much to argue that the Soviet Union fell apart because of the corrupting appeal of American popular culture. The forces that led to the dissolution of the Soviet Union were complex and diverse. It is, however, fair to say that in denying their citizens access to the Western movies, music, and television programs they desired, the governments of the Soviet bloc undermined their own legitimacy. Put another way, a government afraid of popular American television programs like *Ozzie and Harriet* or *The A-Team* seems to be a remarkably weak government that, in time, is likely to fail for a variety of reasons.

American popular culture's role in international affairs has become even more important in the years following the Soviet Union's collapse. New patterns of trade, security, information, investment, ideas, and even of the exchange of entertainment have emerged. These changes have been collectively labeled "globalization" and appeared, at least to many early students of the topic, to be likely to create what President George H. W. Bush called a "new world order" grounded on universal principles of democracy and free trade. Thus, in the absence of a great power to enforce restrictive rules (e.g., as in the Soviet Union), President Bush and others argued that free trade would force every country and region to become a component of a world economy, rather than an economy in itself. If, for example, a region had a comparative advantage in growing rice but lacked the educational system to have a large high-tech industry, it would export rice and import computers from a region that had lots of software engineers but, perhaps, had limited land for rice growing. No country would produce everything it needed within its borders (or the borders of its coalition), at least not efficiently, and so a truly global economy could emerge. Popular cultural entertainment has become an important part of this global economy, and in fact popular culture is the United States' leading export today.[1]

The trade in popular culture, however, has become a source of tension in the post-Soviet era—one that might have been anticipated by the fact that American movies, music, and television programs are perceived to have had a role in undermining the Soviet state. The basis for the contemporary controversy about popular culture is quite simple. As a practical matter, few people care where their rice is grown or where their computer is built. The exchange of rice for computers is generally understood to take place with little moral impact on either society. There may be long-term economic consequences that derive from the imbalance of trade that exists when one society is rich and developed and capable of building computers and another is poor and underdeveloped, of course, and moreover these imbalances may be the result of historical forces like colonialism, racism, repression, and violence that were and remain immoral, but the specific exchange of some rice for a computer is rarely invested with ethical significance.

By contrast, the exchange of cultural goods is almost always laden with moral meaning. People care where their cultural artifacts come from, what values they express, and how they shape the lives of the people who use them. This is true even if the cultural products are as apparently insubstantial as those labeled popular culture, such as movies, music, and television programs. Moreover, as is shown in chapter 3, American movies, music, and television programs reflect American culture and values. This, in turn, brings the ideas, values, norms, and social practices embedded in American popular culture into contact—and often tension—with those of other cultures around the world.

Another source of tension associated with the trade in cultural materials—the fact that change is rarely easy—is addressed in more detail later in this chapter. People become accustomed to certain patterns of life, ideas, and values as normal—as their culture. This is true whether the people live in the United States, North Korea, or Bangladesh. When their norms are challenged, people rarely adopt the "new" point of view easily or quickly (if at all). Instead, as is also discussed later in this chapter, they tend to resist, reject, or dismiss the different ideas as wrong, or immoral, or false. (Consider the ease with which Americans dismiss unpopular ideas as "un-

American" to be a useful example of this general tendency.) If American popular culture actually played a role in the downfall of the Soviet Union, or is believed by some groups or individuals to have been a factor in the Soviet Union's collapse, then it is logical to assume that other governments, cultures, and peoples might be afraid that American popular culture will damage, challenge, or transform their societies. Under such circumstances, American popular culture might be more a source of fear and loathing than entertainment and fun.

Put another way, most people around the world will never visit the United States or meet an American in person. They will never have a Peace Corps volunteer work in their town, village, or city. They may work in factories that produce goods intended for the American market, but their managers will probably be locals, and the rules that govern the factory will be those imposed by the native government, not the United States. And despite the United States' increased global military presence after the terrorist attacks of September 11, 2001, most people live in countries and communities that will never be attacked, much less occupied, by U.S. forces. Accordingly, what people are likely to see of America and what they are likely to know about America will be filtered through the lens of American popular culture. This reality has only expanded in the aftermath of the Cold War as nation after nation and community after community, many of them in areas formerly closed to Western ideas and American entertainment, sprout satellite dishes, video stores, and iPods all linked through the Internet. Accordingly, sociologist Todd Gitlin notes that American popular culture is "the latest in a long succession of bidders for global unification. It succeeds the Latin imposed by the Roman Empire and the Catholic Church, and Marxist Leninism."[2] It is, as a consequence, central to understanding the way contemporary globalization will unfold, both now and in the future.

Understanding Culture, Popular Culture, and American Culture

Since this book focuses on the ways American popular culture influences contemporary globalization, it is necessary to explore what culture is and how it can influence a process as complex as globalization. The question of what culture is and why it matters in social and political life is an old one and is complicated by a literature rife with competing definitions, examples, critiques, and reassertions of culture's significance in human life. It is further complicated by the use of the term in dramatically different ways: as an explanation of a "way of life" for some group or community (the anthropological approach) *and* as a tool for the normative evaluation

5

of particular behaviors or entertainment ("popular" versus "high" culture). Since both types of meanings are used throughout this book in different contexts, a brief discussion of the complexity of "culture" is appropriate before we link culture to globalization.

Anthropological Culture

Core to the notion of culture is the assertion that most human behavior is the result of socialization. For example, while most human babies are born with the innate capacity for language (barring physical disabilities), they do not speak a particular language at birth. Instead, they have to learn one. Sounds themselves are irrelevant; what matters is how combinations of sounds have meaning to the people who share the same linguistic repertoire. This process then continues for other aspects of human life: children, almost always at very young ages, are socialized into the patterns of culture unique to their communities, learning the tools they need for survival and growth from the environments in which they are raised.

Among the many things that cultures teach their members are normative standards of evaluation—of dress, food, behavior, attitudes, ideas, and many other things. One learns that some things/ideas/attitudes/behaviors are appropriate, while others are not. This learning is reinforced by institutions such as laws, courts, police, parents, schools, and religions—any component of the cultural socialization process. Thus culture shapes the attitudes, behaviors, and values of both children and adults, particularly newcomers to a given community (although children, since they have not already learned a set of cultural rules they have to unlearn or alter, tend to be more tractable). Notably, these forces usually work unnoticed: just as children in the cradle never realize they are being taught language as their parents play with them, the agents of cultural socialization embed these attitudes of right and wrong, normal and abnormal, moral and immoral in each generation through an array of means, like pejorative comments or facial expressions, that do not appear as obvious acts of education. Cultural socialization is thus deep. One simply doesn't think about what's right and wrong, for example, because it is obvious and always has been.

The deep-seated nature and generational reproduction of culture give it an additional dimension: cultures are generally resistant to change. Group attitudes about right and wrong, moral and immoral, language and gibberish, or any other feature of socialized experience do not easily change. Indeed, if they did, cultures could not exist across generations. Thus cultures also contain mechanisms for self-defense. These include the shaming of those who transgress the culture's standards, rules governing what should or should not be done in the first place, and the punishment of those who violate the culture's rules. As a consequence of its role in shaping the root values of human societies, culture fights back against those ideas and behaviors that challenge the culture's stability and permanence.

That said, it must be admitted that it is possible to go too far when arguing about the power of culture to shape beliefs, attitudes, and behaviors. After all, even a cursory scan of the ideas, attitudes, behaviors, and values of one's own family and friends, much less the members of the larger community in which one lives, suggests that absolute cultural unanimity does not exist. Most people would likely agree that members of the same family are likely to share a culture, but members of the same family often have dramatically different ideas and values. This fact leads to the obvious question: if culture has such a central role in shaping peoples' core attitudes and beliefs, indeed a role so powerful that it makes many persons reflexively resistant to change, how can there be so much variability in the values of people in the same family and community, much less a state or nation?

Notably, although parents and schools and religious institutions may teach, it does not follow that these messages are learned identically by everyone subject to them. People have different arrays of friends, of social circumstances, and of hopes and dreams, and each of these forces shapes the impact of the agents of socialization in ways unique to each individual. Likewise, parents do not treat every child the same; teachers deal with each generation of students differently; laws change; religions adapt. Accordingly, socialization is at best only partially effective. To say people in a group share a culture, then, is not to say that everyone believes the same thing. Instead, it is to say that people in a given community generally share similar language, values, attitudes, beliefs, and the like. Further, it is to say that people in one community are sufficiently different from people in another community that they can be recognized as sharing a culture, however partial the sharing might be.

As a consequence, then, it is simply not appropriate to assume that there is some fixed, absolute "culture" that determines the behavior/ attitude/style of everyone who lives inside a given community. Instead, culture refers to the root values, ideas, assumptions, behaviors, and attitudes that members of particular communities generally share in an unexamined, automatic way. Variability persists, however. Culture thus influences social and political life without determining it. Culture provides the context in which economic, social, and political life "make sense" to its members. Those ideas and actions that are recognized as culturally appropriate will be supported (for the most part) by members of a given community sharing a culture, even if they do not agree with the specific act. (Smoking a cigarette is considered a personal choice in the United States, for example, and so while most Americans do not smoke, they do not wish to ban smoking either.) By contrast, ideas and behaviors that transgress cultural norms are likely to face sanction and rejection—as happens, for example, when most Americans oppose "communism" without having ever read Karl Marx's *Communist Manifesto* or met an actual Communist. Communism is simply "un-American"; ordinary Americans need no more information than that to make up their minds and act accordingly.

Popular Culture

Even as the term "culture" has this socially defining anthropological sense, it also has an evaluative normative meaning. Put simply, the concept has been used to separate those people who have "taste" and pursue what Matthew Arnold called "the best that was thought and said"[3] from what a character in Shakespeare's *Henry V* referred to as the "base, common, and popular." Indeed, Shakespeare's character, an ordinary soldier named Pistol, actually asks, in challenging someone approaching the position he is guarding, "Discuss with me: art thou officer, Or art thou base, common, and popular?" thus implying a difference in the moral status of people, not just their tastes and pursuits. To be interested in things popular was to be base and common; to pursue "the best of what was thought and said" was to have "culture."

Much of the distinction between "high" and "popular" culture was developed during the Enlightenment. Intellectuals of the time began to pursue universal standards on which to base principles for human life. These principles were to be the product of human thought and exploration rather than a derivation from mystical superhuman sources. Then, since only the educated and the elite were trained to understand the components of "real" beauty, those things that were objectively and universally beautiful (at least according to those who interpreted them) became associated with "high" culture.[4] Everything else became "base, common, and popular."

The social split between high and popular culture intensified and expanded with the onset of the Industrial Revolution in the late 1700s and beyond. As Todd Gitlin has argued, contemporary industrial-era popular culture is a product, usually of large, often multinational corporations providing goods and services for profit. These corporations leverage their marketing and productive capacities to create as large and pervasive a consumer base for their products as possible. They use this power to establish patterns of planned obsolescence, ever-changing styles, and a treadmill of celebrity introductions and exits to promote endless turnover in products that are then marketed and consumed by the population at large. Importantly, this production is essentially secular in nature, meaning that nothing is sacred or holy—everything is available for marketing and consumption.[5] There is, as a consequence, nothing aesthetic or "high" in the pop culture products of the industrial revolution.

The soullessness and mass-produced quality of industrial popular culture led the same theorists who argued that high culture was "good" because it was "aesthetic" to insist that popular culture had no innate value beyond the pleasure it brought to those who consumed it. It was ephemeral, no more meaningful than, as one critic put it, "chewing gum."[6] By extension, there was no value in studying or examining the products, patterns, and norms embedded in the products of popular culture. The "real" values of society were contained in its high culture, not its common one.

The notion that popular culture was without substance, and so was not worthy of careful study or consideration, began to erode in the mid-twentieth century before being rejected outright from the 1960s forward. Drawing on the insights of scholars like Herbert Gans, Mary Douglas, and Baron Isherwood, those interested in popular culture were able to define the cultural meaning of popular mass-produced and mass-consumed items in new and valuable ways. Gans, for example, argued that an item did not lose its value simply because it was mass produced; instead, the people who used it derived meaning and value from it. Douglas and Isherwood added to this insight by noting that communities of individuals—cultures—tend to share common conceptions of what ought to be purchased, used, and consumed.[7] One need only think of the relationship between minivans and soccer moms to see this point: the fact that many people desire minivans because of their associations with children, safety, and utility helps define a particular culture of consumers. Likewise, the revulsion many others feel toward minivans for precisely the same associations helps define another community's culture. Mass production does not eliminate meaning. It simply provides a means by which different groups of people make choices that are meaningful in establishing, reinforcing, and representing particular cultural boundaries.[8] Popular culture thus provides a way for researchers to learn about the values, needs, concerns, and standards by which different communities of people live.

Accordingly, anything used, consumed, or produced by a specific group can be an object of study for a researcher interested in the culture of that society. This study draws on the early distinction between high and popular culture in refining its scope: since the early advocates of high culture used what they saw as a distinction between aesthetic and mass entertain-

9

ment to justify their ideas, this book primarily uses the American mass entertainment media of movies, television, and music to assess the impact American popular culture plays in globalization. As was noted earlier in this chapter, and is discussed in detail in chapter 2, entertainment is a particularly useful tool for examining this question since it is through American popular culture that much of the globe experiences contemporary American culture. These audiovisual media provide the means by which images of the "American" way of life, whether political, social, or economic, are transmitted around the world. It is through these media that the rest of the world sees American values and lifestyle. Moreover, it is in response to images presented through these institutions that much of the dynamic of American popular culture and globalization is expressed.

While the majority of the analysis of the role American popular culture plays in contemporary globalization presented in this book will focus on American movies, music, and television programs, it is important to note that these products are not the sum total of American popular culture—even American popular culture as depicted in American movies, music, and television programs. The fast-food restaurant chain McDonald's, for example, is an American icon that now has franchises in more than one hundred countries; political commentator Thomas Friedman has noted that no two countries that have McDonald's franchises have ever gone to war.[9] Similarly, American soft drink companies like Pepsi and Coca-Cola have a global presence, and the Levi Strauss corporation made the denim blue jean, once a symbol of the American west, an international fashion staple. Hundreds of other examples might be noted. Popular culture works at many levels.

Of particular importance for this book is the elaborate system of product tie-ins that are regularly featured in American movies, music, and television programs. Moviemakers, for example, have learned that a movie audience is effectively captive: short of leaving the theater, patrons cannot flip channels or otherwise avoid seeing the products used in the film. Accordingly, it has become commonplace for movies to feature actors going to specific restaurants—Subway, in the case of the Adam Sandler comedy *Happy Gilmore*—or using particular types of cars (careful viewers of many crime-oriented films will note that the good guys all drive one manufacturer's vehicles while the bad guys all drive another's). The Cadillac Escalade, a giant sports-utility vehicle made by General Motors, became the hottest selling luxury SUV after being featured in numerous rap music videos as a garish and obvious piece of "bling" that became the "must have" purchase for everyone who wanted to show off his or her newly made wealth. When the last of the *Star Wars* movies was released in 2005, advertising directed interested consumers to Web sites where they could purchase and download ring tones and other accessories for their cellular telephones based on or spoken by Star Wars characters. It is thus important to recognize that movies, music, and television programs regularly contain and express many forms of popular culture; in many ways, the product marketing and tie-ins are as important to the money-making ambitions of the producers as the film, song, or show itself.

The marketing and hypermarketing of products through films, songs, and videos and television broadcasts extends well beyond product placement, however. One particularly successful linking of popular and product cultures ties what is seen as the most popular American film type (discussed in chapter 2), the ultraexpensive action-adventure blockbuster, with action figurines and associated paraphernalia that are subsequently offered for sale in fast-food restaurants, in cereal boxes, in retail stores, and on the Internet. The *Star Wars* family of films holds the record for such multidimensional product marketing; in many ways the films are little more than advertisements for products ranging from dolls to light sabers to DVDs that are subsequently sold for years and even decades after the film's release. Even the recent international hit, the *Lord of the Rings* trilogy, offered actual set pieces and replicas of swords, clothes, staffs, and jewelry for sale through the Internet. The popular culture industry is a multiply entwined money-making juggernaut that reaches beyond the direct content of American movies, music, and television programming.

"American" Popular Culture

What does it mean to say "culture" or "popular culture" is "American"? As the earlier section on culture made clear, it is difficult, at best, to claim that a particular group of people share a culture such that each and every individual in it has the same values, attitudes, norms, and experiences. What is true for culture generally is certainly true in the case of a society as complex as that of the United States. The 290 million people who live in the United States come from a vast array of nations, representing every language, religious, and cultural group on the planet. The first people who arrived in the area now called the United States came thirty thousand years ago; hundreds and thousands of people still arrive daily with the hopes of making a permanent home in the country. It is hard, in such a context, to suppose that all these people share a common culture that can be described as "American."

In addition, to describe the culture of the residents of the United States as "American culture" is stunningly arrogant. The Americas, after all, constitute two continents in the Western Hemisphere. These are further divided into four areas: North, Central, and South America, and the island nations of Caribbean America. Well over 600 million people live in more than twenty countries across the region. To refer to any one of these countries or areas as "America," and its inhabitants as "American," is at some level an arrogant act of hemispheric appropriation.

In order to avoid simple-minded assertions that "Americans believe X" or "Sri Lankans believe Y," as if all Americans and all Sri Lankans share the same opinions among themselves while sharing none with others, when examining the notion of "American" culture, this book rests on what Marc Howard Ross has called the concept of "public culture." Public culture refers to the common terms of reference, symbols, rituals, and ideologies within which different groups and individuals press their claims for power, policy, and identity. Such terms are not a matter of private conscience; instead, they can be found, among other places, in public documents, speeches, and campaigns, and political symbols referred to by others as they promote their agendas. Such public cultural symbols constitute a shareable language through which different groups and individuals can press for their goals, define meaning, and create rules and standards of conduct in intersubjectively recognizable—and supportable—terms. Importantly, this sharing can go on regardless of the private values, attitudes, and motives of the actors referencing the public culture. Thus different groups and individuals can express alternative political programs through shared cultural frames. The public culture contains the terms in which political debate and struggle can occur in its particular, limited way in specific polities.[10]

The public culture of the United States is generally termed "civic."[11] That is, the values, ideas, and expectations that people who live in the United States refer to when explaining what they believe, why they believe it, and which programs they favor are usually couched in norms like democracy, individual rights, tolerance, and so on that are seen to cumulatively constitute a civic culture. In particular, it is commonly agreed that Americans tend to focus on several specific ideas and values to justify their plans and programs: liberty, particularly "negative liberty,"[12] the sense that government should leave people alone so that individuals can think and believe and act as they please; political equality, meaning that everyone is entitled to equal political rights; individualism, the idea that individuals have rights that should be protected by government even as most individuals are expected to be responsible for their own decisions and their own fates; democracy, especially in the form of citizens electing others to represent them in government with the expectation that those elected will promote the interests and values of their constituents across an array of local, regional (state), and national (federal) governments; tolerance, the idea that since individuals have rights and responsibilities, and those rights and responsibilities are the most important part of the political and social system, everyone has to let everyone else practice their values in order to preserve the opportunity for themselves; exceptionalism, the idea that the United States is a special nation ordained by God to fulfill an important role in the world; and capitalism, understood as an economic system in which individuals buy, sell, and trade goods and services with the intention of making a profit determined largely by market forces of supply and demand, which establish who gets what, when, and for how much.

This distribution of American public cultural attitudes and values has emerged for several reasons. First among these are the values and goals brought to the east coast of what became the United States by English settlers starting in 1587 (the founding of an unsuccessful colony on Roanoke Island, North Carolina). These early colonists desired, generally, the opportunity to practice their religion as they chose (often excluding members of other religious communities as a consequence); the opportunity to make a living largely free from the restrictions of apprenticeship, indentured servitude, and property restrictions that were common in Great Britain; and the prospect of improving their family's social and economic position. They designed local governments to make and enforce laws that protected individual property rights, promoted participation in government (at least relative to the amount of participation that was allowed in England), and responded to citizen concerns in a timely and effective manner. Admittedly, not every colonist had such dreams, and not every colonial government was quite as democratic as this brief sketch suggests, but in general, and particularly in the New England colonies that led the colonies into the American Revolution, governments practiced these principles. They were profoundly important in imprinting such practices and values on American public culture.

It is important to recognize that these public cultural values were applied differently across the American colonies. The freedoms associated with democracy, economic opportunity, and religious tolerance were not afforded to slaves in the American South, for example. Indeed, many of the men who signed the Declaration of Independence owned slaves despite that document's insistence that "all men are created equal" and that they are "endowed by their Creator with certain inalienable rights." Others who signed the same document believed in the abolition of slavery. Similarly, women were denied the same rights as men in the Constitution. These disjunctions can be explained, but not excused, by reviewing how the people

13

of the time defined the practical implications of American civic values in their lives. For example, slave holders tended to believe their liberty and economic livelihoods were dependent on keeping slaves, while abolitionists insisted that liberty for all men meant freedom for slaves, too. Likewise, women were denied the right to vote and own property in much of the early United States on the grounds that they were not fully rational beings capable of properly enjoying freedom and its associated benefits. The public culture provided the terms on which political and social debate centered even as people came to different conclusions about how cultural values applied in daily life.

The integration of new generations of immigrants also helps explain the emergence of American civic culture. New citizens were usually persuaded to accept the ideals and values core to the notion of a civic culture despite the fact that most new citizens came from very different backgrounds than the original English settlers, and so in many cases did not share the same cultural, political, social, linguistic, religious, and ethnic assumptions held by the early English colonists about the best ordering of society. In part this was the result of the profound economic opportunities the United States provided to its new inhabitants: due to the nation's size, wealth, industrial capacity, and seemingly endless frontier, it was possible for people to come to the United States and find opportunities to work. Indeed, the existence of the frontier made it possible for a person who was unhappy in his or her current state or job to disappear and then reinvent him or herself in a new place, ready to make a new life. Such opportunities reinforced the messages of individual rights and opportunities that were core to the American vision of a civic culture.

The integration of new immigrants into "American" culture was also the result of a conscious practice of civic education by generations of political and social elites in the United States. in the years following the nation's earliest settling. As new populations of people came to the United States, the nation's education and naturalization systems evolved to push new immigrants to learn and accept civic cultural values. Schools taught supposedly "American" values to the children of the newest Americans, for example. Laws were written governing the process of becoming a citizen that required learning U.S. history, "American" values, and English as conditions of naturalization. Industrialist and cultural leader Henry Ford actually required his immigrant employees to take classes in English, history, and hygiene if they wished to keep their jobs in his factories; these employees also had to open their homes to inspection so that Ford's teachers could make sure the employees were behaving like "Americans" if they wanted to keep their jobs. And—as will be discussed in chapters 2 and 3—the mass media also reinforced the values of what it meant to be an American.

Over time, this public culture has come to be labeled "American." Rather than sharing a common ethnicity, language, or some other bond, Americans are seen to be defined by their faith in an ideology—civic nationalism. This ideology is so deeply embedded and unquestioned that some scholars have suggested it should be understood as a civic religion: the cultural values of civic nationalism have become, for many Americans, a sacred text, eternal truths on which judgments of right and wrong, good and evil, ought to be based.[13] Again, these public values are used to justify an array of political programs—but, in general, adherents of both sides of American political debate legitimate their plans and policies in terms of the public civic culture. Public culture is civic even if its practices may not be.

It is important to admit here that the list of variables innate to a civic culture like the United States' is not comprehensive. Any number of additional values might be added to it. Further, when examining public culture it is necessary to keep in mind the prospect that public attitudes and values might not translate directly into policy preferences and programs. As the forgoing discussion of slavery and the status of women in American history suggests, it is possible to derive different specific policy preferences from the same concept. Hence public culture can be shared even if private preferences are not.

As will be seen in chapter 3, the values and ideals of American public culture are expressed through the entertainment media and then marketed across the planet. American public culture is inevitably embedded in the products of popular culture. Issues of culture are thus intrinsically linked to globalization in the modern era.

Grasping Globalization

So what is globalization, and how is the concept used in this book? Manfred Steger has offered a concise, highly useable approach to understanding globalization that both accounts for the many dimensions of globalization and informs the analysis offered in this work. Steger defines globalization as a "*set of social processes* that are thought to transform our present social condition into one of globality." Globality, in turn, is seen as "a *social condition* characterized by the existence of global economic, political, cultural and environmental interconnections and flows that make many of the currently existing borders and boundaries irrelevant." Thus, a combination of economic, political, or cultural factors promote globalization by 1) making it possible to create new and increased ties among people, social networks, and ideas that span traditional nation-state boundaries; 2) linking people together in new ways, making it possible for work or travel or shopping or other activities to take place twenty-four hours a day around the world; 3) advancing the speed of communication and the expectation of instantaneous contact, in effect making global events and issues local ones as well; and 4) shaping and reshaping individuals' ideas and identities as they are exposed to this increasingly complex world. Hence, while globalization is dynamic, uncertain, and insecure, its direction is toward the state of globality—what Steger describes as "interdependence and integration."[14]

Globalization may be a set of processes tending to promote a condition of globality, but it also seems to create movements and reactions in opposition to it. As is addressed throughout this book, the forces shaping globalization seem to both draw people together through trade and increased cultural contacts *and* to anger, frustrate, and frighten many groups and individuals in various (and varied) communities. Political scientist James Rosenau coined the term "fragmegration" to describe the integration-fragmentation dynamic that shapes globalization today. Fragmentation and integration occur at the same time, profoundly shaping the dynamics of globalization. Moreover, fragmegration affects different individuals, groups, sectors of the economy, and communities in varying ways.[15] Thus, whether for economic, political, or cultural reasons, or some combination of these, globalization seems to drive people apart even as it promotes new international connections among people around the world. To understand globalization, then, is to understand how economic, political, and cultural forces that stimulate the growth of shared social institutions and values bring some people together while at the same time pushing others apart.

As will be seen throughout this book, American popular culture is an agent of cultural globalization. It is a conduit by which values, ideas, and experiences in the world at large can become known to Americans, only to be adapted and reflected back out into the world again. Moreover, popular culture is a business run by megacorporations and marketed across the globe. Accordingly, it has an impact on the economic dimension of globalization. This economic activity inevitably links to a political agenda as the sudden intrusion of new forms and modes of communication and entertainment into local communities promotes local tensions. Globalization is not simply *good*. It is multidimensional, dynamic, and transformational in both desired and undesirable ways.

Economic Globalization and American Popular Culture

The economic dimensions of globalization are perhaps the best-understood and most studied feature of contemporary globalization. In fact, so common are the assertions of those individuals and groups who favor economic globalization that Steger argues they have combined to form a powerful political ideology, globalism, to legitimate and promote their preferred policies.[16] Since economic globalization interacts with the cultural dimension of globalization—the primary focus of this book—a brief accounting of this arena of globalization is appropriate here before we move on to the cultural.

One of the central features of contemporary globalization is the degree to which the economic livelihoods of people living in many different countries are now linked through world trade, international finance, and the operations of transnational corporations. This is a remarkable change from the way global economics worked even fifty years ago. For most of the last five hundred years or so, most countries (and, if they had one, their associated colonial empires) pursued their economic interests in competition with the other nations and empires of the world. For example, rather than cooperate to build ships or grow food, nations attempted to grow all the food they needed within their own borders (including the boundaries of their colonies) as well as to produce all the ships they needed themselves. Indeed, the desire to go it alone in economic practices was one of the main stimuli that led the European powers to pursue colonies: lacking sufficient resources and markets at home to keep their industrial factories working, they conquered foreign territories from which they could extract natural resources and to which they could sell finished products. (The United States' expansion across the continent of North America served much the same purpose in the nineteenth century.) The goal of such practices was to protect the profits and jobs of the workers and owners of the home country.

Near the end of World War II, the United States and its allies (with the notable exception of the Soviet Union) decided that such go-it-alone policies were not the best way to ensure their economic futures. They decided that competition for economic resources had in part caused the horrific violence of the First and Second World Wars. They further decided that the economic collapse of the Great Depression in the 1920s and 1930s had been caused and deepened by protectionist trade policies. Finally, they decided that they needed to establish a new kind of economic and political alliance to counter the growing power of the Soviet Union, which espoused Communism as its organizing philosophy. With this as background, they began the process of economic globalization that shapes the world today.

The core of the economic dimension of globalization as developed by the United States and its allies rests on the ideal—if not the perfect practice—of free trade. Free trade is a principle of economic theory that holds that there should be few, if any, restraints on the flow of goods, services, and even people around the world. The theory holds that goods and services should be produced wherever they can be most efficiently made—a concept known as "comparative advantage." This is held to be true whether the product in question is a pound of rice, a computer, or a television program. Restraints on trade necessarily make the prices of some goods and services artificially high and prevent those areas that might make a product more cheaply from having the opportunity to develop. Similar problems emerge if capital, people, ideas, or anything else is constrained from flowing freely by legal or social regulations. While there may be social and political disruptions as industries, jobs, and markets redistribute themselves around the world, free trade is expected to be good for everyone, at least in the long run.[17]

The major powers of the West began the process of expanding trade and reducing barriers among themselves near the end of the Second World War. They agreed to stabilize their currencies in relation to the U.S. dollar, established institutions like the General Agreement of Tariffs and Trade (GATT) and the International Monetary Fund (IMF) to oversee currency exchanges and trade rules for member states, and supported treaties and organizations to enforce the rules governing free trade to which the major powers agreed. In subsequent years, free trade agreements accelerated, and regional free trade zones like the North American Free Trade Agreement (NAFTA) and the European Union (EU) were set up. With the end of the Cold War in 1991, new areas of trade emerged, financial markets were deregulated, and it became possible to invest—and compete for capital—around the world. Services, too, became global as communication technologies like the Internet and cellular phones made it possible to outsource work (e.g., customer service phone operations) formerly done in the corporation's home country. Finally, with the deregulation of financial markets and the emergence of global free trade, new institutions rose to exploit the economic opportunities afforded on a worldwide stage: this was the emergence of the transnational corporations. Companies like General Motors, Honda or Airbus (a joint European enterprise to build commercial aircraft) are spread across the globe, pursuing profit for investors.[18] Relatively free trade is, as a consequence, the dominant mode of global economic exchange today.

Yet free trade has a dark side, a side that has become increasingly evident over time. During the last fifty years, some people have gotten phenomenally wealthy while others—even some who were once well off—have been reduced to abject poverty. For example, as globalization promotes greater economic integration around the world, people whose skills can be replaced at lower costs—as happened in the case of low-skill factory jobs like those in the textile industry in the United States in the 1980s and 1990s—often lose their jobs and even, to some extent, their identities—their ability to perform their role as providers to their families and friends through work they imagine doing for a lifetime. They then lose connection to their extended neighbors in the national community as people move, jobs are realigned, and state policies shift to accommodate the pressures of globalization. Again, this tends to be true whether the industry or economic enterprise affected by globalization is a farm, an industrial production facility, or a music production studio. Each change may serve to integrate the people living in newly developing areas to the larger world (globalization), but each of these processes, and many others, also transform the economic, social, and political order of developing as well as developed nations in diverse ways with varying effects (fragmegration). Economic globalization thus has costs as well as benefits.

In addition, while the United States is the rhetorical leader of the world's free trade movement, its behavior has not always matched its rhetoric. The nation has often worked hard to make sure free trade rules are either limited in their ability to affect important economic actors in the United States or are favorable to the trade in American goods overseas. That is, rather than pulling down trade barriers as such, the United States has kept policies like subsidies to farmers, particularly producers of globally uncompetitive crops like cotton, in place to satisfy the political pressures American farmers of those products have placed on their elected representatives. Similarly, the United States seeks to protect its domestic steel and lumber industries by placing tariffs on foreign goods that might be imported cheaply and thereby disrupt the market for domestic producers. (As will be seen in chapter 4, similar tactics and practices are used by nations seeking to protect their domestic popular culture industries from threats perceived to come from American movies, music, and television programs.) American trade negotiators also seek to insert language into free trade agreements that favors American-produced goods on the global market. Restrictions on trade in certain kinds of computer chips or other high tech devices serve to protect American manufacturers, as do patent and other laws governing the use of inventions created in the United States. Thus, while the United States has been the world's great free trade advocate, it, like other nations, seeks trade arrangements that are favorable to its citizens' interests—not just free trade for free trade's sake.

As was suggested earlier, and is addressed in detail in both chapter 2 and chapter 4, popular culture is a central element in contemporary international trade. As such, it has the potential to provide substantial, enjoyable, affordable entertainment to literally billions of people—the ideal of free trade in general. However, American producers of popular culture have powerful advantages of capital, knowledge, and distribution networks compared to local producers in most of the rest of the world. Accordingly, American producers have the ability to drive local producers of music, movies, and television programs out of business. For economic reasons alone, then, diverse groups and communities may either favor or oppose the global trade in popular culture as economically beneficial or harmful to their interests. Contemporary globalization is inevitably shaped as a consequence of these choices.

Political Globalization and American Popular Culture

The economic changes described above have promoted a series of powerful challenges to the established rules by which global politics have been managed for nearly five hundred years. Accordingly, globalization has political as well as economic consequences. For example, free trade and the rise of transnational corporations are new phenomena in global politics, phenomena that test the power and limitations of nations to pass laws to control their own destinies. In addition, the political notion that government regulation of free trade is harmful for consumers is implicit in the idea of free trade. Finally, it is common for people living in democracies to ask government to take actions that will protect the interests and livelihoods that are at risk; the economic dislocations associated with globalization and free trade have accordingly spawned movements intended to limit the negative economic, political, and cultural consequences of globalization. At the least, such factors establish that globalization has political as well as economic effects that need to be understood in order to assess contemporary globalization.

It is worth noting here that some authors argue that globalization heralds the end of the nation-state. For these thinkers there are few problems, if any, that the market cannot solve more efficiently and fairly than governments can. Thus the answer to almost any social problem (poverty, crime, economic inequity, etc.) is to free markets from constraints and allow them to work: goods and services will be produced and consumed across the globe according to which area can do so most productively and efficiently. By extension, states need to get out of the way—even if they mean to help their citizens, globalists claim that their refusal to accept the logic of the market will ultimately undermine a people's chances for a happy, full, democratic life.[19]

Empirically, however, politics does not appear to be going away to be replaced by benevolent markets. Moreover, a significant anti-globalization social movement has emerged worldwide, suggesting a continuing role for political action in determining exactly how globalization will occur across the planet. Thus, other scholars, recognizing the ideological dimensions of the globalists' claims, have argued that globalization will not eliminate politics. Instead, it will transform how governance works worldwide. Two alternative roles for the state are seen as likely to emerge in the global era. The first comes from the growth of new forms of international organization that transcend traditional state boundaries but have legal power over the residents of member states. For example, since globalization leads to increased contacts among people, it makes sense that globalization has a regional component: links of geography and culture tend to promote contacts over time.[20] The European Union stands as the most robust example of such regional governance systems. Similarly, as communication and knowledge improve, the work of nongovernmental organizations (NGOs) —like those that focus on human rights, environmental regulation, and the like—may also be facilitated.[21] New political relationships, made by states to regulate states and nonstate actors, are thus likely to arise in the context of globalization.

A second role for states derives from their role in the creation and management of globalization in the first place. The neoliberal policies of free trade and increased flows of capital that emerged in the West at the end of the Second World War were, these authors note, the result of choices of specific nation-states at particular moments in time. By implication, other states might follow—or leading states can change policy and thus alter the paths of globalization. State policy further shapes the technological and ecological standards in which trade, communication, and environmental policies (to name a few) are enacted and enforced.[22] The U.S. response to the terrorist attacks of September 11, 2001, has further demonstrated that state control over the creation and deployment of the world's military forces means that states will remain an agent in world affairs for some time to come: the post 9/11 United States has, for example, restricted immigration and asserted its right to use military force to defend itself anywhere it perceives a threat to its interests across the globe. Notably, the United States has been able to take these actions and remain economically and politically powerful regardless of the globalists' claims that such acts violate the spirit and inevitable benefit of free trade. States may change how they do business in the modern world during the global era, but it seems unlikely they are going to disappear.

A third role politics can be seen to play in contemporary globalization has emerged in the form of a loosely coordinated global movement of groups that engage in political protest activity to encourage governments to pass policies that protect people from negative effects associated with globalization. The groups and individuals involved in this movement range from hard-core isolationists who eschew any international contacts among nations to advocates for economic and political justice who fear that the unfettered global pursuit of the cheapest goods will result in outcomes that are harmful *both* to the people who produce products for virtually no earnings *and* to the people who consume these items. This movement seeks to pressure governments and corporations to set and follow rules that protect jobs and livelihoods in developed countries while also protecting health, safety, environmental, and other types of standards in the rest of the world. While this movement has, at present, only a modest influence in the globalization debate, as will be seen in chapter 4, it has perhaps been most effective in limiting the free trade of American popular culture.

As is explored in chapter 4, popular culture is among the most heavily regulated components of international trade, even in the era of globalization. As is also addressed in that chapter, trade in audiovisual entertainment is treated quite differently under international trade agreements than is trade in cars or steel or grain. This, in turn, derives from its perceived importance in cultural affairs. Thus political globalization is linked to cultural—political systems act to protect local cultures and culture-producing enterprises. As such, popular culture is an element of political as well as economic globalization.

Cultural Globalization and American Popular Culture

In broad terms, analysts of cultural globalization focus on the question of how Western goods, services, ideas, values, and media affect local, usually non-Western, cultures once they enter the new markets opened by globalization. Most analysts, relying on a strict view of culture as a set of fixed, rigid ideas and values that resist change, are fairly pessimistic about the likely resulting effects. In particular, three kinds of concerns about the negative effects of the global spread of American popular culture have emerged in the years since the fall of the Soviet Union in 1991: 1) cultural corruption, 2) cultural imperialism, and 3) cultural homogenization. Each is a variant of the other, but all are used by members of different groups, cultures, communities, and nations to resist what they see as the siren call of American movies, music, and television programming.

Those who are concerned that cultural corruption follows from American popular culture build on the research of a school of thought known as the Frankfurt School. As expressed in works of scholars like Theodor

Adorno, Max Horkheimer, and Jürgen Habermas, adherents of the Frankfurt School argued that the Industrial Revolution broke the traditional ties that oriented people to life in their societies. That is, where once people lived in small communities governed by rules established by church, political, and familial authorities who lived in the same small towns, the Industrial Revolution drove people into large cities, where traditional authority structures could not function. When millions of people moved from rural areas to cities to take jobs in the new factories, they were separated from the institutions and values that had previously served as the teachers and enforcers of moral behavior. This separation was important because life in the cities, at least in contrast with the bucolic image of life on the farm offered by critics of town living, was nasty, dirty, and immoral: brothels, crime, and disease flourished, for example, even as new forms of entertainment, like dime novels and the penny press, found markets peddling stories of lust, violence, and exploitation. In turn, life became dominated by new values like consumerism, the pursuit of entertainment, and the satisfaction of individual interests regardless of their social effects. In such circumstances people became profoundly isolated despite living together in huge numbers: lacking patterns of trust and comfort like those embedded in their rural communities, new urban migrants were often left to their own devices to survive. In effect, people's life orientations shifted dedication to the social good of their communities to the autonomous desire to satisfy the self.

This shift from social to private consciousness made people susceptible to manipulation by outside forces. Thus Frankfurt School analysts emphasized the way that new forms of communication, particularly mass communications and entertainment like newspapers, radio, and the movies, could promote false or harmful ideas to their mass audiences: without historical moral anchors like local church and community leaders to offer alternative points of view on crucial issues of the day, all that people living in the mass isolation of large cities could know or care about was what they were told by newspaper publishers, radio broadcasters, movie producers, and other agents of mass communication. Thus two great transformations occurring at the same time, the social changes associated with rapid urbanization and the Industrial Revolution—and, in large part due to the productive capacity and economies of scale associated with industrialization, the rise of mass communication and entertainment to fill the urban market—created a world in which mass media and entertainment could lead to the undermining of moral society in favor of some corrupted new order.

One set of contemporary critics of American popular culture typically

23

espouse a version of Frankfurt School thought known as mass society theory. For adherents of mass society theory, the moral decay of society was a result of the messages and meanings embedded in the communications of mass entertainment.[23] As people were separated (as a result of urbanization) from the social and political institutions that had defined their lives and provided them with meaning, they were exposed to exploitative, manipulative media. The media, it was claimed, served to replace traditional forces in socializing behavior and attitudes: immoral behavior in novels and magazines was mirrored in lustful violence in the real world. Individuals were, essentially, helpless victims of those who could control the messages the media communicated. This is seen to be particularly true for some individuals or groups—particularly children—who are believed to be particularly gullible and prone to manipulation.[24] Thus critics employing mass society theory argue that people need to be protected from "bad" cultural products and messages for their own good, echoing—or perhaps foretelling—the arguments of Soviet leaders about the corrupting influence of American popular culture during the Cold War.

A second group of critics of American popular culture focus on its capacity for cultural imperialism. As a concept, cultural imperialism suggests that the interaction of the different values, norms, and ways of life and social practices that constitute unique cultures will inevitably come into conflict as members of one culture are exposed to the ideas and values of other, quite different, cultures. As a result, one culture or the other will seek to destroy or eliminate the other, whether through outright violence or by undermining the alien culture and installing a new dominant culture in its place. Samuel Huntington, for example, argues that civilizational/cultural boundaries constitute the ultimate cleavages on which political conflict will inevitably arise.[25] In his model, cross-cultural exchanges are more likely to be sources of conflict and resentment than causes for integration and cooperation. Benjamin Barber adds an additional layer of complexity to the arguments of those who fear conflict will derive from cultural global interactions when he notes that globalization, in its drive for integration and coordination, also promotes fragmentation and resistance. The values, products and processes of globalization can and must provoke what Barber calls "jihad"—"bloody holy war on behalf of partisan identity that is metaphysically defined and fanatically defended."[26] Jihad is counterpoised against "McWorld" both *between* societies—the highly integrated globalized societies of the West, for example, and those of the less developed, less linked world—and *within* them (e.g., coastal communities heavily dependent on trade as opposed to upland areas in the same polity). Under such circumstances, increased cultural contacts associated with globalization are likely to generate violence and fragmentation, not the new world order promised by globalism's proponents.

Those critics concerned with the concept of cultural homgenization agree that American popular culture may well dominate the world; however, rather than worrying about American movies, music, and television programming imposing supposedly "American" values on local populations, these critics fear that corporate-produced mass entertainment will ultimately move everyone's values toward those associated with mass consumer capitalism. One scholar has termed this "McDonaldization." Corporations like McDonald's are expected to have such advantages in economies of scale, organization, predictability, and efficiency that, combined with superior marketing, they will drive traditional providers out of business. (The same logic applies if the corporation in question is Wal-Mart, Home Depot, or Starbucks.) In time, then, everyone everywhere will end up eating the same thing, reading the same thing, and wearing the same thing. Under such circumstances, cultural diversity would be lost forever. What is left is a world of soulless consumers just looking for the next thing to buy that is exactly like what everyone else in the world already has and wants until the corporations generate the next "must have" item. One culture, consumer capitalism, and the corporate system that supports it would dominate the world.[27]

Accordingly, whether they fear corruption, imperialism, or homogenization, many people, groups, communities, nations, and cultures around the world can be expected to resist the spread of American popular culture even as American movies, music, and television programming have become a central component in global trade. Indeed, as is addressed throughout this book, many have. In this context, it simply makes no sense to try to understand globalization's recent history or to estimate its likely future without analyzing the critical role American popular culture plays in globalization today.

There are, however, less skeptical analysts of cultural globalization. One group focuses on the concept of cultural hybridization.[28] Roughly defined as "mixing," hybridization has been defined as "the ways in which forms become separated from existing practices and recombine with new forms and new practices."[29] From the point of view of cultural hybridization, such mixing is common. For example, the interaction of Western values, institutions, products, and services does not necessarily lead to the elimination of local norms and desires in favor of rational, efficient Western alternatives. Instead, businesses can adapt their practices to fit the needs of their workers and the culture of their clients.[30] Or Western corporations may develop a profit interest in celebrating and protecting the diversity of the cultures in which they operate.[31] Cultural communication and hybridization is thus seen as a two-way process; Western societies are as likely to be influenced by non-Western ones as non-Western communities are to be influenced by the West. Jan Nederveen Pieterse has referred to the result as a global "mélange."[32] Marwan M. Kraidy suggests that hybridization is the inherent end of globalization.[33]

This interaction of the local and the global has been termed "glocalization" by Roland Robertson. Paying particular attention to questions of identity—how individuals and groups define their values, ideals, and communities—Robertson sees glocalization as a "massive, twofold process involving *the interpenetration of the universalization of particularism and the particularization of universalism.*"[34] Put another way, glocalization describes a process in which established cultures both shape and are undermined by the emergence of a new cosmopolitan culture whose values and ideals are to a large degree determined by the demands of globalization. For example, Robertson argues that "the contemporary capitalist creation of consumers frequently involves the tailoring of products to increasingly specialized regional, societal, ethnic, class, and gender markets—so called 'micro-marketing.'" At some level, this might seem like the respect for local traditions and identities: by micro-marketing their products, international corporations appear to be operating in line with the goals and ideals of the members of local communities. Yet this micro-marketing has the aim of turning locals into consumers in a global economy—which is a transformation in their historical relationship with the world. Glocalization thus works to link local cultures to global ones in new and important ways.[35]

This glocalist dynamic is not painless, however. Indeed, as with all questions of culture and identity, there is often resistance, discomfort, and challenge as "foreign" ideas/products/values/people cross intellectual, economic, and social boundaries. Each challenge to local values is adopted by some, and resented by others. Each new idea that emerges from small communities and enters the global environment can start a movement or a countermovement. (The Islamic concept of jihad offers a useful example of this dynamic, as Barber uses it: it resides in a particular religion, but as globalization has challenged the traditional ideas and values of many Muslims, they have called for jihad against their apparent enemies. This, in turn, has stimulated a worldwide movement to answer the call of jihad and has also brought on an international military, economic, and social coalition of actors to resist it, especially after the terrorist attacks in the United States on September 11, 2001. It has further stimulated a debate within the Muslim world about the proper role of Islam in the modern world.) The

26

global and the local are thus inextricably linked, with resulting dynamics of pleasure, pain, and change.

Popular culture, as cultural artifacts and products that are marketed around the world, stands in the center of the glocalist/hybridized/globalist dynamic. Different groups and individuals can respond to pieces of popular culture from American sources in diverse ways. As is shown in chapter 4, many groups and nations resist American popular culture as an element of globalization. However, as is addressed in chapter 5, these concerns may be misaimed; globalization is a complex phenomenon, and American popular culture is both less fixed and less permanent than is often supposed. In any case, these dynamics shape contemporary globalization.

Conclusion

The economic, political, and social dimensions of globalization described above offer an array of perspectives and expectations about globalization's present nature and future course. These range from the promise of a democratic, free market future to the prospect of cultural global war. This book examines the ways that the messages and mechanisms of American popular culture are a force for fragmegration in contemporary globalization. It focuses on the relationships among the content of American culture as it is refined, shaped, and expressed through the institutions of popular culture and then sent out into the world as representations of American ideals, values, attitudes, and practices. As will be seen, what is the appeal of the American dream for some is repellent to others. What is admirable about a civic culture for one group is proof that people have lost their moral values to other people. What is hopeful in globalism's promise for many is a symptom of the end of uniqueness in another's vision. What is free choice for some is petty consumerism for others. What promises a vision of inexpensive, enjoyable entertainment for some threatens others' livelihoods. Teasing through these dynamics is the task that follows through the rest of this project.

THE GLOBAL SCOPE OF AMERICAN POPULAR CULTURE

This chapter examines how American popular culture is produced and distributed. It further analyzes how the popular culture industry developed as it has. It then assesses the global impact of American popular culture. It examines the degree to which American popular films, music, and television can be seen to dominate world entertainment. It concludes with an assessment of the significance and power of American popular culture as a force in contemporary globalization. Importantly, American popular culture can be seen to have influence even when the production and distribution of popular culture entertainment products is not controlled in the United States. This pervasive, message-rich entertainment venue constitutes a major source of the fragmegration dynamic to be addressed in detail in chapter 4.

The Popular Culture Machine in the Global Era

Perhaps the most striking thing about the shape of the contemporary entertainment industry is how centralized it is in the hands of just a few corporations. Where once many artists, inventors, wealthy amateurs, companies, and coalitions produced the films, music, and television programming that are enjoyed around the world, today this power is controlled by a select group of popular culture-producing giants. Moreover, while not all popular culture is controlled by American-based corporations, the United States' early dominance in the creation of movies, music, and television programming has served to create conditions in which much of the global trade in popular culture is done in genres created in the United States under labels traditionally associated with American companies and performers.

Crucial to this concentration of power and control have been two concepts: synergy and convergence. "Synergy" describes the vertical and horizontal integration of entertainment companies and the products they market. For example, when the same company that produces a performer's album also owns a venue (e.g., a radio station) in which to play and thus market the album, synergy is said to exist. It is enhanced when the company also can place the song in a popular television program it produces or make it the theme song for a movie it has financed; multiple marketing outlets will reach different audiences and hopefully increase sales. This serves to concentrate profit in the controlling company and also lets the company spread the risk of creating a movie, an album, or a television program across an array of businesses: a movie might not make money in the theaters, for example, but it may sell and rent well enough in the post-theater market that, if the same company that produces the movie also controls the companies that produce and rent the videos, it can earn a profit.

Synergy among the producers of popular culture extends into the arena of product placements as described in chapter 1. The soft drink maker Pepsi, for example, has entered into sponsorship agreements with numerous record labels and pop stars; both Michael Jackson and Madonna had major international tours sponsored by Pepsi in the 1990s. (While filming a commercial for Pepsi, Michael Jackson suffered severe injuries when a pyrotechnic explosion set his hair on fire.) Pepsi, in turn, owns an array of fast-food restaurants—including Taco Bell and Pizza Hut—through which it can further promote the music of the stars it sponsors. Pepsi, like most soft drink makers, then seeks placement for its products in other pop culture venues like films and television programs; the association of a big star with Pepsi's products further enhances their marketability and linkages among an array of popular culture items beyond a simple accounting of music, movies, and television programs.

Convergence refers to the long process by which synergy in the entertainment industry has been created. (This will be discussed in detail later in this chapter.) Alternately known as consolidation, convergence implies an inevitable merging of audiovisual production and distribution companies into a few integrated transnational corporations that will dominate world trade in popular culture. The core idea is that through controlling enough products and distribution and marketing mechanisms (synergy through convergence), entertainment corporations can provide consumers with the wide variety goods and services they want at affordable prices.

Most movie, music, and television production is today controlled by eight corporations: Bertelsmann AG; Sony; Time Warner, Inc.; the Walt Disney Company; Viacom; and News Corp. Also of note are General Electric (GE) and Vivendi Universal S. A. Of these, four (Bertelsman AG, Sony, Vivendi Universal, and News Corp) have been historically based outside the United States, in Germany, Japan, France, and Australia respectively. The other four (Time Warner, Disney, Viacom, and GE) are U.S.-based corporations. Each controls the production of a wide range of entertainment ranging from films to music, television, video games, and Internet content.

Bertelsman AG, for example, is a privately owned German media company that operates approximately six hundred companies in fifty-three countries. As a partial sample, in 2005 it owned an array of radio and television stations across Europe, as well as four broadcast-production studios worldwide: FremantleMedia (one of the largest producers of radio and television programming in Europe), Sportfive, teamWorx, and UFA Film and TV Productions Broadway Books. Bertlesman AG's major record production enterprise was BMG, of which it shares ownership with Sony. BMG's labels include Arista Records, RCA, and the Windham Hill Group. It owned partial stakes in AOL Europe, Barnesandnoble.com, and Napster. Finally, it owned such publishing houses and magazines as Ballatine Publishing Group, Bantam Dell, Doubleday Broadway, Crown, Knopf, Random House, *Family Circle*, *Parents*, and *YM*.[1]

Sony, the giant Japanese corporation, is also heavily invested in entertainment industry products. Sony is one of the largest movie studios in the world; its holdings in 2004 included Sony Pictures Entertainment, Columbia Tristar, Sony Pictures Classics, and Screen Gems. The company's music production house, Sony BMG Music Entertainment, jointly owned with Bertelsmann AG, includes, in addition to those companies listed above, Columbia Records, Epic Records, Legacy Recordings, and Sony Classical.[2] Music produced by these companies, in turn, could be distributed through Sony's direct marketing operations, the Columbia House Music Club and "Pressplay," both of which are joint ventures with Time Warner.[3] Sony also owned Sony Pictures Television, which was the final name given to the company resulting from the mergers of Columbia Tristar Domestic Television, Columbia Tristar International Television, and Sony Pictures Family Entertainment. In addition, Sony has a global presence in other arenas, including Sony Electronics and Sony Computer Entertainment America, its video game production and distribution wing.[4]

In 2001, the Internet provider America Online (AOL) merged with

Time Warner to become AOL Time Warner. It was the biggest media merger of all time at $165 billion. It has also become something of a business object lesson in the failure of synergy; by linking entertainment production (Time Warner) with a new form of distribution (the Internet and AOL), the merger was supposed to create a new model for the delivery of entertainment products online. The attempt failed, however, largely as a result of the extraordinary debt the newly merged company acquired. It simply could not market enough products to pay its debts. As a consequence, in time a decision was made to revert to the name Time Warner. Time Warner still owns AOL, however, along with a host of other entertainment companies. In 2004, for example, the merged company controlled the film production studios of Warner Brothers, Castle Rock Entertainment, New Line Cinema, Turner Original Productions, and Fine Line Features. It owned over a dozen television networks, notably the WB Television Network, HBO, Cinemax, Time Warner Sports, CNN, and its variant channels, TBS, TNT, the Cartoon Network, and Turner Classic Movies. It could generate programming for these networks either through its many production arms—Warner Brothers Television, Warner Brothers Animation, the WB Television Network, or Hanna Barbera, among others—or through its control of the Atlanta Braves. These could easily be broadcast by the Time Warner Cable system—as well as advertised in an array of publications ranging from *Time* to *Life* to *Sports Illustrated* to *This Old House* to *MAD* magazine (and many others). It might also promote or distribute its products through AOL, CompuServe, Netscape, or MapQuest, just a few of its Internet holdings.[5]

One of the most famous entertainment conglomerates is the Walt Disney Company. Built from a few cartoon characters first drawn in the early twentieth century, by 2000 the company had grown to have $25 billion in revenues derived from an array of entertainment resources—including, of course, amusement parks like Disneyland, Disneyworld, and EuroDisney.[6] In 2004 in film production and distribution, Disney held Walt Disney Pictures, Touchstone Pictures, Hollywood Pictures, Caravan Pictures, Miramax Films, and Buena Vista Home Entertainment. In the area of music production it owned the Buena Vista Music Group, Hollywood Records, Lyric Street Records, Mammoth Records, and Walt Disney Records. Disney was a major player in the television industry, owning or partially owning ABC, the Disney Channel, SoapNet, ESPN, the History Channel, Lifetime, and E! as well as ten television stations and the television production companies Buena Vista Television, Touchstone Television, and Walt Disney Television. In addition, Disney owned or partially owned thirteen cable and satellite channels around the world. It also owned Radio Disney, ESPN

Radio, and sixty-four radio stations across the United States. Like Warner Brothers, it owned or partly owned sports franchises it could place on its networks: the Mighty Ducks of Anaheim (an NHL hockey team named for a Disney-made movie) and the baseball team the Anaheim (now Los Angeles) Angels. Finally, it had a substantial Internet presence through its ownership of Web sites like ABC.com, ABCNews.com, Oscar.com, Disney .com, Family.com, the ESPN Internet Group, NFL.com, NBA.com, and Nascar.com.[7] In January 2006 Disney announced plans to purchase Pixar, a producer of computer-animated movies like *Toy Story* and *Monsters, Inc.*

Viacom is another media giant, particularly in the fields of film and television. In 2004, for example, it owned the film production and distribution studios Paramount Pictures and Paramount Home Entertainment. Significantly, it also owned Blockbuster Video. In television, it owned or had a significant interest in nineteen networks or cable/satellite channels, including CBS, UPN, MTV, Nickelodeon, CMT, TNN, VH1, Showtime, the Movie Channel, and Comedy Central. It also owned five independent television stations, seventeen CBS affiliates, and eighteen UPN affiliates on which it could provide programming from its television production and distribution companies: Spelling Entertainment Group, Big Ticket Television, and King World Productions. Viacom also owned the Infinity Broadcasting Network, a radio chain of 146 stations nationwide.[8] The company had other entertainment resources that their competitors did not, however, including control of the *Star Trek* franchise. (This franchise spans ten feature films, five television series, and innumerable books, magazines, and collectable paraphernalia, as well as a themed casino in Las Vegas. One source estimates that the combined revenues of the *Star Trek* franchise have exceeded $100 million since its inception in the 1960s.[9]) It also owned seven major book publishers. In the summer of 2005, Viacom announced that it would split itself into two companies starting in the first quarter of 2006. One will concentrate on television production and will include the CBS network, its associated television stations, its radio network, and Paramount Television. The other will include Viacom's cable networks (MTV, Nickelodeon, and Showtime, for example) as well as Paramount Pictures.[10] As of this writing, however, the plan had not yet been implemented.

Rupert Murdoch's News Corp, associated with the Fox label, controls a wide range of entertainment production in the world today. As of 2005, News Corp owned Twentieth Century Fox, Blue Sky Studios, and Fox Searchlight Pictures in the film industry, for example. In television, it owned the Fox Broadcasting Company, the Fox News Channel, Fox Kids Network, Fox Sports, FX, and the National Geographic Channel. It also owned thirty-five Fox-affiliated stations and the British Sky Broadcasting Network, Star TV (Asia), and the U.S.-based satellite provider DirectTV. News Corp also owned five book publishers, with a total of thirty-five imprints, five magazines (including partial ownership of *TV Guide*), and twenty-six newspapers around the world. It also had extensive holdings in sports franchises, owning or participating in ownership of the Los Angeles Kings, the Los Angeles Lakers, and the Staples Center.[11]

Vivendi Universal S. A. is the smallest force in the contemporary production of popular culture, mostly as a result of its sale of the majority of control of the film and television production components of Universal to General Electric in 2004 (discussed below). However, it remains a significant source of global music production under the Universal Music Group, the labels of which include Island Def Jam Music Group, Interscope A&M Records, Geffen Records, MCA Nashville, Mercury Records, Polydor, and Decca. It is also a major source of video game production through its ownership of companies like Blizzard Entertainment, Fox Interactive, Radical Entertainment, and Sierra Entertainment. Finally, it is a significant producer of television programming across Europe.[12]

Perhaps the most surprising major entertainment company is General Electric (GE). GE is one of the largest corporations in the world. It had $152,363 million in sales across all its divisions in 2003 and posted over $16.5 billion in profits for the year.[13] Its eleven major units span a range of areas, including commercial and consumer finance, advanced materials, energy, and health care. GE sells products ranging from dishwashers for individual homes to jet aircraft engines for both commercial and military airplanes. Until 2004 GE was an important but relatively small component of the global entertainment industry; it had acquired NBC and its associated companies through an earlier merger. In 2004, however, GE purchased majority control of Universal from Vivendi Universal, a French conglomerate. (Vivendi retained 20 percent ownership of NBC Universal after GE acquired the company.) After this purchase, GE owned fourteen NBC-affiliated networks and fourteen Telemundo-affiliated networks in 2004. (Telemundo is a Spanish-language network based in the United States.)[14] GE owned several television networks as well, including Bravo, CNBC, MSNBC, NBC, Telemundo, NBC Entertainment (a television production company), NBC News, NBC Universal Cable (a provider company) NBC Universal Sports and Olympics, NBC Universal Television Distribution, NBC Universal Television Studio, the Sci-Fi Channel, and USA. It also owned majority control of Universal Parks and Resorts, Universal Pictures, and Universal Studio Home Video Purchasing Universal. Its control of Universal Studios made it partial owner of October Films,

United International Pictures, and Cinema International BV.[15] As a consequence, GE now sells military aircraft engines to the government and also controls news media outlets through which the use of military forces are reported, as well as entertainment venues in which military products and activities can be promoted.

The Development of the American Popular Culture Industry

The convergence and synergy that led to the dominance of eight corporations in the production of mass audiovisual popular culture was the result of a long history of economic, technological, and social pressures. A brief introduction to this history will help to both explain why these companies have come to dominate the global entertainment industry and establish how American movies, music, and television programming became globally significant even in trade sponsored by non-U.S. corporations.

The film, television, and recording industries arose in the United States in the context of the development of both the media in general and the broader Industrial Revolution. As a consequence, media development was a Western phenomenon in which various competing groups and interests developed, adapted, and sometimes stole technologies and markets to serve capitalist profit-centered ends. The U.S. experience, however, was quite different from Europe's. This difference had profound effects on the way media, including film, television, and recording, developed—ultimately favoring the competitive position of American media.

In Europe, Johannes Gutenberg's invention of the moveable-type printing press in 1436 initiated a revolution in the creation and dissemination of books, pamphlets, and eventually magazines and newspapers. In most parts of Europe, however, printing was heavily regulated by the state; texts were censored, and printers were commonly granted state-sponsored monopolies that served to link the printer's interests with the government's. In addition, printers formed guilds that controlled the industry and limited access to printing by establishing a system of extended apprenticeships. The percentage of Europeans who could read was low, at least compared with the percentage of Americans who were literate. As a consequence, printing expanded slowly in most of Europe—and along with it, literacy and markets for the printed word grew slowly as well.[16]

The history of printing in the United States was very different from that in Europe. While there were early and occasional efforts to regulate what was printed, as well as to limit access to printing technology through apprenticeship systems and taxes on paper, these proved relatively ineffective. Instead, printing spread across the American colonies to serve the needs of a substantially literate population in its desire for Bibles, newspapers, and advertising. For example, from 1790 to 1835, the number of American newspapers expanded from 106 to 1,258 (more than 1,100 percent) even though the U.S. population grew only 400 percent. Likewise, the number of newspaper subscriptions per 100 households grew from 18 or 19 in the 1780s to over 50 in the 1820s. By contrast, the more heavily populated Great Britain had only 369 newspapers in the entire country in 1835—and only 17 were produced daily. The early American media were much more diffuse than the European media.[17]

What was true for the printing industry was true for the industries that followed: telegraph, telephone, radio, recording, film, and television. In general, there was less regulation of the American industries, as compared to European ones; this lack of state-centered control promoted diffusion and capitalism as opposed to state control and monopoly. As a consequence, the American popular culture production companies were particularly well positioned to dominate the international market as it developed in the nineteenth and twentieth centuries.[18]

The film, television, and recording industries are distinguished from earlier media, especially printing, in several important ways, however. These differences need to be recognized before we can analyze these industries in their contemporary contexts. For example, whereas printing spread widely across the United States, promoting literacy and markets nationwide as a consequence, the technologies for making and distributing films, television, and recordings were fairly centralized (albeit not by the state). This was largely a function of the cost and complexity associated with making and distributing these forms of entertainment. Unlike a poem, for example, which is usually the result of one person's creative effort, and which might be produced for profit by a printer who expects only modest sales, movies, television programs, and records are the product of many different people using complex technologies and distribution networks. Movie cameras, for example, are very expensive. So is film. (Digital cameras and other digital recording technology—recent inventions—might alter this calculus over time.) It usually takes an array of actors, extras, writers, producers, editors, directors, producers, and any number of other people to create a film; each one of these people brings a unique set of skills and talents to the film, for which they command a salary—a salary someone has to pay. Once a film has been created, it has to be promoted and distributed. Each of these functions is handled by different groups of people, each of which works with networks that are complex and expensive to use. As a consequence, movies (and television programs and recordings, as will be discussed below) are social products: they emerge from the desire to make a profit in the context of a market with particular preferences and an industry with specific structures and norms.

A Brief History of the Movie Industry

In order to understand why the movie industry operates the way it does today, it is necessary to explore the economic and social conditions that shaped the industry's evolution. Unlike the film industry today, in its earliest days, making movies was highly decentralized, more the product of the various inventors of the technology than of large film companies. Likewise, tinkerers and inventors could make short reel films of horses running or people running and jumping or other live action events, which would then be shown in nickelodeons at theaters and carnivals around the world.

The first major maker and distributor of movies, including multireel complexly plotted films, was the Edison Company. Thomas Edison's company, already an international giant due to its founder's inventive prowess, was able to combine the efficiency of mass production with the marketing advantage of a national and international corporation to turn movies into profit-making endeavors. In so doing, the Edison Company drove many small filmmakers out of business. It also shifted the locus of worldwide moviemaking to the United States—a shift that would be solidified by the early twentieth century when the film industry relocated to Southern California to take advantage of its usually excellent weather and thus, in an era when almost all movies were filmed outdoors, to take advantage of the sun's light and of the region's excellent filming conditions.[19]

By the 1920s the international movie industry was concentrated in Hollywood, California. Most production was controlled by a few companies, such as Universal, Metro Goldwyn Mayer (MGM), First National, and Fox. In addition to film studios, these production companies also tended to own the theaters in which their movies were shown. Stars were signed to exclusive contracts to guarantee the studios profits on the films they showed at theaters they controlled. This combination allowed the studios to generate enormous profits, produce elaborate extravaganzas that no other nation's film companies could duplicate, and take control of the international movie industry. By the end of World War I, for example, American films were shown as much as 80 percent of the time on screens in other countries—particularly those that had not established quotas to protect their domestic film industries. By the 1930s Hollywood earned 35 percent of its income from the overseas distribution of its films—two-thirds of which came from Europe.[20] During this same period a commentator for the British newspaper the *Daily Express* bemoaned that British movie audiences "talk America, think America, and dream America. We have several million people, mostly women, who to all intent and purpose are temporary American citizens."[21] As early as the 1930s, then, American films were internationally pervasive.

The film industry underwent a major shift in financial structure in 1948, when the U.S. Supreme Court declared that the production companies' ownership of theaters constituted an unconstitutional restraint on trade—a monopoly. *United States v. Paramount Pictures,* known as the "Paramount case," led to a significant change in the way movies were produced and distributed—divorcement.[22] By removing a significant revenue stream—ticket sales—from the production companies' control, the Court changed the economic incentives the producers had to invest substantial sums of money in creating new films. Instead, they concentrated on producing likely hits—blockbusters and other movies expected to generate a profit. This opened an opportunity for the reemergence of independent film producers—people who would raise the money to create a movie on their own. The major production companies then entered into distribution relationships with the independent production companies; the major companies contributed some money, but not all, and took responsibility for marketing and distributing movies they did not actually make. Profits, if any, were shared according to the terms negotiated in the contract. In time, most films were created by independent producers and production companies in cooperation with the major film studios.[23]

One consequence of the rise of the independent film producers and production companies was the introduction of a degree of economic vulnerability in making and distributing movies. Independent companies were, as a rule, much smaller than the major studios they replaced in making films. Accordingly, independent producers were much more vulnerable to the vagaries of hits and misses in the film business than the major studios had been; a big hit could make an independent a major player in the movie industry, while a flop could destroy the company. Moreover, a hit could provide a company with the resources to buy another, weaker competitor, while a flop could make a company vulnerable to a takeover. Indeed, especially from the 1970s forward, there was a frenzy of buying and selling movie production companies, leaving a range of very small independent producers, but only a few major players in its wake—the situation described in the first section of this chapter.

In addition to these economic forces, an array of social pressures has shaped the modern film industry. The popularity of films has not always been seen as a good thing. From the earliest days of film, many people have strongly opposed popular movies on the grounds that they were culturally

Table 2.1   Global Film Production

Nation	Average Annual Film Production
India	800
United States	500
France	160
Hong Kong	120
Spain	85
Singapore*	4

Representative of multiple nations with minor film industries.

Sources: Adapted from Better Understand France and the French, "French Movies," www.under standfrance.org/France/FrenchMovies.html (accessed January 26, 2006); Yvonne Ng, "Singapore Cinema: In Search of Identity," *Kinema,* Spring 2001, www.kinema.uwaterloo.ca/yvo011.htm (accessed January 26, 2006); Neil Koch, "Hong Kong Movies FAQ," www.hkfilm.net/hkfilmfaq .htm#11 (accessed January 26, 2006); Jose Maria Alvarez Monzoncillo and Javier Lopez Villanueva, "The Film Industry in Spain," European Audiovisual Observatory, www.obs.coe.int/ oea_publ/eurocine/00001436.html (accessed January 26, 2006).

corruptive—dangerous to the moral order. For example, the *American* magazine worried, in 1909, that "four million people attend moving pictures theaters [*sic*], it is said, every day. . . . Almost 190 miles of film are unrolled on the screens of America's canned drama theaters every day in the year. Here is an industry to be controlled, an influence to be reckoned with." *Outlook*, in April 1916, insisted: "The version of life presented to him [the audience] in the majority of moving pictures is false in fact, sickly in sentiment, and utterly foreign to the Anglo-Saxon ideals of our nation." Similarly, in April 1929 *Commonweal* complained:

> And if the speech recorded in the dialogue (of talking pictures) is vulgar or ugly, its potentialities for lowering the speech standard of the country are almost incalculable. The fact that it is likely to be heard by the less discriminating portion of the public operates to increase its evil effects; for among the regular attendants at moving picture theaters there are to be found large groups from among our foreign-born population, to whom it is really vitally important that they hear only the best speech.[24]

As popular forms of entertainment and communication, movies faced criticism for failing to uphold high standards of conduct and values.

In response, efforts were made to censor and otherwise control the industry and its products. In 1930, in an effort to forestall externally imposed censorship, the major film producers, under the leadership of U.S. General Postmaster Will Hays, created a production code that remained in force, with declining levels of success, until 1968, when it was replaced with the ratings system still in effect in the United States today. The Production Code was intended to govern the behavioral and moral content of movies. Thus, for example, depictions of sexuality were to be limited, if allowed at all, and characters with "good" values were to be victorious over those who were "bad." In the end, the Production Code helped create the supposedly "American" movie. In shaping the audience's expectations, it pushed the studios to adopt particular formulas, which they then repeated again and again, all to the delight of that same audience.[25]

Another round of social pressure hit the movies in the late 1940s and early 1950s: McCarthyism and the Red Scare. In the context of the Cold War competition between the United States and the Soviet Union, Hollywood found itself on public trial to test its "American-ness." Actors, directors, writers, and others were called to testify before Congress—particularly to the evocatively named "House UnAmerican Activities Committee" (HUAC)—about whether they were, ever had been, or knew members of the Communist Party. Those who refused to testify, or who were identified as party members, found themselves blacklisted and denied the opportunity to earn a living. Others, like Screen Actor's Guild president Ronald Reagan, became political activists; Reagan joined the conservative wing of the Republican Party after testifying to Congress against many of his fellow actors and Hollywood professionals. (Reagan parlayed this experience into an active role in Senator Barry Goldwater's campaign for president in 1964, his own election as governor of California in 1966, and election and reelection as president of the United States in 1980 and 1984.) Hollywood got the message: its films espoused anticommunism throughout the 1950s.

In 1968, in the midst of changing social standards about sexuality, the proper roles for women and minorities in society, and other issues, the motion picture industry perceived it was likely to face another bout of social and political pressures to regulate its products. In response, the Motion Picture Association of America (MPAA) created a ratings system for the movies. This was intended to allow filmmakers to experiment with complicated adult themes while providing parents and community members with sufficient information to make informed choices about which films they and their children went to see. In effect, G and PG movies would tell safe, traditional "American" stories, while R-rated films might provide a zone of freedom for some topics and stories that might not otherwise be produced.[26] In time, a PG-13 rating was added for movies too violent or sexual for a simple PG label; likewise, an NC-17 rating was established for those films whose content was considered to be too adult for any children to attend at all. (PG-13 films are not supposed to cater to children younger than thirteen without a parent or guardian's permission; NC-17 films are not supposed to admit anyone under eighteen. The "XXX" rating of porno-graphic films is a marketing device for that industry, not an official MPAA rating.) This effort at self-regulation has been only moderately successful; as the need to develop the PG-13 and NC-17 ratings suggests, filmmakers have continued to stretch the limits of what is socially acceptable in the movies.

The Production Code, the reaction to the Red Scare in the 1950s, and the imposition of voluntary ratings in the 1960s were particularly impor-tant to the creation and sustenance of the "American" movie. In large mea-sure, the conventions and genres established in the early days of the movie industry can be seen to have survived the internationalization of the indus-try. The pressures of these events worked to sustain the "American" movie well beyond the time it was an exclusively American phenomenon. Thus even as foreign companies buy "American" production companies (conver-gence) they purchase the expertise and experience of filmmakers shaped by making American movies for a global audience. The effect of early U.S. dominance of the industry let it establish many of the conventions and genres in which movies are presented. It also meant that the labels on many, if not most, of the films distributed around the world are associated with the United States, not other countries. Regardless of how "American" a given film is, then, in terms of production, money, actors, plot, or audi-ence, it is often recognizably American in form and genre.

A Brief History of the Recording Industry

Like the movie industry, the recording industry has faced a series of technological, financial, and social pressures that have led to its contempo-rary form. Technologically, the recording industry is the product of Thomas Edison's invention of a "talking machine" in 1877. (It was Edison's patenting of this machine that brought him the funds to move into the film industry a few years later.) This device used wax cylinders as the recording medium. Speakers or musicians played or shouted into an acoustic horn that scratched marks into the cylinder that could later be sensed by a nee-dle and amplified through another acoustic horn into sounds loud enough to hear. Quality was poor.[27]

Phonographs began to be marketed to a mass audience in the 1890s. These early machines included the capacity for owners to record their own music or speech. Given the low quality of these recordings, however, a market quickly developed for prerecorded discs on which highly skilled performers largely overcame the limitations of the media and created im-pressive recordings. This preference was reinforced when, in the years prior to World War I, recording discs (as opposed to cylinders) were invented; while these could not be recorded on, they provided sound quality superior to that presented on cylinders. By 1919 almost two hundred companies were selling 2 million phonographs per year; total record sales in 1921 surged past 100 million.[28]

As quickly as the phenomenon of recorded music as mass entertainment rose, however, it very nearly collapsed just as fast. Two factors, the emergence of radio as a source of entertainment and the Great Depression, nearly destroyed the recording industry. (Radio would eventually reinvigorate record sales, as is discussed below.) Radio as a form of entertainment began to expand in 1922. As the year ended, there were 670 stations licensed by the federal government, and sales of radios and radio parts grew to $60 million. By 1924 such sales had expanded to $358 million. Importantly, a new style of entertainment came to dominate radio broadcasts: live performances, usually of comedy shows, soap operas, or mysteries/dramas. Recorded music had little, if any, role in the early days of radio. And once the Great Depression hit, and people had virtually no money to spend on entertainment niceties like recorded music, record sales collapsed. There were only 6 million record sales in 1932, for example, more than 94 million units below the peak sales of 1921. Indeed, the only bright spot for the recording industry lay in the emergence of a new technology—the jukebox. By 1939 there were 225,000 jukeboxes playing 13 million records; by 1942 that number had nearly doubled. Otherwise, radio—which was free for listeners because its programming was paid for by advertisers—had taken over the entertainment market in the United States.[29]

When television gained significance in the 1950s, radio rediscovered recorded music. Rather than offering general programming aimed at a large audience, radio stations began to specialize in particular forms of music, such as jazz, classical, or country. Of particular importance was the growth in popularity of rock and roll. Arriving at the same time as a large generation of teenagers known as the baby boomers, rock music linked radio and markets in new and immensely profitable ways. The industry took advantage of a new technology—the 45-rpm record that was smaller and more durable than older 78s—and aggressively marketed rock music to the baby boom generation. From 1955 to 1957, for example, record sales increased from $277 million to $460 million. This was then followed by the shift of rock music to LPs—long-play albums on which performers could explore musical complexities in rock and other genres and that could take advantage of the higher fidelity, stereo sound, and audio quality available on FM radio bands. As a consequence, the industry saw increasing sales (again). For example, the Beatles' album *Sgt. Pepper's Lonely*

Hearts Club Band (1967) sold 7 million copies in LP, an unheard-of number for rock music prior to that time.[30] Later developments, like the audio cassette and the compact disc, only added to total music sales—and profits.

In the 1990s and into the twenty-first century a fundamental challenge to the recording industry's control of its product emerged: MP3s and digital recording and copying technology. As the computer revolution advanced, computers became capable of copying and storing information held on CDs—including music and other recordings. With the spread of the Internet, these then became available for easy transportation around the globe, whether to be downloaded into private digital music players or into another person's computer. Significantly, this sharing could occur outside the recording industry's control—or profit. The long-term effects of this technology on the industry have yet to be determined, but the industry has taken it seriously enough to begin to prosecute those it believes have inappropriately stolen copyrighted material like music. Ironically, the rise of MP3s and digital technology has enhanced the industry's ability to have its product distributed around the world; however, lacking an economic incentive to allow this distribution for free on the Internet, the industry is trying to stop this change. Whether it will be successful remains to be seen.

In addition to these technological challenges, the recording industry has faced a number of economic challenges that have shaped it as well. Like films, recordings are the product of many individuals, ranging from performers to studio engineers to marketers to distributors to producers who raise the funds to pay for all these functions. Over time, the networks of people involved in making, marketing, and distributing have become increasingly complex. The first great period of recording industry consolidation came during the Great Depression, mirroring what occurred in the film industry during the era when recording companies were taken over by other entertainment companies. Thus, for example, RCA (Radio Corporation of America) took over Victor, a major producer of phonographs, in 1929. The ensuing corporation was known as RCA-Victor. Another record company, Brunswick, saw its phonograph and record division taken over by Warner Brothers, one of the dominant movie production companies, in 1930. And in 1938, the Columbia Broadcasting Service (CBS) bought Columbia Records.[31]

As happened with the film industry, as various producers succeeded or failed in the marketplace, music production was consolidated in a relatively small number of studios—particularly those listed earlier in this chapter. Thus as independent producers created and marketed new sounds lacking a proven market record (e.g., rock and roll or rap), established labels either purchased the upstart labels or started their own in competition for the entertainment dollars.[32] Media convergence proceeded apace.

An additional pressure led to the consolidation of the music business: the complexities of marketing music for sale, whether in the United States or internationally. In the 1930s and 1940s, making and distributing a recording was relatively simple: manufacturers contracted with distributors to place their products in retail venues, where they could be purchased by consumers. The invention of the jukebox, however, complicated this simple process: in addition to dealing with distributors to retail outlets, record companies also had to integrate subdistributors who worked to place and maintain (and record the number of times a song was played on) jukeboxes in thousands of venues across the United States. Then, shortly after jukeboxes were integrated into record distribution, record clubs were created to market records directly to consumers through the mail (in the late 1950s). Another layer of complexity was thus added to the making and marketing of recordings. Each new marketing strategy brought new challenges, making it increasingly hard for those who created records to control their marketing and distribution. Chain record stores (e.g., Tower Records, Sam Goody) demanded special pricing deals with recording studios to account for their volume of sales; video companies needed to be formed (or contracted) to produce, market, and distribute music videos; and the expansion in the number and sophistication of dance clubs—many of which played music videos as well as music—created new demands for record industry action.[33] Thus, as was the case with the film industry, this complexity and sophistication promoted the creation of large businesses to support its operations, rather than local control. Large business dominance of the music industry was never complete, but it was substantial both in the United States and throughout the rest of the world from an early date.[34]

In addition to these financial concerns, the recording industry has, like the film industry, faced an array of social pressures that have shaped its character. As music evolved in the early twentieth century, for example, it developed the fast rhythms of Dixieland and the innovative harmonies of jazz. In response, people began dancing differently; gone were the formal patterns and prescribed movements of ballroom dancing. In their place rose free-form dancing, often at a fast pace and mimicking, in various degrees of specificity, sexual contact. Persons of conventional morality were shocked, seeing in this new explicit music and dancing the corruption of Western civilization. Accordingly, they pressured music companies and radio stations to censor or otherwise control the suggestiveness of "new" music. In one particularly humorous example, the Cole Porter song "Let's Put Out the Lights and Go to Bed" was renamed "Let's Put Out the Lights and Go to Sleep" before being aired on radio.[35] Songs like Billie Holiday's "Love for Sale" would later be banned altogether for its allusions to prostitution.

Notably, and quite different from the film industry, music producers and distributors have also faced indirect regulatory pressure from the U.S. government. This is the result of the fact that radio (and, as will be discussed, broadcast television) is regulated by the federal government through the auspices of the Federal Communications Commission (FCC). On the principle that the airwaves are public property (a movie camera or set is not available to all people all the time, for example, but air waves are there for anyone who has the technology to harness their use), the federal government licenses the use of specific frequencies to radio station owners. In other words, a radio station owner gets a license from the federal government to broadcast on a specific radio band. Only the licensed radio station is allowed to broadcast on that frequency in a given area known as a "market." The license also regulates how powerful the radio station may be, thus limiting its effective range and allowing the same frequency to be used in neighboring markets. In exchange for the exclusive right to use a specific frequency—which the federal government enforces by seeking out and penalizing any broadcasters who fail to get a license or broadcast without a license—the station owners must agree to a series of limitations on their freedom to do business. While these limits have varied over time, they have included the number of stations one individual or company is allowed to own and a requirement that a certain amount of programming serve the public interest (such as news or participation in emergency broadcasts in times of war or other crisis). Of particular importance are regulations governing the moral content of a station's broadcasts: the federal government insists—at the penalty of losing one's license or, at a minimum, serious fines—that broadcasters must uphold high moral standards in their programming. Offensive language and controversial speech were thus effectively banned for much of the history of radio—which, since music companies needed their products played on radio to expand their markets, worked to limit how scandalous most music might become. And since many of the radio stations on which the music was being played were themselves owned by or a member of a network owned by one of the giant media conglomerates (synergy), concentration of ownership was reinforced.

These government-based limits were not absolute, however, since music sold directly to the consumer was not subject to FCC regulation. The rock-and-roll explosion in the 1950s and the subsequent music movements of the 1960s offered a strong challenge to the limitations embedded in FCC rules—especially once producers discovered that sexually explicit music and music about drugs sold well. FM radio, in particular, also provided an avenue for more "adult," or "blue," music. As a consequence, more and more performers offered more adult, challenging, and even offensive lyrics, ranging from 1970s hits like Blue Oyster Cult's "Don't Fear the Reaper" (a song commending the virtues of suicide) to Madonna's 1980s classic "Like a Virgin," which most decidedly does not applaud the virtue of virginity. Such challenges to conventional morality only increased as the music industry fragmented and differentiated into new genres like hip-hop, rap, and Latin music. A significant gap often emerged between what one might hear on cleaned-up or obscured versions of songs on the radio and what was actually on a given album.

It was in response to discovering the gap between what was expected, based on radio play, and what the actual content of an album was that Tipper Gore, wife of then-U.S. senator (D-Tenn.) and later U.S. vice president Al Gore, took action that led to the most significant contemporary attempt to regulate the content of music in the United States. Tipper Gore and a number of allies formed the Parent's Music Resource Center (PMRC) to lobby Congress to find that offensive music was pornographic and should be restricted, at least in sales to children. They claimed that violent, sexually explicit music contributed to the decline of the American family and the moral decay of society in general. To support their contention, in 1985 they issued a list they called the "Filthy Fifteen" that included songs like Sheena Easton's "Sugar Walls" and Twisted Sister's "We're Not Gonna Take It," which the PMRC claimed were harmful due to their explicit references to sex and violence.[36]

Rather than face congressional sanction, the major record companies adopted a voluntary labeling system in which they placed stickers on albums that contained offensive material. The idea was to forestall regulation by providing parents with important information they could use to exercise informed control over what their children listened to. Subsequently, Wal-Mart announced it would not carry any albums deemed offensive; this led many major producers to create two versions of their products—one for Wal-Mart, and the one the performer actually intended to create.

Cumulatively, the technical, economic, and social forces that shaped the development of the American music industry encouraged its consolidation with other music houses, as well as with movie and television production studios. The major producers had advantages of fiscal and technical resources and expertise, marketing skill, licensing agreements, and royalty management that allowed them to survive when minor producers could easily fail. The end result was the dominance of American music producers, and American musical forms, in international musical production and distribution.

A Brief History of the Television Industry

As was the case with both the film and music industries, television has been affected by a series of technological, fiscal, and social developments that have shaped its contemporary role in global entertainment—and linked it to the audiovisual media powerhouses discussed in the first section of this chapter. Television is the most recent of the technologies discussed in this book. Television signals, like radio, operate on radio frequencies. Television grew as an entertainment medium only when the technologies necessary to send pictures in radio waves and to receive and interpret those signals and convert them into visual images were invented in the 1930s. The first broadcasts began in 1939, and by 1940 there were twenty-three television stations broadcasting to approximately 10,000 television sets around the world—mostly in New York and London. These broadcasts were quite primitive, and as a practical matter television was put on hold during World War II. The postwar economic boom in the United States, however, led to the dramatic expansion of the American middle class. This expanded class demanded new forms of entertainment. Television fit the bill, and the number of television sets in the United States grew over 700 percent in just the years 1951–1953.[37]

Early television programming borrowed from radio the practice of having performers present live on stage. In many cases, radio hits simply transferred to television; in others, the format crossed over. Accordingly, television was filled with soap operas, quiz shows, talk shows, and variety performance shows. New programming was offered every week, almost all of it live.[38]

These early broadcasts were usually local. The capacity to offer coast-to-coast broadcasts only developed in 1957. If producers wanted to distribute a program across the nation, they had to film the program as it was displayed on television and then distribute the resulting kinescopes to other stations for presentation. Given the poor quality of the original television signal, and the mediocre quality of the set receiving and displaying the picture, the kinescopic copy was inevitably quite poor. Only the invention of videotape, in 1956, made it possible for distribution of quality programming across the nation: videotape could capture action as it was being performed and then could easily be edited into a final product without first being shown on a television screen. The resulting quality was much higher than that of kinescopic technology had been, promoting shared programming across networks of television stations.[39]

The 1970s, 1980s, and 1990s each saw significant technological breakthroughs in the way television was broadcast, experienced, and evaluated. Cable television was the first of these developments. Cable television led to a dramatic change in the way many Americans experienced television; rather than receiving a signal through the air, the television signal was literally piped directly into a set from a central distribution point through a long wire. There were several advantages to this technology that led to its rapid expansion in the United States, particularly in urban and suburban markets, where there was sufficient population to make profitable the distributor's investment in laying cable, purchasing programming, and sending it direct to viewer's homes. For example, cable signals did not suffer the kinds of quality degradation that broadcast signals did; sunspots, storms, and distance from the station did not cause major signal problems in cable transmissions. Likewise, the advent of cable programming offered new opportunities to create and distribute programming independent of the major television networks; as a consequence, new niche programming networks like Home Box Office (HBO, movies) and ESPN (sports programming) found a spot in American homes. Cable television quickly expanded into American homes, bringing with it a profusion of programming above and beyond that which was available on the traditional networks.

The rise of cable television was followed by the invention and widespread adoption of two technologies that would change the way people used television quite dramatically: the videocassette recorder (VCR) and the remote control. The VCR made it possible for people to tape programs and watch them at their convenience. (It also made it possible for people to fast-forward past commercials, an issue addressed below.) Moreover, both VCRs and most cable systems came with remote controls, which enabled viewers to change channels or program with no more effort that the energy associated with the flick of a thumb. Gone were the days when changing channels meant getting up and walking across the room, probably including the need to adjust the "rabbit ear" aerial antenna through which broadcast signals were brought into the television receiver. As a consequence of high-quality cable programming, a profusion of programming alternatives (both cabled in and recorded on VCR tapes), and a small amount of effort, it became easy to "surf" an array of entertainment choices. Viewers were no longer at the mercy of the broadcast networks for either their programming or their schedule. Television became a servant of the consumer, rather than the opposite.

The 1990s saw the widespread adoption of satellite programming services across the globe. While satellite broadcasting of television began in the 1970s, the early technology was awkward to use: it required the installation of a large, unsightly dish in a householder's yard through which satellite signals were collected and transmitted to a converter attached to the family's television. By the 1990s, however, the technology evolved, and dish sizes became small. Satellites dedicated to providing programming to these small dishes were launched. Notably, these satellites were capable of carrying even more signals than could be piped through a cable wired directly into a house. As a consequence, the satellite companies led a push for even more programming to be made available—multiple movie channels, music channels, and even dedicated sports channels for golf or tennis. Niche programming and fragmentation as a consequence of technological capacity and consumer demand describes the contemporary television environment.

In addition to these technological developments, television has faced a series of financial pressures that have shaped its current form. In order to understand the nature and shape of these pressures, it is necessary to link the history of television to the history of radio, from which most of the television industry's business practices evolved. When radio stations were first being established across the United States, it was relatively common for a single corporation to own many stations nationwide. This practice derived from the synergy of company wealth, the start-up costs of radio stations, and the ability of entertainment companies to create and deliver products on stations they owned. A prime example of this was RCA, which owned two chains of radio stations, including more than one station in each of the major media markets in the United States. Notably, in the 1940s these single owner networks were broken up by an order from the Federal Communication Commission (FCC) and a Supreme Court ruling that no one owner should hold more than a few radio stations across the country, and no more than one in a single market.[40]

A crucial component of the radio chains, whether owned by a single corporation or stood as independent units, was the radio network. A network is a contractual affiliation between a series of radio stations and a production company to present the production company's programming on the contracted stations. Radio networks share programming produced by a central production company such as the Columbia Broadcasting Company (CBS), the National Broadcasting Company (NBC), or the American Broadcasting Company (ABC). (The two chains of radio stations owned by RCA were affiliated with NBC, for example.) Thus even many independently owned stations receive much of their programming from the same production company. Rather than having to generate their own programming, then, radio stations broadcast programs produced elsewhere.

In order to make this contractual relationship work, early American radio executives developed an innovative scheme to finance their operations. Unlike movie theaters, where patrons pay an entry fee to see the film, radio is broadcast free on the public airwaves. It can be picked up by anyone with the appropriate device. The innovative financing scheme hit on by the early radio pioneers was to have advertisers pay for the programs, which would then be presented to the public for free. It would be as if you could get your groceries for free simply for watching a series of advertisements in the grocery store: the purpose of the radio program was to deliver an audience to an advertiser. The higher the number of listeners, the greater the fee the stations could charge for advertising time. Profit was generated from advertisers rather than from patrons.

In exchange for free programming from the network producer, local, or chain radio stations had to allow the central network to control a certain amount of advertising time on the local station. Put another way, if the radio station anticipated selling fifteen minutes of advertising in a given hour, it might be forced to cede five minutes of that fifteen-minute total to the network. The network, rather than the local station, earned the profit from the five minutes of advertising it booked; the local station earned revenues from the remaining ten. The local station thus forewent some of its potential earned revenue (from the five minutes of advertising time it ceded to the network) in order to avoid the substantial costs associated with creating radio programming. By 1945, even though most were independently owned, 95 percent of radio stations in the United States were affiliated with a broadcast network.[41]

As television expanded it adopted the basic business practices of radio, including the use of networks to produce programming. Television stations were independently owned and operated, but received at least half of their programming from central production companies organized as CBS, NBC, and ABC (among others). (Other programming was actually purchased by advertisers and provided to stations independent of the networks; thus networks and advertisers cooperated in some venues and competed in others to control television programs.)[42] In either case, programming was provided to consumers free of charge (for the most part) in exchange for the network receiving the right to sell advertising on the local station, or for the advertiser's exclusive right to have their name and product embedded in the show.

Over time, the costs of producing television programs grew as casts, plots, sets and special effects became more complex. As the price of making television shows grew, the prospects of being supported by an individual sponsor diminished. In turn, the significance of network production of television programming increased. Only the networks had the array of marketers, advertising executives, promoters, developers, directors, actors, writers, and other parts of the television production process to make the production of television programming economically viable. Accordingly, only they had the economies of scale and expertise to continue producing television programs. As a consequence, the networks largely replaced the advertisers as direct developers of programming in the 1960s.[43]

A further change in the economics of television began to take shape starting in 1954, when the television networks made deals with movie companies to present films on television. These filmed products were very popular, and as was discussed earlier, Hollywood already had a large stockpile of writers, directors, film equipment and professionals, actors, extras, and good weather for producing films. Once videotape was invented, it became easy to provide pretaped, rather than live, programming to the members of a television network. As a consequence, the production of many television shows shifted to independent producers in Hollywood just as the production of movies had; in fact, in many cases the same producers might be involved in making a television drama and a movie blockbuster. Networks largely stopped producing material themselves and instead focused on purchasing the rights to products others created and then marketing these in a schedule distributed out to their network-affiliated stations. Thus it is common today for a producer to sell programs to several different networks, which in turn distribute the programs they choose to purchase to their stations. As a consequence, a "network" show can suddenly reappear on another network if a competing network purchases the rights to the program.

Between 1957 (the start of true coast-to-coast network broadcasts) and the 1970s, the television industry was dominated by three major networks that broadcast (usually) pretaped programs (news and sporting events were often, although not necessarily, shown live) through their affiliated television stations: ABC, CBS, and NBC. In the 1990s, Fox Television began a broadcast network. Independent stations existed, usually in local areas, and the Public Broadcasting System (PBS) was created by congressional mandate to provide kinds of programming, unaffected by the need to sell commercial time, that was unavailable through mainstream networks. The broadcast networks were dominant, however—a position they would retain so long as television signals were received at home over the airwaves.

Just as cable and satellite television changed the technical environment of the television industry, they also changed its business context. Starting in the 1970s, cable, and then satellite, companies found a market in collecting the broadcast signals of the networks (and other stations) and sending them packaged together directly into individual homes. (Cable and satellite companies pay fees for the right to transmit these accumulated signals.) While these companies generated the bulk of their revenues from subscriber fees, they, too, had incentives to require advertising time on broadcasters' programs: in advertising their products the cable and satellite companies earned additional revenue; broadcasters agreed to this exchange as part of the incentive package by which the broadcaster got the cable or satellite company to add their particular channel to the cable or satellite offerings. As a consequence, cable (and later satellite) companies became competitors for advertising dollars. This competition was particularly intense as the number of channels and networks increased: new networks were forced to compete for space on cable or satellite bandwidth, encouraging them to exchange favorable subscription and advertising rates to the cable and satellite companies. Network, broadcast television was forced to compete for revenues in ways it never had before.

Along with increased competition for revenues came reduced viewership for broadcast television. A combination of the enhanced signal clarity of cable and satellite signals and the multiplication of niche channels that followed the increased transmission capacity of these new technologies drew viewers away from traditional, broadcast networks and towards cable and satellite programming. Movie, sports, news, and other specialty channels drew increasing shares of the viewing audience. In many cases, these niche channels provided superior service to the traditional broadcasters: at the start of the first Iraq war, 1990–1991, for example, the only network with reporters still in Baghdad was the Cable News Network (CNN). By the end of the war, CNN was America's most watched news network. Indeed, in time even traditionally broadcast television would be viewed by most consumers only after it had been collected and retransmitted as part of a cable or satellite package. By 2000, viewership of the traditional networks had declined precipitously even as the distinction between "broadcast" and "other" television had substantially blurred.

A further set of reforms, in 1996, augmented the position of telecommunications companies in the television business. Prior to 1996, telephone companies, which, like cable companies, had strung millions of miles of wires from central locations to consumers' homes, had been barred from providing television services to those same customers. The 1996 Telecommunications Act lifted this ban, making it legal for telecommunications companies like AT&T to purchase cable or program production operations.[44]

Ironically, the rise of alternatives to broadcast television—satellite, cable, and the like—has actually encouraged media consolidation. As the number of channels has proliferated, the margin of profit per channel has grown quite thin. As was the case with the movie and music industries, it was only the major producers who had sufficient resources and talents for marketing and synergy that could increase the chances for a profit in any individual channel or program. Accordingly, a combination of technical and economic forces encouraged the merger process that led to the contemporary business context of popular culture addressed earlier in this chapter.

Like movies and music before it, the television industry has also found itself under repeated attack as a force for social evil and moral chaos. As early as 1949, for example, the *Saturday Review* worried,

> Here, in concept at least, was the most magnificent of all forms of communication. Here was the supreme triumph of invention, the dream of the ages—something that could bring directly into the home a moving image fused with sound—reproducing action, language, and thought without the loss of measurable time. Here was the magic eye that could bring the wonders of entertainment, information and education in to the living room. Here was a tool for the making of a more enlightened democracy than the world had ever seen. Yet out of the wizardry of the television tube has come such an assault against the human mind, such a mobilized attack on the imagination, such an invasion against good taste as no other communications medium has known, not excepting the motion picture or radio itself.

Similarly, just five years later (1954) the *New Republic* opined:

> Seeing constant brutality, viciousness and unsocial acts results in hardness, intense selfishness, even in mercilessness, proportionate to the amount of exposure and its play on the native temperament of the child. Some cease to show resentment to insults, to indignities, and even cruelty toward helpless old people, to women and other children.[45]

Notably, these attacks occurred despite the fact that, like radio, television broadcasting was regulated by the FCC—and for the same reasons (e.g., public ownership of the airwaves, monopoly licensing in exchange for protection of markets, and the like). Indeed, as was the case for radio, the FCC announced decency standards for television programming similar to those embedded in the Hays Code for movies: sexual conduct was to be avoided; individuals were to behave with decency and dignity or, if they did not, were to be the "bad guy" of the story; bad language was not to be used. Accordingly, when the top-rated *I Love Lucy* showed star Lucille Ball's bedroom in one episode (itself a fairly shocking event at the time), it showed the room containing only twin beds placed several feet apart despite the fact that Ball was actually pregnant, her pregnancy was written into the show, and her real-life husband, Desi Arnaz, was her on-screen husband and the program's co-star as well. Likewise, other popular shows of the era, like *Father Knows Best* and *Leave It to Beaver*, reinforced conventional morality as delimited in FCC regulations.

Social changes in the 1950s and 1960s challenged conventional morality, particularly when it became clear that "new" ideas, behaviors, and values were big audience draws. Rock music, in particular, pressured television executives to stretch the boundaries of social acceptability to present dynamic performers who brought huge ratings. For example, *American Bandstand* presented popular musicians and bands live on stage as teenagers danced, often provocatively by the standards of the time, and Ed Sullivan, a host of a variety show, allowed Elvis Presley to perform—but only televised his performance from the waist up as Presley's gyrating hips were perceived to be too sexually suggestive for the television audience. Over time, a distinction emerged between programming aimed at adults— generally to be broadcast after 9 pm eastern time—and children's programming, which might occur earlier in the day. Later programs were allowed to be more sexually explicit and adult-themed, although outright nudity was still banned. Likewise, language limitations were loosened, leading one comedian, George Carlin, to offer a routine called "The Seven Dirty Words You Can't Say on TV" lifted directly from the FCC's banned list.

Notably, as the cable and satellite industries expanded they were effectively unregulated for content. Like a record that a consumer purchases and then brings home, cable and satellite programming are not as effectively regulated as broadcast programming is: it is brought directly into the home by the consumer—who can, if he or she wishes, simply turn the service off if the images or programming is offensive. This is different from broadcast television, which is available for anyone with a TV. The distance between what the FCC can regulate and how most people receive their television programming explains why some satellite and cable companies offer pornographic or extremely violent programs through their services: the FCC lacks significant authority to prevent such programs from being distributed through cable or satellite broadcasts.

There has been a recent turn towards FCC enforcement of morals regulations on broadcast television and radio, however. This resulted from an incident at the Super Bowl on February 1, 2004, in which Justin Timberlake, a pop singer, removed a patch that was covering pop singer Janet

Jackson's right breast during the halftime show. This event, which was quite mild compared with much of the programming available even on broadcast television in the later evening, much less on cable or satellite networks, nonetheless caused a substantial outcry from many people across the United States. As a consequence, the FCC launched an investigation of the incident and leveled a total of $550,000 in fines on CBS for the violation. (The maximum indecency penalty the FCC can assess is $27,500; CBS' parent company, Viacom, owns twenty television stations nationwide; $27,500 × 20 = $550,000. Notably, the FCC did not fine CBS's affiliate stations, which number more than two hundred.)[46] The FCC then turned its attention to radio broadcasts: a number of network programs, including several by nationally prominent radio star Howard Stern, were noted for their apparent obscenity and fined.[47]

Little in the way of FCC enforcement seems likely to change the basic dynamic of media consolidation in the movie, music, and television industry, however. Indeed, in passing the 1996 Telecommunications Act, Congress intensified, rather than limited, corporate convergence in the audiovisual entertainment industry. In addition, as is shown in the next section of this chapter, the economic, technical, and social pressures on the production of movies and music and television described above both served to give American programming the opportunity to create the dominant genres of much of the world's trade in pop culture and to build transnational corporations that could leverage their resources into dominance of world trade in popular culture.

Movies, Music, and Television from the USA to the World

Just how pervasive is American popular culture in the world entertainment market? There are many ways to assess the relative dominance of the products of American popular culture in world entertainment. This section offers an analysis of the pre-eminence of American movies, music, and television programming in global popular culture. It also notes the areas and genres in which American popular culture has been unable to gain a market foothold.

To take films as an example, there are a number of ways to illustrate the dominance of American movies in the world market. However, it is important to note that as a result of the hybrid way in which films are produced today (discussed earlier in this chapter), with independent producers seeking studio financing as well as lower costs by searching for international actors, venues, and markets for their films, it is rare that a movie will be "purely" American. American-born actors might be filmed in

Canada, for example, or international actors might be used in a film financed by an American studio. Thus assessing what is or is not an "American" movie is a judgment call; here, several criteria are used: the nature of the financing, the locale in which the film was set, the nationalities of the central actors (and, where evident, the nationalities of the characters the actors were portraying), and the type of movie it is (e.g., film noir, big budget blockbuster, and so on). It is therefore possible for the director and actors of a given movie to be international but the movie to be American in type and financing; such hybridity is, today, the norm rather than the exception.

As of the end of 2004, most of the top grossing films of all time, worldwide, were either made by American or American-based studios, starred Americans, had themes and values recognizably in line with American public culture, or were set in a locale definably American. The list includes the all-time top grossing film, *Titanic*, with worldwide ticket sales at $1,835,300,000, *Jurassic Park*, *Independence Day*, *Star Wars* (three of the then five parts), *The Lion King*, and *Forrest Gump*. The only movie in the top twenty-five clearly *not* "American" was the Australian American movie star Mel Gibson's independently produced and released *The Passion of the Christ*. Likewise, the hybrid cast, financing, and themes of the *Lord of the Rings* series (all three parts) and the *Harry Potter* movies (two of which were in the top twenty-five as of 2004) might or might not be seen as "American"; these films follow the conventions of the blockbuster movie laid down by American studios and American financing but their plots and casts are international. Even removing the *Rings* movies and the *Potter* movies from consideration, however, means that nineteen of the top twenty-five grossing movies in history were definably "American"—or 76 percent. As of the end of 2005, an additional *Harry Potter* movie had moved into the top twenty-five while *The Matrix* fell out; this change left eighteen of the top twenty-five movies of all time, or 72 percent, as inarguably American.[48]

In addition, the flow of money in the world entertainment market has increasingly favored American films in recent years. For example, American films took 85 percent of European film revenues in the early 1990s, grossing $1.7 billion of total film receipts of $2 billion. This dominance occurred despite the fact that France alone produced an average of 150 movies per year during the same period—suggesting that American movies were vastly more popular than their local counterparts. Indeed, by the early 1990s almost 60 percent of French spending on movies was for attendance at American films. For example, when the American megahit *Jurassic Park* opened, it occupied fully one-quarter of all movie screens in

France. Likewise, in Germany, American movies grew from one-third of the market to two-thirds of the market between 1972 and 1991. By the end of this time frame, American movies controlled more than 80 percent of the European market collectively. In return, European movies accounted for less than 2 percent of American ticket sales.[49] Thus, even in competition with European films in the European market, American movies expanded in importance throughout the post-WWII era.

Looked at from another perspective, American films can be seen to dominate a surprising array of nations' moviegoing. Benjamin Barber, in a survey of twenty-two countries' movie watching in 1991, found that either *Dances with Wolves* or *Terminator 2* was the top-grossing movie in fifteen of a group of countries ranging from Argentina to Austria, Brazil, Chile, Egypt, Hungary, Malaysia, and Poland. Of the remaining seven countries, an alternate American film was the top grosser in five. Only Italy and Finland had a non-American movie win the box office title; in each case, an American film was second. Similarly, 63 percent of all imported films in India were imported from the United States. Even Iran, which censored most foreign films as antirevolutionary, admitted *Dances with Wolves* and *Driving Miss Daisy*. Each found substantial audiences.[50]

As might be expected, given the dominance of American movies in the international market, U.S. films are also dominant in the post-theater market in the form of DVDs and videotape. The top-selling DVDs of all time, for example, are *Finding Nemo* and *Shrek 2*, while the top-selling DVDs of 2004 were largely American products: *Shrek 2*, the *Star Wars* trilogy, *Spider-Man 2*, *The Day After Tomorrow*, *Elf*, *Brother Bear*, and *American Wedding*. (As was the case with the top twenty-five all-time list, the only exception to this rule was Mel Gibson's *The Passion of the Christ*; *The Lord of the Rings: The Return of the King* and *Harry Potter and the Prisoner of Azkaban* were hybrid movies on the list as well.)[51] This list was generally mirrored by an accounting of the thirty top-selling DVDs of all time in Australia: *Finding Nemo* was first, followed by two of the three *Lord of the Rings* movies, *Shrek*, *Shrek 2*, and an array of American movies.[52]

It is important to contextualize the nature of American movie dominance lest it appear that everyone everywhere is only attending movies starring Americans or based in the United States. In particular, the most popular American movie exports have tended to be action adventure films and dramas—precisely the kind of blockbusters intended by their creators to generate vast profits at the box office and in DVD or video sales. These, in turn, rest on formulas designed by Hollywood producers to match the desire of most Americans for entertainment despite the fact that, as a whole, Americans come from so many cultural and social backgrounds that producers cannot assume the audience has similar educations, values, knowledge, or opinions. In this context, movie producers create films that appeal across class, culture, and ethnicity to the fullest extent possible by adopting simple, good versus bad plots usually filled with beautiful people in beautiful places who are in constant action to create happy endings against difficult (but never impossible) odds. These factors, linked to mythic stories and archetypal characters played again and again in different stories and exploiting the wizardry of contemporary special effects, work to create a product—a film—that, done well, is virtually universal in appeal. Notably, this appeal transcends the borders of the United States: the technical wizardry and mythical context of the *Star Wars* movies, for example, makes as much sense in Asia at it does in Iowa. Accordingly, given the historical dominance of U.S. filmmakers in world cinema, American action adventure movies are globally appealing almost as a consequence of being made for an American audience alone. Dramas, too, can have broad reach, but it is usually not quite as extensive as that of action adventure movies.[53]

By contrast, American comedies tend not to do as well in international markets. Films aimed at children are also generally less successful in global commerce.[54] A glance at the top twenty-five grossing movies of all time confirms this assessment: only the *Shrek* movies, *The Incredibles,* and *Finding Nemo* make the list as children's movies—and each has enjoyable content for adults. No non-animated comedies are on the list.[55] As a practical matter, comedy, as well as standards for appropriate entertainment of children, are highly culture bound: comedy relies on shared knowledge, assumptions, and conventions that the comedian makes fun of, for example; while how we ought to entertain our children, and with what content, is a highly variable and contentious issue within the United States itself, much less across the world. Unlike action adventure movies, which easily cross internal and external cultural boundaries, then, comedies and children's entertainment are less global. Accordingly, as is discussed later in this chapter, it is through action adventure and similar movies that the international film-going audience experiences American popular culture.

Music, too, has been an area of U.S. dominance of world markets, although American pre-eminence has not been absolute. As was the case with American movies, there are a number of ways to assess the pre-eminence of American music in world entertainment. Of the top twenty-five selling artists of all time (as of December 2001), for example, eighteen were American—ranging from the top American (third overall), Garth Brooks, with 104 million album sales, to Elvis Presley (86.5 million), the Eagles (83.5 million), Madonna (59 million), Michael Jackson (58 million) to, perhaps surprisingly, Kenny G, with 45.5 million album sales. Only the Beatles (number one with 164.5 million sales), Led Zeppelin (number two; 105 million), Pink Floyd (number seven; 73.5 million); Elton John (number nine; 64.5 million), AC/DC (number ten; 63 million), the Rolling Stones (at number fifteen with 53.5 million) and U2 (number twenty-five; 45 million) broke the American stranglehold on the top twenty-five list.[56] Notably, each of these non-American groups made their fortunes playing American music—rock and roll. Accordingly, the distinction between "American" and "non-American" may be fairly artificial in this context. The American musical style of rock and roll is clearly the most successfully marketed music format in the world.

A review of the top-selling albums of all time confirms this view of the dominance of American music. Of the twenty-four albums that have had at least 15 million in worldwide sales, thirteen were the product of undeniably American acts: the Eagles' *Their Greatest Hits* (28 million) is the number-one selling album of all time, while Michael Jackson's *Thriller* is number two with 26 million sales. Other American groups on the list include Billy Joel, Fleetwood Mac, Boston, Hootie and the Blowfish, Garth Brooks, and Guns n' Roses. As was the case with the top-selling groups of all time, the top-selling non-American albums were made in genres created by Americans: rock (Pink Floyd's *The Wall*; Led Zeppelin's *Led Zeppelin IV*; the Beatles' *The Beatles*) and country (Canadian Shania Twain's *Come on Over*).[57]

Of course, not all music is produced in the United States. Other nations and cultures have distinct musical forms. However, the fact that not all music is produced in the United States by Americans for the world market is important here only to the degree that it contextualizes the scope of American dominance of the global music industry. American pre-eminence is substantial, not total—particularly focused in the rock and country genres. Accordingly, it is to rock and country, and to a lesser extent rap, that one's attention should be turned to assess the way(s) people around the world are attracted, repelled, lured, and horrified by the appearance of contemporary globalization as expressed by the United States. In other words, it is in American rock, country, and rap that American music expresses its values, worldview, and desires to a global audience. It is through these genres that any assessment of the fragmegrationist effects of American music must be framed.

The dominance of American rock, country, and rap is perhaps most evident in the direct tie-in between music and television created in 1981 with the formation of the cable network MTV, Music Tele(V)ision. In their endless search for venues in which to promote their products, music companies, and artists hit upon the idea of filming videos to accompany the songs that were playing on the radio. These videos were, in effect, mini-movies, and took advantage of the synergy of media consolidation to link television and film directors with musical groups to create visually exciting accompaniments to particular songs. In addition, the videos served as advertisements for the songs and albums—just as radio play had been invented to encourage people to purchase the singles and albums from which the songs were drawn. In effect, watching a music video is watching a commercial. The genius of MTV—which is owned by media giant Viacom—is that having watched commercials for songs, artists, and albums (the videos, which music companies paid MTV to show in the first place), viewers would then watch formal, traditional commercials for which the network would be paid just like every other network. This was a money-making breakthrough: everything, whether commercial or video, was paying MTV a fee for airtime.

An idea this profitable was sure to spread, and spread it did. Just ten years after its creation MTV was available in 201 million households in seventy-seven countries ranging from Australia to Brazil to Hong Kong. MTV Europe grew from 3 million households in 1988 to 14 million in 1991 and then 37 million in 1992.[58] By 1995 almost every country in the world (barring most of Africa and a few countries in South America, along with a scattering of nations elsewhere) had MTV or indigenous, but essentially duplicative, music television networks.[59] While the network adapted its playlist to local tastes and preferences, it concurrently provided a platform on which American music was linked to global television across the world. It was thus positioned to play a central role in the fragmegration process of contemporary globalization.

American programming was similarly pre-eminent on non-music television screens around the world. For example, for every dollar spent internationally on purchasing television programming, 75 cents goes to U.S. companies. The bulk of these 75 cents goes to the motion picture and television production studios that, as was described earlier, dominate the production of television programming. In fact way, these studios generate at least 25 percent of their revenues from international programming.[60]

Much of this imported programming has been feature films intended for broadcast on television. One study of European television, for example, showed that 80 percent of program imports were feature films; of these 53 percent were American. The percentage of American movies shown on European television screens grew from 46 percent to 53 percent between 1988 and 1991. In Norway, 100 percent of films showed on the commercial television station TV Norge during these years were American in origin;

Sweden's TV3 broadcast American movies 81 percent of the time. Commercial television stations in France and Italy likewise broadcast American movies at least 73 percent of the time in the same period. Meanwhile, the percentage of domestic movies shown on these same stations in the period declined approximately 10 percent.[61]

Television series have been another area in which American programs have been successfully marketed globally. In Europe, only the United Kingdom produces a majority of its own programming; in general, 83 percent of television series shown in Europe were from elsewhere—particularly the United States and Australia. Commercial television stations in West Germany from 1988 to 1991, for example, showed imported television series 99 percent of the time; in other European countries, even non-English speaking ones, American and Australian programming was similarly popular. Between 1988 and 1991, imports of American television series grew from 36 percent to 56 percent of total programming, while domestically produced European series declined from 37 percent to 16 percent.[62]

One particularly popular American television genre that, as one commentator explains, has "been seen across the globe wherever a TV set is to be found," is the soap opera. With their high production values, pleasant visual settings (often involving people and places of great wealth and privilege), fast pace, use of conventional narratives already well established in the audience's minds through Hollywood movies (good versus evil, etc.), and melodramatic style, soap operas are able to overcome what Barker refers to as the "cultural discount" of a foreign program: the preference peo-

Table 2.2   Fictional Television Program Production in Europe

Country	Hours of Fiction Produced, 1996
Germany	1,689
United Kingdom	1,058
France	690
Spain	459
Italy	221
Other	93
Total:	4,210*

Source: Adapted from European Audiovisual Observatory, "Germany Leads European Production of TV Fiction," May 25, 1997, www.obs.coe.int/about/oea/pr/00001138.html (accessed January 20, 2006).

*The major televisions stations in the five major markets of Europe broadcast 50,000 total hours of fiction programming in 1996. Domestically produced programming constituted 8.42 percent of total fiction broadcasts in these markets.

ple have to watch stories told in their local language, set in local conditions, and making use of culturally relevant materials. In effect, soap operas function like action-adventure movies: they are sufficiently universal in plot, look, and style that they have become a universally appealing genre. Thus nighttime American soaps, like *Dallas* and *Beverly Hills 90210,* have been extremely popular worldwide. American daytime soaps, too, have found a global audience. One commentator notes that in September 1996 he was able to watch *Days of Our Lives, The Bold and the Beautiful, The Young and the Restless,* and *Santa Barbara* (as well as *Beverly Hills 90210*) while visiting South Africa.[63] The contemporary drama/melodrama *The West Wing* has likewise found a substantial international audience.

Recently, the widespread diffusion of satellite dishes worldwide has served as an important force in the spread of American television across the world. It can be broadcast into politically repressive countries from more open ones and does not rely on expensive networks of cables to link viewers to product. Star TV, a satellite network wholly owned by Rupert Murdoch's News Corporation (which, in turn, owns the Fox Television Network and associated movie, music, and television production facilities), has a substantial presence in Asia. For example, formed only in 1991, it now has more than 300 million viewers in fifty-three countries ranging from China and Japan to India, Indonesia, Australia, and even Iran and is watched by at least 100 million people each day.[64] Similarly, Eutelsat, which provides satellite programming across Europe, the Middle East, and North Africa on its Hot Bird and Eurobird satellites, provides services to over 52.6 million of the 119.4 million households with television in its area of operations. Notably, the company claims that subscriptions for satellite services increased at three times the rate cable subscriptions did between 2002 and 2004.[65] Satellite television is obviously playing an increasingly important part of the global television market.

Satellite television has brought an increased presence of American television programming. Star TV, for example, broadcasts several ESPN channels and other American networks like the History Channel.[66] Sky, another News Corporation-owned satellite system serving the United Kingdom and Ireland, has extensive U.S. contacts: Animal Planet, several Discovery Channels, National Geographic, E!, the Cartoon Network, Nickelodeon, and, of course, several music TV channels.[67] As satellite systems proliferate, they need to fill the immense bandwidth on which they broadcast. Ready made and already proven popular (on movie screens), American programming provides easy filler. Under such circumstances it is reasonable to expect American television programming to proliferate globally in the coming years.

Table 2.3   History of Imported versus Domestic Programming Worldwide

Percent Imported Programming	Countries
> 10%	United States, Soviet Union, Japan, China, India
10–30%	Indonesia, South Korea, Philippines, Pakistan, Cuba, Vietnam, France, United Kingdom, Italy, Germany, Australia
< 50%	Singapore, Tunisia, Ecuador, Ireland, Cyprus, Iceland, New Zealand

Source: Adapted from Dietrich Berwanger, "The Third World," in *Television: An International History*, ed. Anthony Smith with Richard Paterson (New York: Oxford University Press, 1998), 189.

What the world sees of American television, then, is dramas and melodramas, including soap operas, some news, some game shows, some reality programming, and videotapes and DVDs of American movies and programs. To the degree that these television genres, in combination with movies and music, can be seen to have a uniquely American content, they provide the fodder that both advocates and opponents of the spread of American popular culture use in their arguments and actions. To the degree that the United States is seen as the leading force in the movement toward the condition of globality, reactions to the products of American popular culture inevitably become part of the globalization debate.

Conclusion

As a consequence of the business, technological, and social factors noted throughout this chapter, the production of mass popular culture has always been centered in the United States, even as Americans have reached out to the rest of the world for ideas, money, and markets. In addition, much, if not most, of the music, films, and television programming generated by the major popular culture corporations carries an American label regardless of the nation of origin of the company that owns it; moreover, much, if not most, of this programming—especially the programming that has sufficient backing to be marketed and distributed around the world— derives its life and context from the economic, social, and technological forces that led U.S. companies to take a global lead in the production of popular culture. Accordingly, American popular culture is a global phenomenon that is as embedded in the context of globalization as is any other facet of our contemporary era.

"AMERICAN" POPULAR CULTURE

To write (or read) a book on the effect(s) American popular culture has on contemporary globalization is to assume, perhaps without being aware of it, that there is something uniquely "American"—as laid out in chapter 1— about the movies, music, and television programming made or developed in the United States and consumed around the world. Chapter 1 introduced the notion that American public culture was seen to contain an array of values, norms, and practices that tended to distinguish Americans from other people. In particular, American public culture was shown to be "civic": members of the political community share support for key values that are intended to promote the dignity and rights of all individuals. Such values were seen to include particular forms of liberty, political equality, individualism, democracy, tolerance, exceptionalism, and capitalism.

As described in chapter 1, however, Gitlin's notions of popular culture as a secular enterprise and of the imperative of profit to transnational corporations would seem to militate against there being an identifiably American core to pop culture's content. Accordingly, since American values and American norms might offend people who do not share them, and who would then, in turn, choose to not buy a movie ticket, purchase a CD, or watch a television program, the corporation's bottom line provides powerful incentives to remove offensive content, whatever its source.

Yet, as is shown below, an identifiably American core remains in many, if not most, of the movies, music, and television programs produced or in genres created by American companies and artists. This chapter explores the "American-ness" of American popular culture through the analysis of why national culture can be reflected in popular culture, through summaries of academic studies that link popular culture and American culture, and through description of the many formulas, genres, and conventions that shape American popular culture products in specific and predictably American ways.

Popular Culture and the Nation-State

Despite Gitlin's conception of popular culture as secular, there are good reasons to assume that the products of the American popular culture industry are shaped by American culture. Whatever its mode of creation, popular culture can be seen to reflect the values of the nation from which it emerges. As analyzed by Ernest Gellner, this is the result of the industrial revolution that made the creation of mass-produced popular culture possible in the first place. For Gellner, preindustrial agrarian societies were noteworthy for their bifurcation of two classes of people: high culture elites trained to think and reason and use language in abstract ways divorced from the particular context of use (writing, for example), and low culture masses, for whom words were used only to express specific meanings.[1]

By contrast, after the rise of industrialization, people no longer lived in small kin-related communities their entire lives. They did not know the people they lived near or with whom they worked—instead, whole populations were displaced to new population centers—cities—in search of work. Moreover, that work was itself very different from operating a plow while walking behind a mule. In an industrial community, achieving a goal requires more than walking from one end of a field to the other. Instead, running a complex machine or managing money or overseeing others as they work requires a sophisticated understanding of others' ideas, expectations, and goals; people in an industrial society need to understand how their work connects together with the work of an entire system of processes, actions, and actors if they are to create a car, balance a corporation's accounts, or coordinate the efforts of an entire factory floor. As a consequence of this need, Gellner argues, the masses had to be brought into high culture (literacy, the capacity for abstract thought and speech, etc.) to make the Industrial Revolution possible. Accordingly, education and social systems had to be changed to accommodate the new economic reality: universal education, at least to the level of literacy and abstract thought, became standard; social and legal codes that kept people in closed communities instead came to promote migration from rural areas to cities; and family ties could no longer define a person's place in society.[2]

For Gellner, importantly, high culture is not culture neutral. Access to high culture is not just a matter of being educated, literate, and capable of understanding instructions on how to operate a machine because one understands the principles on which the machine operates (abstract reasoning). Instead, high culture "has to be articulated in some definite language, such as Russian or English or Arabic, and it must also contain rules for comportment in life; in other words, it must contain a 'culture.'" Thus, he continues, "Modern industrial High Culture is not colourless; it has an 'ethnic' colouring, which is its essence. The cultural norm incorporates expectations, requirements and prescriptions, which impose obligations on its members."[3] In the end, then, the products of high culture are necessarily embedded in particular cultures. This is true whether the product is language, a car, or popular culture artifacts like movies, music, and television programs.

American Civic Culture and American Popular Culture I

There is empirical support for Gellner's theoretical linkage of national and popular cultures. Allen McBride and Robert K. Toburen, for example, in their work "Deep Structures: Polpop Culture on Primetime Television," offer a useful and interesting explanation of how the values of American civic culture are expressed in American popular culture.[4] McBride and Toburen analyze the content of fifteen of the twenty most popular television programs from the 1992 broadcast year. (They did not examine programs that lacked a continuing story line, like news magazines or clip shows such as *America's Funniest Home Videos*.) Thirteen of the programs were situation comedies; the others were hour-long dramas of various sorts.

The specific focus of their analysis was conflict: how it arose and how it was resolved, by whom, and when. For McBride and Toburen, conflict serves as a useful indicator of the cultural values of a given community. Different cultures can be expected to both initiate and resolve conflicts differently. In a traditional community, for example, conflict would likely emerge when an individual challenged his or her assigned place in the system, and the conflict would likely be resolved through appeal to community standards and norms. In an individualist society, by contrast, simply challenging hierarchical norms would likely be insufficient to start a conflict, and an appeal to comply with group values is unlikely to satisfy a person motivated by the desire to improve his or her personal lot in life.

McBride and Toburen's central finding is consistent with the idea that the United States has a civic culture organized around the rights of individuals. They show that individualist values dominate both conflict and conflict resolution on popular American television programming. In the programs they studied, most conflicts were between individuals, at least one of whom was usually seeking some personal benefit for him- or herself or a friend or loved one. The conflict was usually resolved through interpersonal negotiation, bargaining, and cooperation—although the fact that many of the shows involved family relationships guaranteed that many conflicts were resolved through an appeal to an authority figure like a parent. In any case, McBride and Toburen show that the core civic value of individualism is omnipresent on popular American television shows.

Conrad Kottak's analysis of Brazilian television provides additional confirmation of the individualism apparent in American television programming, even as it offers some additional insights to this finding.[5] Kottak notes, for example, that compared to American programming, Brazilian television is more focused on the importance of extended traditional families in Brazilian life. Rather than showing adults who live far away from home and do interesting or important jobs, for example, Brazilian programs show adults living at or near home and interacting with their family members instead of bosses, social leaders, or members of the broader community. Similarly, Brazilians have less expectation of privacy—family members, servants, and others can easily walk into or out of homes or overhear personal conversations through the usually open doors and windows of Brazilian homes. This reality is, he notes, reflected in Brazilian television. Brazilian programming emerges from a web of social interdependence and accountability, while American programming derives from the deep individualism of American life.[6]

Kottak also sees the value of political equality reflected very differently in Brazilian and American television. Issues of social and economic class, for example, are largely absent from American programming (even though they certainly exist in American life) even as class and status are central to Brazilian television. Few American programs make class a focus of their story lines: the characters in American programs rarely, if ever, link their social and economic status to political or financial factors beyond their control even if the shows focus on working-class families or characters. Likewise, better-off characters like doctors and lawyers are usually seen to have achieved their status by their own hard work—not as the result of some racial, ethnic, gender, or class bias. By contrast, Kottak notes that Brazilian society is deeply divided by issues of class and status. People with university degrees are legally entitled to different treatment under criminal law, for example, and social superiors expect their social inferiors to get out of their way in line or in demands for government and social services. These social attitudes and legal norms are common in Brazilian programming, reinforcing the class inequality that is core to Brazilian society. Held in comparison with the values of American civic culture, then, the class and racial foundations of Brazilian programming highlight and expose the egalitarian ethic that is one of the defining characteristics of American public culture is reflected in American popular culture.

Kottak is also insightful on the relationship among capitalism, tolerance, and race in both Brazilian and American societies. In the United States, for example, race is a fairly rigid category that is ascribed to a person at birth. It is fixed through some combination of color, appearance, parentage, and culture. In the United States, however, black characters have been both more common and more popular than they are on Brazilian television, even when the major audience for the U.S. program is white. *The Cosby Show*, for example, was both the number-one show in the United States for a number of years in the late 1980s and early 1990s *and* was one of the most distributed programs worldwide. Its story lines revolved around typical family situations, not the complexities of living as a black family in a racist nation. The parents had jobs—as a doctor and a lawyer— which they had earned as a result of their hard work, and from which they were able to provide their children with a healthy and comfortable home. They lived in a large New York City home and interacted easily and comfortably with a diverse range of Americans. In other words, the Cosby family was self-sufficient, individualist, egalitarian, and tolerant—all of which combined to make them nonthreatening and even acceptable to mainstream Americans. Likewise, white Americans tolerated and even celebrated this vision of an employed, educated, and successful African American family. Put another way, it is hard to imagine a television show being as popular as *The Cosby Show* was if the family were dysfunctional and headed by a single woman working several jobs or receiving welfare who decried her fate as a black female in a racist America. The context of American public culture can thus be seen to shape both the content of American popular culture and the conditions under which it is likely to be economically successful.

Timothy Havens has offered an extended analysis of *The Cosby Show's* popularity as "The Biggest Show in the World." For Havens, *The Cosby Show* was noteworthy for its ability to address issues of race, racism, and economic inequality in a way that was recognizable and appealing to audiences worldwide. Thus, rather than making economic hardship and social exclusion a central theme of the show (a theme that would be hard to pull off given the economic and social status of the show's parents, in any case), the program addressed questions of race and discrimination in indirect ways. For example, the Cosby's son, Theo, had an "Abolish Apartheid" sticker on his bedroom door. Show plots included discussions of the significance of the civil rights movement both in the past and in contemporary life. African American art hung on the home's walls, while jazz and blues (musical forms often associated with black performers) played in the house. In other words, *The Cosby Show* could appeal to diverse audiences because it provided an appealing vision of a happy, integrated African American family enjoying the full promise of American life. That this program was packaged in an upper-middle-class family that has benefited from capitalism and American opportunities only made it more likely to be produced and disseminated through the institutions of American popular culture.[7]

Importantly, apartheid, civil rights, jazz, blues, and other references were easily recognizable around the world, making *The Cosby Show* a good candidate for international appeal. More broadly, the cultural conditions that shape the civic character of American popular culture function to enhance the appeal of American programming worldwide. Scott Robert Olson explains that American popular culture, as a result of its unique mix of cultural factors, "has a competitive advantage in the creation and global distribution of cultural taste." This advantage is transparency, which he defines as "any textual apparatus that allows audiences to project indigenous values, beliefs, rites and rituals into imported media or the use of those devices." Thus, Olson continues, "This transparency effect means that American cultural exports, such as cinema, television, and related merchandise, manifest narrative structures that easily blend into other cultures."[8]

To return to *The Cosby Show* for a moment, Havens finds exactly this kind of transparency in the reaction of international audiences to this top-rated American program. Drawing on other research, Havens quotes a resident of Barbados as noting, about *The Cosby Show*, that "Black people in this show are not isolated, no fun is made of Blackness, and the characters are shown as leading wholesome moral lives." Similarly, a black South African viewer simply explains, "The show makes me proud of being black." Another black South African even sees hope in *The Cosby Show* for educating and persuading white South Africans to treat blacks with dignity and respect: "The Cosby Show . . . is saying, 'Come on, you white guys [in South Africa], the blacks are not so bad as you make them out to be. Look at us, we are having a good life and normal problems here in America. Give those guys down there a chance. Let's change for the better and live together, not apart." Havens even finds non-black audiences identifying with the Huxtables: a Lebanese Shiite man notes, "American blacks are a little like us. They have big families."[9] American stories and contexts as depicted in *The Cosby Show* are thus both American and transparent across a wide variety of cultures. This combination makes it relatively easy for American popular culture to spread across the globe—particularly when it is distributed through the corporate fiscal, production, and marketing resources described in chapter 2.

Another feature of most popular American television programming—and of most American movies and, to a lesser extent, music as well—is the prevalence of the happy ending. This contrasts sharply with many European-produced works, like those of the Swedish director Ingmar Bergman or the Italian filmmaker Federico Fellini, whose works almost always depict disturbing, even painful, stories that, like real life, often, if not always, end badly—even bizarrely. In European movies and programs, bad guys are not always caught; lovers do not always bond; good people do not always learn lessons about life from which they can grow into better people. On America's televisions and movie screens, however, problems almost always resolve themselves in the allotted time: The situation comedy ends with a homily about family love; the cop show's bad guy goes to jail; the hero of the action-adventure movie is reunited with his or her child/family/buddies. As is addressed below, even *Titanic*, the most popular movie of all time, manages a happy ending amidst the horrors of that ship's sinking: the heroine loses her lover to the frigid waters of the North Atlantic, but she is improbably rescued as a sole survivor in a sea of corpses, escapes her hated fiancé, marries for love, and has a wonderful family—all while keeping her ship-borne love in her heart forever.

The happy ending is a central feature of American popular culture for several reasons, not the least of which is the role played by social forces like the Production Code, the McCarthy hearings, and FCC regulations discussed in chapter 2. Put simply, the early producers of American movies sought to put an American stamp on their work and mandated that the good guys, however defined (white-hatted cowboys, police detectives, and the like) *had* to beat the bad guys in all their films.[10] This mandate expressed itself in endless serialized films shown to millions of audience members year after year after year. It set an audience expectation that was adopted in the Production Code and could be challenged only at the risk of running afoul of public and political pressure (as the film industry discovered during the McCarthyite Red Scare scandals of the 1950s). Moreover, once routinized, this formula served as the foundation for producing the endless number of television shows and movies needed to fill the growing market for popular culture. The happy ending thus makes both business and political sense as a central feature of American popular culture.

The happy ending makes cultural sense as well. The happy ending serves to emphasize the importance of the individual in determining his or her own fate and happiness—and thereby manages to undermine the role of class, education, fate, or any other factor in shaping human lives. The happy ending is, in large measure, the contemporary popular culture manifestation of the myth of the self-made man expressed in such nineteenth-century venues as the Horatio Alger stories. Horatio Alger wrote hundreds of dime novels in which anyone, no matter his life circumstances, could succeed through hard work, perseverance, and dedication. Thus, by extension, class was irrelevant: a poor boy could become rich through effort. In fact, one's station in life was ultimately one's own responsibility: since everyone could succeed, failure to succeed was the obvious result of one's laziness. Happy endings teach Alger's lesson to contemporary audiences: Bruce Willis might have to run (improbably) across broken glass in his bare feet while fighting the (heavily armed, well-trained, numerous) bad guys in *Die Hard*, for example, but because he is willing to do it, and committed to his task, he is able to defeat the (expressly) European terrorists who are holding his wife and her co-workers hostage. Similarly, Scarlett O'Hara may have had her house burned down and lost her lover by the end of *Gone with the Wind*, but "tomorrow," she says, "is another day," as she swears she will never be hungry again. No problem is too big for the individual to overcome; no limitation is determinative of one's fate. The happy ending is American public culture made real on screen.

At least one other feature of American popular culture programming deserves attention here: the product tie-ins that are embedded in much of it. In his study of the television program *Dawson's Creek*, for example, Will Brooker found that the program's producers had created a virtual community in which the show's fans could continue to participate in the program's story lines outside of broadcast hours. The producers created a virtual town with restaurants, a library, coffee shops, and other characters beyond those actually shown in the program. Notably, the purpose of this imagined community is commercial: the site features numerous linkages to other programming in the WB, *Dawson's Creek*'s cable network home, and also provides users the opportunity to link to the J. Crew and American Eagle clothing company Web sites, where they can purchase the same outfits that the show's stars wear. Similarly, the site provided lists and links to the popular music prominently featured in each week's show; viewers could purchase and download their selections without ever leaving Capeside, their virtual home. While Brooker found that only a small percentage of viewers, whether in the United States or internationally, visited this site, his analysis suggests the many levels through which American movies, music, and television programming carry diverse forms of distinctively American popular culture to a global audience.[11]

American Civic Culture and American Popular Culture II

Following the survey of academic research linking American popular culture to the values of American civic culture, this section of this chapter offers a series of extended analyses of representative examples of American movies, music, and television programs that have been popular worldwide. Rather than just relying on the broad descriptions available in academic research, then, this section offers a detailed examination of the ideals, values, and themes contained within American popular culture.

American Movies

This section offers an extended commentary on three American movies—*Titanic* (1997), the highest-grossing film of all time; *The Patriot* (2000), Mel Gibson's tribute to the American Revolution, and *Blade Runner* (1982), a dark dystopian vision of a future in which the values of American public culture combine to create a nightmare, rather than a fantasy, of a globalized world. Any number of films might have been presented, of course, and the analysis offered here should not be seen as comprehensive. Instead, what follows is intended as an exegesis of how American culture is expressed in movies, using these three films as particularly useful examples.

Titanic: *Class and the American Dream*

Titanic's success was stunning. Many people rushed back into the theater to watch the film a second and third consecutive time despite the movie's extraordinary length of well over three hours. It set numerous box office records on its way to smashing the all-time gross mark at almost $2 billion in ticket sales alone.

This success is seemingly out of proportion to the story. Essentially a love story framed in the foreshadowing context of the *Titanic*'s doomed ocean voyage, the movie follows the trials of Jack (played by Leonardo DiCaprio) and Rose (played by Kate Winslet) as they meet, fall in love, and struggle to survive as *Titanic* sinks. Jack is supposed to be a down-and-out working-class youth trying to return to America; he only gets on board the ill-fated ship because he wins a third-class ticket in a last-second poker game. Rose, by contrast, is the daughter of an aristocratic British family

73

that has fallen on hard times; she is to be married to an American million-aire to restore the family fortune. Where Jack is lucky to be on *Titanic* at all, Rose is berthed in the lap of luxury in her first-class accommodations.

Despondent over her pending forced marriage, Rose decides to commit suicide by jumping off *Titanic*. Jack, who has snuck onto the first-class deck, saves her by threatening to join her in her plunge. The two quickly establish a relationship as the poor-but-talented Jack sketches Rose, reads her poetry, and otherwise acts like a perfect romantic hero. By contrast, Rose's fiancé is a petty, disinterested, possessive man of little integrity or merit to recommend him other than the size of his bank account—which he himself did not earn. When Jack's relationship with Rose is discovered, conflict ensues—Jack is imprisoned and nearly drowns as *Titanic* sinks (before being saved by Rose, returning his earlier favor), and Rose and Jack spend the last hour of the movie slowly moving toward the back of the sinking ship—the place where they had met just a few days before. They barely survive *Titanic*'s final plunge beneath the waves and share a last good-bye moment before Jack freezes to death in the frigid waters of the North Atlantic. Rose is rescued, but when she has the opportunity to re-sume her former life by joining her fiancé (who has survived by claiming a small child was his and using this excuse to join one of the few boats *Titanic* manages to launch before it sinks) on a rescue vessel, she hides. She tells a questioner that her name is Rose Dawson—Jack's last name, not her own. Love has survived tragedy.

Whatever the merits of this story—and it is told effectively, with good acting and stunning special effects—it is hardly unique or innovative. Ac-cordingly, something else must account for its popularity. Here, the analy-sis focuses on the ways the values of American public culture emerge in the movie and provide the transparent foundation on which others can build their interpretations of the film's significance in their lives.

Notably, at least part of the movie's appeal can be seen to lie in the everyman-versus-privilege story that characterizes Jack's relationship with Rose's fiancé (Cal). Jack, despite his status as a poor working-class kid, is romantic, loving, engaging, poetic, artistically talented, self-sacrificing, heroic, and, above all, happy. Like Horatio Alger, Jack is self-made, self-confident, and successful in the most important ways: he risks his own life to save Rose, risks his personal safety to maintain a relationship with Rose despite threats and humiliations, tries to save several passengers (including children) as *Titanic* sinks, and insists to his last breath that Rose must live no matter what. By contrast, despite his supposedly superior parentage, Cal is shown to be deceitful, manipulative, and uncaring—whether for Rose or for the young child he claims is his in order to escape in a lifeboat (he immediately hands the child off the second he takes his seat). He orders his butler to kill Jack. Whereas Jack is a skilled artist, Cal has no interest in art or other social finery. Having money, clearly, is not the same thing as having class.

Not only is having money not the same thing as having class, but having money is seen to undermine the true development of human character. Cal is not the only character whose life of privilege has served only to promote selfishness. Rose's mother is horrified by the thought of a life without wealth and essentially prostitutes Rose to Cal to ensure the family fortune. Most of the first-class passengers treat Jack badly when he is invited to a dinner party. By contrast, the one first-class passenger the audience sees who was born middle or working class, Molly Brown (later to be called the Unsinkable Molly Brown for her actions as *Titanic* sank) treats Jack with dignity and mocks the values of the alleged upper class. She alone is willing to return to the sinking ship to try to rescue dying passengers; her elite boat mates are paralyzed by fear. Similarly, when Rose visits the third-class cabin with Jack she is immediately embraced and immersed in a web of dancing, friends, and shared food and drink. The message is clear: the rich are snobs, while only the poor are authentic, decent people.

As was discussed both in chapter 1 and earlier in this chapter, the sense that class is not the key to happiness or even a guarantee of good behavior is central to American public culture. Jack has had to live by his wits, uncorrupted by the luxuries of wealth. Jack may be working class, but he has a heart of gold. He will clearly be successful and happy wherever he might go. Cal, of course, will never be happy, and indeed the film notes, as it closes, that Cal kills himself during the Great Depression. A central theme in the film is thus that class—the control of wealth—is unimportant. Indeed, class provides no constraints on either behavior or opportunity: since Jack can win Rose's heart, the barriers of class mean nothing.

Like the Horatio Alger stories, Jack's story further emphasizes the moral importance of individualism in human life. Jack is a plucky, optimistic individualist who gains admission to the ship on his own wits and talents, figures out how to stop Rose's suicide attempt on his own, charms his way onto the first-class deck, and is even invited to a formal dinner (which he attends wearing a borrowed tuxedo that, since this is a love story, fits perfectly and looks beautiful). All he has are his talents and his intelligence. With them, however, he is able to establish a rapport with most of the first-class passengers and be invited back again and again despite the disapproval of Cal and of Rose's family. In the end it is only Jack's and Rose's individual spirit and desire that accounts for their survival of *Titanic*'s final fateful plunge into the ocean. Likewise, it is Molly Brown's spunky character, formed outside the halls of privilege and sloth, that makes her heroic. Individuals, not social backgrounds, matter.

Yet even as *Titanic* suggests that class is not important for a good life, it tempts its audience with a vision of great wealth. Life in first class is very good: china plates; crystal glasses; expensive meals, art, and displays. The people are beautiful, as are their clothes and jewelry. Simply in terms of the lure of material possessions, then, *Titanic* has an obvious appeal.

It is in the context of the ostentatious wealth of first class that Jack's easy entrée into such ranks needs to be understood. Class, education, training, and opportunity are not structurally limited only to those who go to the right schools or are born into the right families. Instead, all one needs is quick wits, charm, individual creativity, and, to a large extent, the courage to imagine yourself in first class in the first place. Likewise, those in the upper classes need to be tolerant of the diverse skills and talents distributed throughout society if they are to enjoy a full and rich life.

Taken together, this account of *Titanic's* popularity rests on the values and variables of American popular culture. The irrelevance of class, the importance of individualism, the lure of capitalism, the need for tolerance, and the distribution of talent across society are all foundations of American public culture. In reflecting them, *Titanic* told a story that reached out to the world. The world responded.

The Patriot: *Extraordinary Individuals and the Making of Liberty*

Perhaps no element of the story of the American Revolution is as culturally meaningful and persistent for Americans as the perceived role that citizen soldiers played in achieving American independence. Popular mythology holds—indeed insists—that it was ordinary people like farmers and small businessmen who, when the nation called in its time of need, left their land and their towns to volunteer to fight the British oppressor. Then, when the time of crisis passed and victory was won, these simple civilians gave up their service, returned home, and resumed the quiet lives of dignity and productivity they had enjoyed before the war interrupted them.

This myth is deeply embedded in American life. It is taught in schools, reproduced in books, and, as is discussed below, made the focus of major films. As such, the myth can be seen to be popular because it neatly conjoins the liberal and exceptionalist streams of American public culture and provides a model that others can follow: if only we all behaved as our patriot forebears did, the myth suggests, the nation would be strong and secure. It also provides a reason to trust that those who are exercising power in the name of freedom: like the militias of old, moral men and women will put down their arms when the job is done. They wish liberty for themselves and will do nothing to harm others' enjoyment of it.

That the myth is, in fact, not true is irrelevant. It survives to be told again and again. One particularly effective representative movie of this genre is Mel Gibson's 2000 film, *The Patriot*. As the film opens, Benjamin Martin (Gibson) is a member of the South Carolina legislature debating whether to send troops to join George Washington's forces in the North. Despite (or perhaps because of) his prior military experience in the French and Indian Wars, Martin is a strong opponent of joining the fighting. He reminds his fellow legislators that the war will be fought among their homes and families, that it is impossible for them to protect their children from the sights and sounds of violence. Instead, he advocates negotiation and peace. Despite the passion of his appeal, however, he loses.

Martin changes positions when British forces occupy his farm, arrest his oldest son (a soldier in the American army), and kill another of his sons. He takes his two oldest remaining sons and attacks the British squad escorting his oldest son to prison. Martin kills all the British soldiers and rescues his oldest son. Now a confirmed partisan, Martin organizes a militia that hides in the swamps of coastal South Carolina and makes highly successful, if brutal, raids against British units and supply lines on a hit-and-run basis. The militia is mostly composed of farmers who, like Martin, would have preferred to be left alone but who were swept up in the fighting as British forces abused their rights and liberties. In addition, one is a slave who ultimately hopes to win his freedom. Another is a local preacher, linking God to the project of universal human emancipation. This diverse group spends the war harassing the British and ultimately plays a crucial role in the defeat of British forces in the South. Then, once the British surrender at Yorktown, Virginia, Martin returns home to rebuild his life. Arriving back in South Carolina, he finds his old militia compatriots, including the now-freed former slave, working to rebuild his house. One informs him that they knew they had to start rebuilding the country somewhere; his house seemed like a good place to start. The war, then, is over.

There are a number of dimensions of *The Patriot* that express values, attitudes, and beliefs that appeal to and inspire those who share American civic culture. Furthermore, many of the film's themes are popular within the broad parameters of American political culture. In particular, questions of motives and outcome that are central to *The Patriot* are also crucial to understanding the link between American civic and popular cultures.

In terms of motive, Martin seeks only to be left alone. He has no ambitions or desires beyond raising his family as he sees fit. His actions are seen as pragmatic, appropriate, and moral. As such, he is the archetypal individualist—a man interested only in pursuing his personal goals, with no desire to impose his preferences on others.

The Patriot also promotes racial tolerance. When the slave joins the unit, he is welcomed by all his fellow soldiers—except for one openly racist, intolerant soldier. Over time, however, as the slave proves his worth in battle and chooses to stay with the unit even after he has served long enough to earn his freedom, the intolerant soldier changes his mind and embraces the African American as a full member of the unit. Ultimately, it is these two characters who take the lead to work together to rebuild Martin's home. Differences are thus overcome through the means of hard, shared work.

Cumulatively, *The Patriot* takes the liberalism and exceptionalism of American political culture and links it to the revolutionary myth of the militia all over again. Martin as mythic hero—and thus cultural example of ideal behavior and values—is an individualist and a democrat. He believes in the power of hard work and individual morality. His courage provides a model around which his community can form for action. Then, at the height of his power, his innate goodness and trustworthiness demonstrate themselves, and he goes home, leaving behind the trappings of power he accepted only as a necessity. He will again be that which he apparently always wanted to be: a gentleman farmer, husband, and father—an American icon.

Blade Runner: *The Emptiness of Consumer Capitalism*

Ridley Scott's 1982 *Blade Runner* offers a strikingly different vision of American life and civic values than does either *The Patriot* or *Titanic*. *Blade Runner* presents a dystopian vision of a globalized future. Yet, as will be discussed, its dystopia is every bit as derived from the content of American public culture as the other two films discussed above are. It simply offers a negative vision of the way American attitudes and preferences might play out over time. As such, it provides a useful introduction to why some people might react negatively to the American values presented in popular culture.

In the world of *Blade Runner,* society has been transformed into a disconnected mass of polyglot consumers with no evident purposes or goals other than consumption. Set in a future Los Angeles where it always rains—a symbol of the general alienation that characterizes the mood of the film as humans have managed to change even the environment from its "natural" order—*Blade Runner* hinges its story around the actions of a police officer, Decker (Harrison Ford) who works in a special unit designed to track down and kill androids (called replicants) who return to Earth. In this future, humans have begun to colonize other worlds. Much of the dirty work of colonization—whether it is working in hostile environments, serving the needs (including sexual needs) of human workers, or serving as soldiers in various wars—is performed by androids. Most of the time this is a good deal for humans: much of the hard, dangerous work of colonization and combat is taken on by machines.

The replicants are sentient, however. They are aware of the moral implications of the things they do. They are also aware of their own mortality: they have an internal clock that limits their lives to only a few years. A primary tension in *Blade Runner* is the story of a group of replicants who return to Earth to confront their maker—the Tyrell Corporation and its genius owner, Dr. Tyrell—to force him to adjust their life clocks so they can extend their lives. Decker works to find and kill them—a task he ultimately completes only because one of the replicants, Roy, chooses not to kill Decker when he has the chance. Instead, in an affirmation of the value of life, Roy saves Decker and then dies.

Significantly, *Blade Runner* is striking in its lack of any direct examination of the politics and social life that ground its vision. There are not even any oblique references to the powers that be in the film. Instead, the dystopia it offers, and the lessons it draws about a particular human future, has to be teased out of the background—which is its ultimate political point.

Of particular importance in this vision is the dominance of the global/galactic megacorporations. Tyrell Corporation is clearly one of the megacorporations that run society. Its power is symbolized in its towering obelisk of a building that rises, along with those of other megacorporations, above the crowds and rain of Los Angeles. Yet this dominance seems so well entrenched that no one finds it remarkable. For example, it is never evident that there are courts or other mediating structures to link citizens to government through consent, consideration of opinion, or the protection of rights. Instead, Decker and his fellow agents seem to work largely at the will of the Tyrell Corporation. Their agency exists only to solve problems caused by Tyrell Corp., and they kill replicants on crowded streets with little consideration for the safety of innocent civilians. Indeed, even Decker never challenges the logic of his work: a problem exists that has to be solved, and even when Decker falls in love with a replicant and works to save her life, he never considers that laws might be changed to make Tyrell accountable for the problems it causes. No discussion ever occurs about the need to limit Tyrell's power, either.

The anonymity of the mass population is another important dimension of the vision of the future *Blade Runner* offers. The streets literally teem with people: individuality is lost in the rain and decay of lower-level Los Angeles. One can buy artificial replacement body parts for only a few credits. No one appears to be going anywhere in particular or doing anything important. What action there is on the street is offered by the endlessly circling electronic billboards that advertise cola and other products for consumption. There is no other end to life than that of shopping.

An important example of the anonymity of the mass is the language of the street. Most people speak a language amalgamated from a mix of German, English, Japanese, and Spanish. The face and garb on the model on the floating billboard is clearly Asian, probably Japanese, and the mix of people on the streets constitute a true melting pot: styles, trends, languages, ethnicities—are all commodities to be exchanged and merged in a giant marketplace. Notably, most people pass each other without consideration or concern: this identity swapping is less a source of collective identity than a facilitator of indifference.

The artificiality of life serves to emphasize the anomie of the community. It also serves to highlight the irony that, while all other life is artificial—eyes, pets, and the like—artificial human life, the replicants, is banned from Earth. In *Blade Runner*, pets are illegal—at least natural ones. If people own pets, they own replicants. (One can only imagine Tyrell Corporation's lobbying efforts in supporting such a law.) And, as was previously noted, one can buy artificial body parts, such as eyes, on the street. Only humanoid replicants are bad. Everything else is acceptable, regardless of its artificiality.

Blade Runner thus offers a vision of the dark side of American public culture. Individualism inspires isolation, not participation. People are anonymous, not engaged. There is no exceptionalist crusade to make things better and spread truth and justice across the world because there is no group, organization, or government with any kind of social conscience with which one might work if one desired to make the world a better place. At the root of all this empty existence is the dominance of consumer capitalism. When freedom becomes the freedom to shop for whatever one might like (including life itself), life holds no meaning or value. When liberty becomes nothing more than the freedom to choose one from a series of options on the shelves of street vendors, it is an empty concept.

American Television

Three programs are examined here: *Star Trek*, *The West Wing*, and a short-lived cult hit, *Max Headroom*. *Star Trek* offers perhaps the single clearest example of an idealized vision of American public culture leading to universal—literally—happiness. *The West Wing* is an immensely popular television drama around the world, and *Max Headroom*, like *Blade Runner*, depicts a world in which the individualism and capitalism that are at the heart of American public culture create a dystopia—the opposite of *Star Trek*'s utopia.

The Universe of Star Trek *and the Universe According to* Star Trek

Star Trek, originally broadcast on NBC from 1966 to 1969, was a ratings failure that has since achieved iconic status. Its episodes have been re-broadcast for decades, its fans have developed a global subculture, and its creators have spun off ten movies and four television series from the original series. Much of the continuing popularity of this science fiction program lies in its vision of a globalized, ethically driven, rights-respecting, democratic future—American public culture made manifest on a galactic scale.

While most fans and casual observers of the *Star Trek* phenomenon focus on the characters, stories, and technology that lie at the heart of the series' storytelling, it is also important to note that this action takes place in a well-developed political-social context: the Federation. The Federation, organized along lines similar to the United States' political structure, is the political agency that those in Star Fleet—Kirk, Spock, McCoy, and their collegues—serve. Star Fleet is the military arm of a political order made up of a federation of planets that elect representatives to a central governing council. The Federation—formally titled the Federation of Planets—is organized along classic federal principles: each member planet has broad discretion to enact its politics as it pleases; however, the central authority does hold certain powers through which it can establish and enforce peaceful relations and protect the safety of its members from both internal and external threats. The existence of Star Fleet is one such power.

The parallels with American federalism extend beyond the name and the existence of a central governing body, however. In addition to electing representatives to the Federation's governing body, planetary members elect a president and a Federation council. These leaders make policy that is then ratified (or not) by the Federation's elected officers. These officials operate in the context of the rule of law and are bound by their oaths to respect the rights of all people to self-determination. Indeed, during the course of the series and films several senior political and military officers are arrested and otherwise removed from office for violations of their legal responsibilities. In many ways, then, the Federation manifests the ideals of

81

American democracy in actual practice. The world of *Star Trek* corresponds with what many contemporary politicians and other leaders claim America is today.

The key to the Federation's success is warp technology. Warp technology allows humans to travel faster than light, and in the aftermath of the first human warp flight, they establish first contact with an alien species—luckily for the humans in this case, the rational, peace-loving Vulcans. The development of warp technology and the first contact with an alien species transforms global politics. Warp technology and the integration of the Earth's economy with the galactic one leads to a revolution in power generation and the provision of goods and services. All basic human needs can be met easily. Hunger, poverty, disease, and other curses are cured. Indeed, there is so much wealth and social benefit associated with the new technologies that even psychological disorders are cured in all but the most extreme cases. Finally, the diverse communities of Earth integrate and establish global governance on liberal democratic principles.

Once the transformation of Earth was underway, humans set out—like Puritans coming to America—to bring their way of life to the galaxy at large. After a slow process of exploration, interaction with other species, and wars, humans sponsor the creation of the Federation as a coalition of species and cultures that share relatively common values and political practices and work together to promote and defend these ideals against internal threats—officials and others who would use their power for their own good—or external ones—political and military competitors like the Romulons and the Klingons. Importantly, Star Fleet is civilian controlled and is subject to legal restrictions on its actions. Thus, even the Federation's warriors are democratic and rights oriented. In its political, military, social, and economic dimensions, then, the Federation is a shining symbol of the capacity of technology, integration, and procedure to bring nearly universal benefits to all who embrace its vision.

At the core of this ethical expansionism is a concept the show's fans developed only after the original series went off the air: IDIC. IDIC stands for "infinite diversity in infinite combinations" and is used to represent the way the many cultures of the Star Trek universe can respect each others' particular practices and values while working together in a collective, healthy way. Many of the show's plots deal with the struggles to both accept others and explain when it can be appropriate to intervene in diverse cultures.

The *Star Trek* vision of a global—indeed galactic—democratic future is profoundly optimistic, mirroring the claims of contemporary globalists. People are not displaced by technology; they are empowered by it. Disruptions in a former way of life do not cause pain; they are liberating. There are no fundamental tensions among cultures and communities; all can be bridged successfully. Life in the Federation is not simply rich; it is reward-ing. Technology and politics work to free the human—broadly under-stood—soul from pain, want, and repression.

This vision of the relationship between globalization and democracy is as pure an example of American public culture made real as has ever been presented in popular culture—with the obvious exception of its depiction of the corrupting role of capitalism on social morality. Tolerance promotes order, growth, opportunity, and education; democracy and a respect for rights ensures freedom; and individuals pursuing their dreams leads to so-cial harmony. The world of *Star Trek* is that of an idealized America pro-jected onto a galactic stage.

The West Wing *and the Democratic Experiment*

The West Wing offers an idealized, compressed vision of the workings of American democracy. It deals in detail with the processes of politics in the United States. It has featured episodes on the filibuster, the appoint-ment of Supreme Court justices, the use of force in international affairs, the problems of racial violence in America, support for human rights overseas, the invocation of the Twenty-fifth Amendment of the U.S. Consti-tution, a terrorist attack on the United States, and the attempted assassina-tion of the president. Each of these, and many more, have offered extended commentaries on the formal rules and informal practices of American de-mocracy. They have also invoked the ritualistic aspects of the presidency as President Bartlett calls the parents of American troops wounded in combat, lights the national Christmas tree, gives the State of the Union Address, and offers his annual pardon of a Thanksgiving turkey. To watch *The West Wing*, even casually, is to be offered an object lesson in the workings of American government.

The world of *The West Wing* is an exceptionally tolerant and diverse one. President Bartlett is Catholic; two of his senior aides are Jewish. Most of the rest are Protestant. Bartlett's personal aide is an African American male, an obviously subservient role for a black character; however, for the bulk of the show's run, the powerful chairman of the joint chiefs of staff was an African American man as well. Women, too, play important roles in the Bartlett administration, ranging from the first lady to press secretary to national security adviser to staff person. They fight as effectively and as passionately for their causes as do their male counterparts. The administra-tion even nurtures recovered alcoholics. Notably, this diversity melds together almost seamlessly to create a cooperative and successful harmony of committed, caring individuals dedicated to achieving their goals on be-half—they say—of the American people.

Indeed, it is only when they fail to respect the inherent decency and dignity of everyone everywhere that the Bartlett administration finds itself in trouble. In an episode dealing with a terrorist attack on the United States, for example, Leo McGarry, the president's chief of staff and one of the show's main characters, ruthlessly interrogates a Muslim White House employee who happens to have the same name as a suspected terrorist. As he conducts this questioning, McGarry questions the employees' patri-otism and assumes his guilt on the basis of his skin color and religion. Tellingly, however, when the employee is found innocent, McGarry is ashamed. (Notably, in a sign of religious and personal tolerance the em-ployee returns to work after his interrogation.) Likewise, it is only when the staffers demonize their political opponents or when the president him-self loses faith in the American people (as he did by covering up his illness during his first election) that the administration gets into trouble.

The story of *The West Wing*, then, is the story of the best parts of Ameri-can civic culture played out with sufficiently realistic touches to make the politics seem real. It bears little to no relationship to how the U.S. presi-dency actually works, of course. The people are too attractive, everyone is too smart and too selfless, the staffers have far too much ease of access to the president, people sublimate their agendas to the good of the group far too easily, and above all everyone spends too much time talking to and about everyone else to accurately simulate the frenetic, disjointed experi-ence of working for the president of the United States. Likewise, the show offers little insight into how laws are actually developed and passed; the tedious hours of drafting, revising, reconsidering, and negotiating that go into the legislative process for just one of the hundreds of significant laws passed every year would make stunningly boring television. Instead, in *The West Wing* the audience sees noble people trying hard to follow the Consti-tution and do what is right. They see how Americans want to believe their government functions as a manifestation of their deepest cultural hopes and beliefs.

Max Headroom *and the Dark Side of Consumer Capitalism*

Max Headroom, a short-lived television series aired on ABC in 1987 (and subsequently shown in reruns on the Technology Network), was a remarkable example of the synergistic crossover desired by transnational corporations; the character who titles the show, an electronically animated

84

head who speaks in jerky fits and starts, was originally introduced to American audiences as the spokesperson for Coca-Cola commercials. When Max Headroom become a pop sensation, a television series was conceived as a means to further exploit the character's popularity.

Both in cause and in content, *Max Headroom* offers a different vision of the way American public culture might express itself in political and social life—a take more close to that found in *Blade Runner* than in *Star Trek*. Subtitled *Twenty Minutes into the Future*, the series is explicit in its attempt to imagine a plausible future from current context. Moreover, despite being derived from an explicitly commercial source, the series weaves a complex set of stories around the theme of corporate-political greed and corruption.

The series' star, and Max Headroom's real-life alter ego, Edison Carter, is an enterprising investigative journalist working for Network 23. With the help of his human supporters, and his computerized self (Max), Carter explores and exposes various corporate and political malfeasances. One plot, for example, centers on a new technology the evil Network 66 had developed that put its viewers in a hypnotic trance and guaranteed their continued viewing of the network's programming. Another involves a contractual relationship between a network and a terrorist organization that allows the network to broadcast terrorist attacks as they occur. Yet another involves the efforts of a political leader to stamp out his generation's version of the homeless, called blanks.

Unlike *Blade Runner*, the political system is front and center in *Max Headroom*. In contrast with *Star Trek,* however, the world of *Max Headroom* is not benevolent and rule bound. Instead, various political leaders conspire with corporate officials for political and personal advantage. The reason for this collaboration is clear: in a chilling yet believable extrapolation from current practice, in this future, networks run political campaigns. Networks choose potential officeholders and manage elections. The person elected to office is the candidate representing the network with the highest ratings at a given time. Hence the need for popular programming: it is on the basis of a program's viewership that political power is allocated.

The linkage of the political and the corporate does not necessarily construct anomie among the public, however, as it did in *Blade Runner*. While there are large numbers of relatively apathetic and ignorant people in the community, others are active and prepared to work for change. It is Edison Carter's crucial role to expose the various plots and prevarications of the wealthy and powerful so that ordinary citizens can react and so the state can intervene. Thus, after Edison's stories are aired, there is usually some kind of public demand for change or improvement. Of course, by implication, if a story is not aired—either because it is suppressed or simply missed—no one cares. Democratic passion is still possible—but only when it is activated by a television exposé. While the members of the political system ultimately believe more in Edison's values than they do in the ideas and ideals of society's elites, theirs is usually a passive support rather than an active one.

Thus *Max Headroom* offers a fairly bleak vision of the way American public culture works. Most people are, most of the time, isolated individuals staring at television screens, absorbing whatever information (or misinformation) that the networks beam at them. Few people have meaningful relationships with each other and the broader social world; instead, consumption—whether of television programming or the products the television networks advertise—replaces human relationships. That there is any resistance to these corporate powers is, of course, a testament to the enduring power of the promise of American public culture, but a significant portion of the show's narrative appeal lies in the credibility of its vision of an American life dominated by isolated, meaningless consumption. Both *The West Wing* and *Max Headroom* are thus plausible in the context of American public culture.

American Music

It is not as simple to offer an extended analysis of the way American public culture manifests itself in popular music as it is in the case of American films of American television. Individual pieces of music are usually quite short to fit the time available on commercial radio, and the medium rewards brevity and simplicity rather than complexity. In addition, most songs, even when collected into albums, are rarely linked thematically in the way that television programs and films are. Consequently, individual pieces of music lack the substance to provide a solid foundation for analysis.

Rather than focus on a particular song or group of songs, the analysis offered here is based on the careers of performers in each of the genres in which American music has been particularly successful worldwide: rock, country, and rap. No claim is made that these performers are the best of their genre or era, nor is what follows representative of the whole of each genre. Each of these performers has been hugely successful, however, and has shaped his or her career to fit the expectations of the global marketplace.

Deconstructing Britney Spears

Britney Spears is one of pop music's most successful performers. Born in 1981 in Kentwood, Louisiana, Spears's career has been a product of the popular culture industry since her earliest days in show business. At eight years old she auditioned for a role on Disney's *Mickey Mouse Club* television show; when she was turned down for being too young, she contacted a New York agent. She spent several years honing her skills at a New York summer theater program before finally winning a part as a cast member of the *Mickey Mouse Club* at age eleven. She played on the *Mickey Mouse Club* for two years and used her experience on the show to make connections with agents and music industry executives throughout the entertainment community.[12]

Spears's breakthrough came in 1998 when she released her debut song, "Baby One More Time," from her album of the same name. This success was followed by a string of hits including "Sometimes," "(You Drive Me) Crazy," "Oops . . . I Did It Again," and "Lucky." Her debut album sold 13 million copies, and her follow-up album sold at least 9 million. Subsequent albums have not done quite as well, but Spears has remained a star of substantial marketability, whether in films, on television, or on radio, since her breakthrough in 1998.[13] Most recently she has starred in a moderately successful reality show with her husband, Kevin Federline, although as this is being written her career is on hiatus due to her pregnancy and childbirth.

Spears's appeal, it should be noted, is out of proportion to her actual vocal talent. Her songs are remarkable for the amount of engineered special effects they contain; her voice alone, it appears, is insufficient to draw an audience. Likewise, on stage Spears uses taped backup vocals to cover her lapses during her active, dance-filled shows. Even her relatively subdued outings, such as the music video for her title-track song to accompany her acting debut in the film *Crossroads*, has her dressed in tight shorts and close-fitting, midriff-baring shirts. It is the package of marketing, sex appeal, personal talent, and the talents of the songwriters, producers, and technicians that has made Britney Spears a star, not her individual skills alone.

What matters here, however, is less Spears's talent than the way her career reflects the values of American public culture for consumption around the world. Notably, despite the virtual army of people needed to turn a relatively weak-voiced person into an international superstar, Spears's career is presented as the result of individual hard work and accomplishment—a testament to what anyone with a dream can achieve. Thus, despite the fact that Spears writes virtually none of her own material, and her acting debut *Crossroads* was a moderate success at best, Spears's official biography presents her achievements and plans as her own. "I've loved every step of this journey I'm on," her official Web site quotes her as saying. "I love singing and dancing and acting and songwriting. . . . It all energizes and inspires me. . . . I can't imagine ever reaching the point where I've hit the wall. . . . There's always something new and challenging to tackle."[14]

In addition, Spears's videos are awash in the images of the goods associated with consumer capitalism, stardom, and the benefits of wealth. Characters drive expensive cars, live in and visit expensive hotels and apartments, and otherwise live what many would call the good life. Her private life supplements this video reality with trips to expensive resorts and restaurants and access to homes, planes, and some of the most exclusive places in the world. Indeed, her private life has morphed into her public career: she and her husband have starred in a reality genre show, *Chaotic,* which is broadcast worldwide. The cumulative message is one of success through individual effort—one is rewarded in proportion to one's effort. This is the essence of American individualism.

Through it all Spears maintains that she is *not* a product of the entertainment industry. She insists her choices are her own, and thus that what the audience sees is the authentic Britney Spears. Again returning to her official biography, Spears insists that in her latest album, *Me against the Music,* "'I had the freedom to explore and experiment with some of the most exciting people in music. In the end, that allowed me to make a record that is a pure reflection of where I am right now."[15] Likewise, in responding to suggestions that her clothing choices are too provocative, especially for the younger female audience that constitutes the core of her fan base, Spears argues (in this case in an interview with *Esquire* magazine): "That's just a weird question. . . . I don't even want to think about that. That's strange, and I don't think about things like that. Why should I? I don't have to deal with those people. I'm concerned with the kids out there. I'm concerned with the next generation of people. I'm not worried about some guy who's a perv and wants to meet a freaking virgin."[16] She thus presents herself as rich, famous, successful, and authentic—a living embodiment of the American dream.

A final component of Spears's appeal has been her articulation of the Horatio Alger story: small-town girl made good who somehow doesn't lose her values (although this last point may be in jeopardy, as will be discussed). Spears presents herself as an all-American girl for whom the trappings of wealth and luxury are ancillary to her real love—the music. Like the hero in Alger's stories, Spears appears to have lifted herself from rural Louisiana to fame through the sweat of her own labor—despite the fact that it took a family commitment of enormous time and money to support Spears's work in New York, endless auditions, and other efforts in pursuit of her career. Where one starts is unimportant, her story suggests; all that matters is hard work, pluck, and talent, and anyone with those attributes can make it in America.

Notably, Spears's career also suggests the constraints American public culture places on its stars. Spears's popularity has declined in the last year, at least in part due to her marriage to Kevin Federline—a professional dancer who essentially abandoned the woman he was living with, who was pregnant with his child, in order to move in with Spears. Their reality show depicted a chain-smoking Spears often shot in the green glow of night-vision photography. The show came after Spears's brief, immediately annulled marriage to a longtime friend. Put simply, Spears's recent behavior has violated the Alger myth of hard work leading to a good life. Interestingly, Spears's latest album, *B in the Mix*, had no promotional support on release and debuted well outside the top one hundred albums in the United States.[17] American public culture can thus be seen to frame the path toward and the limits of celebrity in popular culture.

The Making of Garth Brooks

Garth Brooks is the most successful country performer of all time and in fact is the most successful solo artist ever. He has sold over 100 million albums in the United States alone and over 3.5 million tickets to hundreds of live performances around the world. He had fourteen albums enter the Billboard Pop and Country charts and had twenty-one number-one singles. Seven of his sixteen albums debuted at number one. He also won two Grammy awards, sixteen American Music Awards, eleven Country Music Association Awards, the Recording Industry Association of America's Artist of the Century Award, and a Golden Globe—along with many other accolades. Notably, all these accomplishments were compressed into the twelve-year time span from 1989 (the release of his first album) to 2001—the release of his last.[18]

Brooks made his reputation singing an array of songs that touched on and ennobled the lives of the common person. Songs like "Friends in Low Places" and "American Honky-Tonk Bar Association" make a virtue of being working class while suggesting that better-off, better-educated people are snobs unwilling to get their hands dirty in real, important work. "The Thunder Rolls" and "Callin' Baton Rouge" offer views of passion—both negative and positive—that many people responded to. And "The Dance" and "If Tomorrow Never Comes" remind listeners of the importance of family and family life across time and tragedy. Cumulatively, Brooks presented an image of country music as the music of ordinary people's lives and times.

89

Notably, the apparent authenticity of Brooks's music was every bit as much the product of a popular culture machine as was Britney Spears's. For example, the country music industry rests on a system of songwriters who author pieces that then are made available to established performers for selection and recording. These songs are often formulaic and rest on thematic and musical conventions that have proven to be highly marketable over time. Particularly well-established stars can put songs on hold so that even if the star cannot record the song in the immediate future he or she can release it later—even years later. Thus, while individual stars may write some of their own music, few develop the bulk of their own material once they are successful.

In addition to this songwriting help, Brooks—like Spears—was noted for his elaborate stage shows. He was the first country artist to adopt rock-and-roll show effects, including lasers and fireworks, into his act. Brooks also made a practice of exploring the whole stage, running and leaping off equipment or substages, and even using harnesses to fly above his audiences. But Brooks did none of this himself, of course. An army of technicians, roadies, backup singers, band mates, and innumerable others (truck and bus drivers, accountants, advance people, hairdressers, stylists, video directors, and style consultants, to name only a few) were needed to make a show like Brooks's possible. The singularity of Brooks's success was thus a fiction: it was the result of the interaction of many parts of a well-oiled entertainment machine.

The fiction of Garth Brooks's public persona was most clearly evidenced in his decision, in 1999, to present himself as an entirely new artist, Chris Gaines. This idea stemmed from Brooks's casting to play a character named Chris Gaines in a to-be-produced movie called *The Lamb*. Gaines was to be a rock-and-roll singer with many personal problems. Brooks decided that in order to prepare for the role, he should actually create Chris Gaines as a "real" figure in the entertainment industry. As a consequence, Brooks adopted a façade as Gaines and recorded *Garth Brooks in . . . The Life of Chris Gaines,* a collection of Gaines's greatest hits (and music for the movie). While the album sold 2 million copies, Brooks's audience was not ready for this plasticity in character. He released one more album—*Scarecrow*—and then retired from the music industry.[19]

As was the case with Britney Spears, the question here is not so much whether Garth Brooks has an exceptional musical talent as it is how Brooks's persona manifests the values of American public culture. Like Spears, Brooks's popular character is one of individual hard work and accomplishment leading to success beyond anyone's imagining. Like Britney

Spears, Garth Brooks presents himself as an example of an American dream come true.

Unlike Spears, however, Brooks is more focused on the class dimension of American life. Or, put another way, his career is grounded on reinforcing the meaninglessness of class. Brooks's appeal, in an extension of Horatio Alger's or Jack Dawson's, rests on an explicit articulation of the moral superiority of the hardworking average Joe versus both the well-off snob and the undeserving poor. Songs like "Friends in Low Places" have Brooks describing an encounter with a former girlfriend as she hosts a black-tie dinner; her reactions, and those of her guests, are those of horror and shock that Brooks's character would dare intrude in their "ivory tower." As he leaves the party, Brooks's character says he didn't want to cause trouble, but since he has been treated so badly, his ex should "kiss my ass." Performed live, the line inevitably received roaring approval from the audience. Similarly, the "American Honky-Tonk Bar Association" mocks those "standing in a welfare line" who "reach for handouts" in defense of the authentic values of the bar-visiting members of the "American Honky-Tonk Bar Association": "the hardhat / Gunrack, achin'-back / Over taxed, flag-wavin', fun-lovin' crowd."[20] Such are the values of real Americans, Brooks asserts—and in response, Americans made him the most successful solo performer in recording history. Other songs, like "Much Too Young (To Feel This Damn Old)" and "Two of a Kind, Working on a Full House," extol the virtues of working-class life. By contrast, the wealthy and the educated are wimps. Accordingly, in what is ultimately a reinforcement of the classlessness of American civic culture, Brooks's career rests on undermining class as an important variable in shaping the lives of Americans and others around the world by insisting that working-class people are real, while others are phony and not to be envied.

It is worth noting that Brooks is also much more focused on questions of social and political tolerance than Spears is. For example, Brooks sings highly patriotic songs—"The Dance" is an homage to fallen American heroes that touched many Americans shortly after the Alfred P. Murrah Federal Building was destroyed by Timothy McVeigh in April 1995. His take on patriotism is not jingoistic, however: for Brooks, the focus is on the sacrifices of the victims and their rescuers, not the savage horror of the enemy. Brooks also acknowledges the racial and ethnic discrimination that has been a prominent feature of American history. This sensitivity is most apparent in "We Shall Be Free," Brooks's gospel-inspired tribute to the downtrodden and ignored, the poor and the abused. "The Change" offers a similar call for moral and social reform to improve the lives of society's most defenseless.

Thus Brooks presents a more sophisticated, more subtle translation of American public culture in his chosen popular culture venue. His individualism reinforces the meaningless of class in America. In so doing he offers a vision of a system in which ordinary people need not struggle to improve their economic and social conditions since, as a practical matter, the "better off" are in fact really worse off because they are disconnected from the kinds of social interchanges that constitute real friendship and real work. When the system has been unfair, however, Brooks is quick to promote tolerance and moral change to make the world a better place. This is Americanism with a human face sent around the world through the power of song—and the American popular culture industry. It in large measure accounts for his extraordinary global success.

Tupac Shakur and the Making of a Rap Archetype

Tupac Shakur was born Lesane Parish Crooks in June 1971 in New York City. His mother, Afeni Shakur, was a member of the Black Panther Party who had served time in prison while pregnant with Tupac on allegations of setting bombs; she was released just a month before Tupac was born. His godfather was the Black Panther leader Geronimo Pratt. Shakur claimed never to have known who his father was.[21]

The circumstances of his birth would have a major impact on Shakur's brief life. His family was very poor. His stepfather was a drug dealer and he and his sister moved, with their mother, often. With no fixed address or permanent connections to established neighborhoods, Shakur turned to poetry and acting to fill his time. He continued these pursuits when the family moved to Baltimore, Maryland, in 1984. During his sophomore year in high school he was admitted to the Baltimore School for the Arts.[22]

The family's stay in Baltimore did not last long, however. Unable to find a job, Shakur's mother moved the family to the Oakland, California, area. There, after several years on the FBI's most wanted list, his stepfather was arrested and sentenced to sixty years in prison, while his drug-addicted mother was unable to provide much of a home. Shakur moved in with a neighbor and started dealing drugs and working the streets.[23]

He also developed his interests in rap music. He made friends with other rap performers and in 1990 joined the rap group Digital Underground as a dancer and part of the road crew. He enjoyed only moderate success performing with this group but by 1991 was able to release his first solo album, *2Pacalypse Now*. Its moderate success prepared the ground for his second album, *Strictly 4 My N.I.G.G.A.Z*, which spawned two number-one hits. This success was followed by two additional popular albums, *Me against the World* and *All Eyes on Me*, the first double CD in hip-hop history. It went on to sell more than 9 million copies.[24]

2Pacalypse Now set the pattern for Shakur's music—and public reactions to it. While he was capable of writing songs of great sensitivity and kindness, for the most part his music was wrapped up in images of violence, especially by and against police officers. This was often extended to women as well. Guns were prominent in his videos, as were material possessions. When one person claimed that *2Pacalypse Now* encouraged him to murder a Texas police officer, then-U.S. vice president Dan Quayle said the album had "no place in our society."[25]

Shakur's musical persona was mirrored in his private life—to an extent strikingly in contrast with Britney Spears or Garth Brooks. In 1991 Shakur was arrested for jaywalking in Oakland; during his arrest he claimed to have been brutally beaten and afterwards settled a $10 million lawsuit against the Oakland Police Department for $42,000. In 1993 he shot two police officers he believed were unjustly attacking a suspect in Atlanta, Georgia. Charges were dropped when the police officers were found to have been intoxicated and in possession of stolen weapons. In an even more serious incident, in December 1994 Shakur was arrested, tried, convicted, and sentenced to four and half years in prison for sexually assaulting a woman in a hotel room. (In fact, *Me against the World* was released while Shakur was in prison; when it hit number one on the charts it made him the first artist in music history to have a top-selling album while serving a jail sentence.) Notably, just before his verdict in the sexual assault case was announced, Shakur and three other men were shot multiple times in a robbery at a music studio. Shakur was shot five times, robbed of thousands of dollars in jewelry, and left for dead. He appeared at his assault sentencing in a wheelchair, still recovering from this attack.[26]

Shakur's problems did not end with his subsequent eight months in prison. He was a central figure in a long-running dispute between East and West Coast rappers, many of whom believed members of the other side were violently hostile toward them. He accused other rappers of being tied to the mafia and insisted that yet others were no-talent hacks. These various hostilities were rumored to be the reason for Shakur's murder in a drive-by shooting in Las Vegas in September 1996, but nothing was ever proved. Rap had lost one of its earliest superstars—and the creator of many of the lyrical and visual conventions of "gangsta" rap.[27]

As was the case with Britney Spears and Garth Brooks, what matters here is less Shakur's talent or moral status and more his relation to American public culture. Like *Blade Runner* and *Max Headroom*, Shakur's persona is a representation of the dark side of American life. In his case, individualism led to conflict rather than cooperation; consumer capitalism drove a striving for glory and possessions as ends in themselves, not tools for creating a better life; and tolerance meant only the acceptance of those in one's own gang or posse. As a consequence, the universalist values at the core of American public culture became particularist and exclusive. Freedom became the freedom to consume, to hate, and to dominate. Liberty became the right to do whatever one wanted to do without limit or consequence. Equality results from the violent protection of whatever is one's own. Shakur's music and life reflect the values of American public culture in their dark dimensions.

Formulas in American Popular Culture

As a practical matter, there is no way to create as much programming as has been described in this chapter in an accessible, audience-friendly way without, in effect, telling the same story over and over again, each time perhaps making mild adjustments to setting, stage, character, plot, and moral to distinguish one product from another. Thus even as American political and social values are manifested in American popular culture, they are enmeshed in formula-driven products that link those same political and social values with images, themes, and content that often anger and frighten people both in the United States and around the world. Understanding these stereotypical formulations in which American popular culture is presented to the world is an important part of understanding how American popular culture feeds the fragmegrationist dynamic that is at the center of contemporary globalization. (As an aside, it was formulas and conventions such as those addressed in this section that caused Soviet leaders to refer to Western and American culture as corrupt during the Cold War.)

Take, for example, the issue of the violence that is central to many of American popular culture's products. Violence has been a part of American popular culture since well before the emergence of modern electronic entertainment. The shock value of violence has been demonstrated to be an effective means of drawing and keeping an audience. Violence, including sexual violence, sells. Images and themes of violence also play a useful role in distinguishing good characters from bad ones, particularly in the time-compressed formats of movies, television, and music. (One need only see or hear a description of someone committing an act of violence against an obviously innocent person or animal to know, instinctively, that the person committing the act is the piece's bad guy.)

For these—and many more—reasons, violence is a central feature of

American movies, television programs, and even music. The inevitable plot of an action-adventure movie—pick one; they are all quite literally the same—illustrates the thematic and commercial utility of violence and its global appeal: a hero—almost always male—stands as a lone individual facing some great evil. (In some cases the hero is reluctant; in others, anxious.) Usually heroes are people with some special training or power—for example, Special Forces veterans or, depending on subgenre, inheritors of some mystical force that shapes their lives—although in some cases they are recognizably ordinary. The odds are usually overwhelming, and the stakes high: a child is being held hostage or the safety of the world hinges on the victory of the hero or any of a number of outcomes hinge on the hero's success. Then the bloodbath begins. The hero slaughters untold numbers of the enemy and either escapes unharmed or is wounded only enough to enhance the dramatic tension. In this modern era of computer graphics much of this destruction is accompanied by extraordinarily vivid explosions, graphic depictions of decimated flesh, and a soundtrack that drives the action at a frenzied pace. All this violence, of course, is depicted as necessary for achieving whatever goal the hero must accomplish; anything less and the child dies or the world explodes or evil conquers the innocent.

Notably, the plot of such action-adventure films is recognizably "American": it emphasizes the individual's powers and rights over the group's; it (usually) shows heroic action in defense of what are often offered as or assumed to be American values or the American way of life, and so on. It is also transparent, to use Olson's phrase; the plot is so established in films that audiences around the world can recognize it instantly, and the visual spectacle of dramatic special effects offers a lure to the movie that few non-Hollywood products can offer; movies made elsewhere lack the financial backing and the technical support to create such elaborate images. There is no "cultural discount" in watching a spaceship explode; it is its own meaning.

What is true for movies is equally true for television programs and even music. According to one report from the University of Michigan's Medical School, the average American child sees eight thousand murders depicted on television before finishing grade school. Given American children's TV consumption, they may see an average of ten thousand rapes, assaults, and murders each year.[28] Indeed, given the rise in popularity of television programs like *Law and Order* (and its variants) and *CSI* (in all its variants), as well as the inevitable production of copycat programs on other networks, popular American television programming—especially the programming popular around the world—is awash in violence. Notably, shows like *CSI* take as much advantage of computer graphics in presenting violence as films do; through computer animation the audience sees bullets penetrate skin, shatter bones, and slice through arteries, leading to arcs of blood spurting across the screen and splattering across walls. While it might be argued that the violence inherent in such crime shows humanizes the victims—that it is intended to make the audience feel the suffering and fear of innocent people—the effect is ultimately dehumanizing and pornographic. Audiences get to witness horrific acts of violence in a detached, clinical way, as happens, for example, in the opening scene of the debut episode of the 2005 television program *Killer Instinct*: a woman paralyzed by a spider bite is viciously raped and murdered before the first commercial break. The appeal is to the prurient interest in order to grab and keep an audience— whether in the United States or elsewhere around the globe.

Popular American music is embedded in depictions of violence, too. Rap music, in particular, has been cited for its emphasis on violence. As was discussed earlier, for example, a "war" broke out between East Coast and West Coast rappers that led to, among other things, the deaths of several rap stars and producers. Both Tupac Shakur and Christopher Wallace, also known as Notorious B.I.G. or Biggie Smalls, are alleged to have been murdered by partisans of either side. These partisans were alleged to have been motivated by the violent and machismo-laden lyrics of so-called gangsta rap. Rap has also been criticized for linking violence and the acquisition of wealth; for example, the video accompanying the rapper Fifty Cent's song "L'il Bit" depicts an ambitious gang member who uses women to lure various gangland bosses into situations where the star can murder his way to the top of the organization. And, of course, rap has been attacked aggressively for its descriptions of violence against women; an obvious example is the rap superstar Eminem (Marshall Mathers), who in one song imagines slitting the throat of a cheating wife named Kim who has a child named Hailey—the names of the star's ex-wife and daughter. The album on which this song appeared won the 2001 Grammy award for Best Rap Album.

It would be wrong to note only rap's reliance on violence. Violence has been a centerpiece of rock and roll as well as country music. In the Doors' hit "The End," lead singer Jim Morrison imagines murdering his father and raping his mother. Garth Brooks, in his country hit "Papa Loved Mama," describes a jealous man driving his eighteen-wheel truck into the motel room where his wife is cheating on him, killing both his wife and her lover. The Dixie Chicks joyfully sing about murdering Earl, the wife-beating bad guy in their number-one song "Goodbye Earl." Unlike the husband in "Papa Loves Mama," the wife and friend who kill Earl get away with their crime and prosper after his death. Violence is thus not the exclusive province of rap music.

Concerns about the content of American programming only expand as other conventions of American popular culture are introduced for discussion. Sex and sexuality are common themes in movies, music, and television programs. Moreover, the depictions and uses of sex and sexuality in American popular culture tend to push lines and challenge social norms for the same basic reasons violence is a convention: sexuality is enticing, engaging, and likely to hold an audience—particularly when it tests social limits of good taste or typicality. Nudity in film—especially female nudity—has become quite common, even in films rated for teenagers (PG-13 and above), to say nothing of the pornography industry, which produces thousands of hours of film and television programming per year. Sexual activity is also pervasive in American movies: in film after film, actors meet and bed one another quickly and readily. Such couplings are rarely consequential: few people get pregnant or are infected with venereal diseases; people connect because they want to "hook up" and then move on. In addition, even sexuality in mainstream, non-pornographic films is being depicted in increasingly graphic ways. Movies like *The Brown Bunny* have shown established award-winning actors engaged in explicit sex acts. In almost all cases these events are presented in individualist, hedonist, self-interested terms; sex and nudity are as much marketing devices as they are integral to the plot.[29]

Sex and sexuality are equally present, although perhaps less explicitly, on television (barring pornographic broadcasts on satellite channels). Both daytime and evening soap operas depict sex in a casual, common way, with characters changing partners at mind-boggling speeds. One famous episode of the popular comedy series *Seinfeld* was organized around a contest to see who among the program's cast could resist masturbating for the longest period of time. Entire series—notably the HBO hit *Sex and the City*—have been organized around the sexual adventures of the program's stars. And while nudity is very common on cable and satellite broadcasts, it has become increasingly common even on broadcast television, where programs like *NYPD Blue* show actors fully nude while entwined with various partners. Like movies, television is as much awash in sex and sexuality as it is in violence.

Music, too, has taken advantage of the marketing power of sexuality and sexually provocative imagery. The apparent sexual energy and movements of rock and roll have been a matter of public concern at least since Ed Sullivan ordered the cameras on his 1950s-era show not to film Elvis Presley's gyrating hips during the star's first televised performance. In retrospect, such concerns see quaint. Lyrics like those in the peppy Beach Boys' hit "I Get Around," which asserts "and we've never missed yet with the girls we meet," have evolved through the Beatles' classic "Why Don't We Do It in the Road?" and beyond. Kelis, in the recent rap song "Milkshake," is virtually a prostitute advertising her sexual skill and superiority when she asserts: "My milkshake brings all the boys to the yard, / And they're like it's better than yours, / Dam right, it's better than yours, / I could teach you, but I'd have to charge." The Bloodhound Gang managed to create an entire new vocabulary of implied sex acts by describing their desire to "power drill the yippee bog / With the dude piston" and to "put the you know what in the you know where" in their rock song "Foxtrot Uniform Charlie Kilo"—the military call signs for the letters F, U, C, and K. The disco classic "Lady Marmalade" explicitly asks: "Voulez-vous coucher avec moi?"—do you want to sleep with me? The country classic "Help Me Make It through the Night" insists: "I don't care what's right or wrong / I won't try to understand / Let the devil take tomorrow / 'cause tonight I need a friend."

The link between music and sexuality is nowhere more explicit than in contemporary music videos—among the most globally popular and duplicated of the products of American popular culture. Song lyrics that are already aggressively sexual are regularly framed in highly erotic or sexually suggestive images and situations. From Madonna's "Like a Virgin" video, in which she rolls on the floor wearing a wedding dress and making moaning sounds and describing herself as being "like a virgin, touched for the very first time," at her lover's caress, through the Pussycat Dolls' "Don't Cha," in which scantily clad women tease a potential boyfriend with provocative dancing and questions like "Don't cha wish your girlfriend was hot like me? / Don't cha wish your girlfriend was a freak like me?" music videos have traded on sexually stimulating imagery to sell their products. Indeed, there has been something of a "race to the bottom" as once-scandalous images (Madonna kissing an African American statue depicting Jesus Christ, which brings the figure to life, for example, in "Like a Prayer") become bland. The next video, then, needs to capture the attention of an audience that has, quite literally, seen it all.

Issues of sex and sexuality do not stop at the depiction of heterosexual sexuality, of course. Accordingly, American popular culture also employs other controversial aspects of sexuality, such as homosexuality and trans-gendering, as it seeks to keep and build audiences for its products. The first mainstream American television program to feature a leading male character who was gay was the 1970s comedy *Soap*. Another 1970s show, *Three's Company*, revolved around the efforts of a straight male character to pass as a gay man in order to live with two female friends whose landlord was opposed to sexual cohabitation. Each of these shows was controversial in the United States, as were subsequent programs like the popular 1990s comedy *Will and Grace*, which also featured central characters who were gay. The 1970s film *Dog Day Afternoon* features Al Pacino as a bank robber motivated by the desire to raise funds for his homosexual lover's sex-change operation; twenty years later, Robin Williams and Nathan Lane played a gay couple of long standing who run a business together in a highly sympathetic portrayal of homosexuality in *The Birdcage*. Notably, the business is a nightclub in which men perform dressed as famous women in an elaborate cross-dressing extravaganzas.

Lesbianism, too, has been a common feature of American popular culture's products. What was once shocking—the 1982 film *Personal Best*, in which Mariel Hemingway's character engages in a torrid affair with another woman, or Roseanne's sister, in Roseanne Barr's eponymous 1980s situation comedy, kissing another woman on America's TV screens—has today become commonplace. A cottage industry of *Girls Gone Wild* videos, allegedly recording the antics of college-aged women across America as they kiss and fondle and expose one another's breasts, has sprung up, and the woman who is perhaps Hollywood's most famous lesbian, the comedian Ellen DeGeneres, has her own daily talk show. Music videos, particularly rap and rock videos, regularly show their male stars surrounded by groups of women touching and kissing each other. If anything, contemporary American popular culture seems to celebrate lesbians—at least in the case of attractive women who appeal to men (or other women) by making sexual contact with other attractive women.

Even issues of transgendering are regular, if not common, elements of American popular culture. The shock rock star Marilyn Manson often appears on stage wearing a plastic body suit that makes him appear both nude and without genitalia, and an earlier generation of rock stars, the members of the band Kiss, made themselves famous by wearing outrageous costumes and elaborate makeup. Actress Hillary Swank won an Academy Award for her portrayal of a woman who is ultimately beaten to death for hiding her gender behind male clothes and restrictive undergarments in *Boys Don't Cry*. Another Academy Award–winning film, *The Silence of the Lambs*, records the efforts of law enforcement officials to find a serial killer who, it turns out, wants to undergo a sex-change operation but is rejected as psychologically unstable. In American popular culture, boys will not always just be boys.

At least one other aspect of sex and sexuality needs to be addressed if the link between American popular culture and global reactions to it is to be understood: its link to violence. Sex and sexuality are, of course, among the most emotionally charged aspects of human life; given the extraordinary tension that accompanies human sexuality, it is perhaps not surprising that violence is one aspect of the experience of sex. Linked to the evident marketing appeal of violence, the sex and violence dimension of American popular culture should be expected. Thus, as many of the examples of movies, music, and television programs listed above suggest, violence is a regular part of the depiction of sexuality in the products of American political culture. As was noted earlier in this chapter, Hillary Swank's character is beaten to death for hiding her sexuality, and Al Pacino's character is willing to rob a bank and risk killing innocent people in order to fund his lover's operation. In other cases, the sex-violence linkage is more purely prurient, as is the case in the opening scene of *Killer Instinct*: its sole purpose is to shock and horrify its audience with the image of a paralyzed woman being raped and murdered. Whether as an accurate expression of the pains and tensions of human emotions, or as a virtually pornographic tool of exploitation and audience appeal, violence is often linked to sexuality in American popular culture.

Violence and sexuality are not the only elements that combine to attract audiences to American popular movies, music, and television programs, of course. Several others deserve attention. Take, for example, the role of gender in American popular culture. The question of what roles men and women ought to play in society is a regular source of controversy in social and political life around the world. American popular culture has certainly employed issues of gender in its products; these images and themes have been and continue to be controversial both in the United States and across the rest of the globe.

At least four stereotypes of women's roles in society can be identified in American movies, music, and television. One is the woman as sex object. In this role, women serve as little more than eye candy for the sexual enjoyment of the audience. Cheerleaders at football games; gratuitous lesbian (or female-nudity-only) sex scenes in films, music (and their associated music videos), and television programs; and the classic character of the "dumb blonde" with large breasts who cannot add or subtract all fall into this category of stereotype.

A linked stereotype is that of woman as victim. In this role, females are dominated, often through sexual violence, into accepting the will of an authority figure—usually, although not always, a man. This role is often linked to women who have challenged social norms (e.g., refusing to accept a husband's demands, or going out to a bar alone and meeting an abusive male). The lesson is that to be safe a woman should comply with society's rules and expectations. (There is an exception to this lesson, the strong woman, to be discussed later.) Otherwise, pain and suffering follow.

Another common gender stereotype in American popular culture is that of the traditional wife and mother. Explored and ultimately enshrined in such 1950s television classics as *Leave It to Beaver* and *Father Knows Best*, this image usually depicts a woman whose life is devoted to her family. She is the master of the private realm of family life, working endlessly to cook, clean, care for the children, and support her husband as he interacts with the outer, public world. Admittedly, over time this role has evolved along with the American family—Carol Brady, in the 1970s TV hit *The Brady Bunch*, had to deal with a blended family, for example—but the basic pattern of the role has remained relatively unchanged. The woman's reward for accepting her domestic place is a life of relative physical luxury (a nice car, a nice home, etc.) if not complete emotional and intellectual satisfaction. The contemporary programs *The Sopranos* and *Desperate Housewives* offer modern interpretations of this established stereotype.

A final female stereotype is that of the "power woman," which usually comes in one of two forms: the superwoman who balances family and career to be a success in the world at large, or the victimized woman who throws off her oppressors and becomes a new, strong person. The first version is usually shown as a woman in a position of authority, such as an attorney or a judge or a business executive, or, in the case of the 2005–2006 television show *Commander in Chief*, president of the United States. The second is a woman who learns that there are other ways to live and so escapes whatever forces—usually a man or a society bound to traditional values of women's domestic subservience—have been controlling her. In either case, the women are shown to wield power, to overcome challenges placed in their way by men, and, often, to be sexually assertive and power seeking.

For males the range of gender roles tends to be more limited. As a rule, men are either 1) strong and assertive or 2) wimpy and effeminate—even implicitly or explicitly homosexual. Those males who are seen to have appropriately "male" values tend to be in positions of authority or athletes; in both cases they are characterized by their endless pursuit of sexual conquests. By contrast, "failed" males hold weak positions at work, are dominated and mocked by colleagues and families, or are incompetent at sexual gamesmanship. While there has been a noticeable shift toward an acceptance of gay male characters, particularly on television programs like *Will and Grace* and *Queer Eye for the Straight Guy*, these characters almost always conform to the effeminate notion of homosexuality—and so, by extension, make the life of a non-assertive heterosexual male all the more complicated by allusion to gayness. (Rap music, by contrast, is noted for its expressive homophobia.) Other conceptions of maleness rarely make it to the screen, the CD, or the multiplex.

Family is also another dimension of human life treated in fairly conventional form by American popular culture—when it is addressed at all. As was discussed in chapter 2, one of the striking things about American popular culture is the relative absence of the family: the characters in many shows and movies, as well as those described or shown in music and music videos, often have no—or virtually no—association with their families at all. Instead, they live lives of independence and self-satisfaction rather than familial obligation and respect.

When families are depicted in American popular culture, they tend to appear in three forms, two of which are profoundly dysfunctional and the third of which is, at best, improbable. The first form is at the root of many, if not most, situation comedies. It centers on hapless and incompetent fathers, faithful and persistent wives (if they exist in the show; many such programs feature only divorced or widowed fathers) who really hold the family together, and an array of loud-mouthed, basically disrespectful children who provide the family tensions around which the show revolves. The children, in turn, may or may not be biologically related to either or both parents. If the program admits that parents have parents themselves and includes the grandparents in the program, the grandparents are as often a burden as a help—an adult version of the show's children. (See, for example, the CBS long-running hit *Everyone Loves Raymond*, or the Fox series *The Simpsons*.) Every half-hour some problem is introduced, chaos ensues, and order is restored through the love everyone actually feels for each other.

A second dysfunctional family form appears on one of the most globally popular forms of American programming, the soap opera/melodrama, especially on television. Such melodramas regularly use the family as their dramatic focus; however, families in the serial universe are not mutually supportive bastions of strength to help each other through a troubled world. Instead, soap opera families are internally competitive and vicious. Brothers—and for that matter fathers—scheme to sleep with each others' wives and girlfriends; sisters—and mothers—engage in a constant barrage of gossip and criticism that intends only undermine another's self-confidence and self-worth and so enhance the gossiper's chance of sleeping with the gossipee's husband or boyfriend. While the members of the family are often alleged to have important jobs that generate great wealth, no one actually ever goes to work; everyone spends time attacking and manipulating each other emotionally as well as sexually. (The trend toward wealth in families, particularly on television, has led to a relative doubling in the salaries paid to TV fathers of contemporary programs versus those of the 1950s.)[30] Thus, while everyone is well-dressed and has expensive possessions, family is an obstacle, not a key, to happiness.

The third typical family form in American popular culture derives from the power woman stereotype. In this convention, the mother is often important and powerful and well off; her problems, such as they are, come from struggling to find time to balance the competing pressures of job, family, and—if she is married or dating—romance. More often than not, however, the family is relatively harmonious with happy children and a satisfied spouse—even if the families are blended among two (or more) divorced/widowed couples. Unlike the 1950s, when father knew best, in contemporary television and movies, housework is now a shared responsibility, as is care of the children. The end result is well-adjusted children enjoying a middle—or better—class lifestyle.

Race and ethnicity are yet another area of human life in which American popular culture broadcasts stereotypical, often offensive, images and themes. Indeed, many of these stereotypes predate the emergence of electronic media and stand as legacies of the racist and ethnically discriminatory policies that the United States has adopted and defended throughout much of its history. Thus, in general, whites (especially white Anglo-Saxon Protestants, Wasps) have been shown to be the best-educated, most effective, most law-abiding members of society. They are seen to fill most positions of authority in the political, economic, and social systems, and it is through their actions that the plots of movies or television programs, or the commercialism of modern pop music, are carried forward. Notable exceptions to these patterns have been Catholics, Jews, and gay people; they, along with poor, usually Southern, whites constitute the only Caucasian groups that American films, music, and television programs consistently mock or assign cultural stereotypes to. None of this should imply that whites are only presented in heroic or positive terms; many films, television programs, and pieces of pop music make it clear that whites, typically men, are the bad guy of the piece. However, when whites are presented as evil, their evil is rarely ascribed to their cultural background—unless they are Catholic, Jewish, gay, or Southern. Instead, they are responsible for their crimes—or their heroism—as individuals. It matters less what color they are than it does who they are as people.

The situation is not as positive or hopeful regarding the popular culture images of members of other races and ethnicities in America, however. African Americans, in particular, have been subject to centuries of savage, horrific portrayals in U.S. social and political life—images that have been perpetuated in contemporary popular culture. One image, for example, is that of the black male as criminal. Established during the era of slavery as a means to justify the violent control of black males, as well as a tool to frighten white women into compliance with their husbands' and fathers' threats that leaving the house made them vulnerable to attack by black men, the image of the black male as an out-of-control, sexually aggressive predator has recurred throughout American history. Indeed, the first major multireel movie, D. W. Griffith's *Birth of a Nation*, was based on *The Klansman*, a novel that depicts the horrors of black violence against innocent white women in the aftermath of the U.S. Civil War. Its heroes are members of the Ku Klux Klan, who save the women from an attack by evil blacks. (*Birth of a Nation* is still considered a classic groundbreaking film.) Contemporary popular culture is awash in images of violent black males, whether as sports stars, gang members, prisoners, or drug dealers. Ironically, an entire genre of rap music, gangsta rap, exploits and reinforces this imagery throughout the United States and the world, having inspired gangsta rap wannabes in Japan, India, and elsewhere. Likewise, an entire cable network, the WB, seems aimed at reinforcing stereotypical images of African Americans through its broadcasts of conventional, formulaic comedies in which black adults and children do little except insult each other for half an hour. Sympathetic portrayals of professional African American men are few and far between. (The comedian Robert Townsend mocked the limited range of roles available to African Americans in his film *Hollywood Shuffle*.)

The situation for African American women is hardly any better in popular culture—with one substantial exception, the daytime talk show host Oprah Winfrey. Black women are regularly shown as un- or underemployed, usually single mothers who are inevitably lifetime welfare recipients. (Former U.S president Ronald Reagan once famously referred to such women as "welfare queens," implying that they were living lives of comparative luxury on government handouts.) These women are also generally depicted as drug or alcohol addicted. Alternatively, particularly in rap videos and music, they are depicted as objects of sexual desire who exist, mostly, to satisfy the sexual demands of various male partners. Only rarely are sympathetic images, such as the wife on *The Cosby Show* or those associated with Oprah Winfrey, who has become one of the wealthiest people in entertainment, manifested in American popular culture—despite the fact that in the real world, an African American female, Condoleezza Rice, has become the U.S. secretary of state.

The lives of Latinos and Latinas are similarly dire, at least as depicted in American popular culture. Early images were the grossest form of stereotypes of an alien "other" with which few Americans would have ever come into contact. Thus the male image of the Mexican bandito, which was a staple of Western movies and television programs in the 1930s, 1940s, and 1950s, morphed into a 1970s cartoon character selling the snack food Fritos by singing, "Ay, ay, ay ay, I am the Frito Bandito" while stealing various victims' snack chips. This, in turn, linked to the 1980s and 1990s conventions of Latinos as gang members, drug dealers, and drug lords in innumerable movies, television shows, and songs set against the context of the international drug trade. The only other types of Latinos allowed were prisoners—usually arrested for gang and drug activity—and, in a few cases, police officers intent on rescuing the neighborhoods in which they grew up from the ravages of the drug trade.

Latinas are given even less diversity in their presentation in American popular culture. The earliest images of Latinas in U.S. films centered on the character of Carmen Miranda, an attractive woman who became a famous entertainer while wearing seductive clothing and a bowl of fruit on her head. Since then, most Latinas have been shown to be sexual attachments of the men in their lives, and thus—given the distribution of Latino characters—members or associates of gangs engaged in or managing the drug trade. They are seen to raise the men's children. On occasion one woman is shown to resist or challenge the corrupt values of the local community, but more often than not, Latinas are active participants in the criminal lives of their men. Indeed, there is not a single major sympathetic portrayal of a Latina in contemporary American popular culture.

There is really only one stereotype of Asian Americans in contemporary popular culture—that of a hard-working but potentially dangerous person, whether he or she is a nerdy hard-working student, an entrepreneur, or a crime boss. This is ironically related to earlier depictions of Asians, particularly during World War II, as devious, dangerous people who attacked the United States without warning on December 7, 1941. This, in turn, derives from Anglo fears of Asian migration in the nineteenth and early twentieth centuries; as Asians immigrated to the western areas of the United States in the aftermath of the Civil War, usually for economic opportunities associated with the gold rush or the building of the transcontinental railroad, local Anglo-Americans passed restrictive rules against Asian employment and access to education, and other regulations limiting the freedoms of Asian immigrants. These were later codified by the U.S. Congress to include limitations on the numbers of Asians who could immigrate to the United States as well as laws that barred Asians from owning property or becoming naturalized citizens of the United States. The three images— hard-working student/entrepreneur, devious enemy, or alien scare—are similar in their portrayal of Asian Americans as undermining the American way of life. In each case there is the sense that, whether student, enemy, or immigrant, Asians are so different that they will work to replace American ideals and values with their own—that they will not become fully American. This is also true in the rare cases where Asians are villains, such as Japanese gangsters—the Yakuza; the Asian menace is out there, the stereotype explains.

Native Americans are perhaps the only ethnic group that has seen a full-scale reversal in its characterization in American popular culture. Early in the history of electronic media, Native Americans were "savages" who brutalized settlers, who wanted to make new lives for themselves in the American west. At best, if they cooperated with Anglos, Native Americans could serve as scouts and supporters, never leaders, of Anglo troops and wagon trains; at worst, Native American tribes were bloody raiders of innocent villages or alcoholics on reservations. All this has notably changed since the 1970s. It is now rare to see a negative portrayal of a Native American in American popular culture. If anything, the images of Native Americans have become stereotypically positive as tribes are presented as environmentally sensitive, peace-loving people who acted only in self-defense against rapacious Anglos.

Another stereotype deserving of attention here is the vision of crass, consumerist capitalism that is at the root of most programming in American popular culture. Whether it is rap music videos filled with Cadillac Escalades, ever-larger gold crosses proclaiming the wearer's Christian faith, other sources of "bling-bling," or the luxurious setting of Southfork Ranch in *Dallas*, most American movies, music, and television programs create fantasy worlds of extraordinary wealth. Even television shows set among the allegedly poor—*Roseanne* and *Grace under Fire* stand as useful examples—have their families living in relatively large houses surrounded by refrigerators, microwave ovens, dishwashers, televisions, VCRs, cars, and other assorted consumer goods that are, in much of the world, unimaginable extravagances. As a consequence, American popular culture presents a vision of Americans as wealthy, consumerist, and selfish.

A final dimension of American popular culture worth discussion here is its preponderant use of English as its medium of communication. Throughout most of its period of dominance in world entertainment, American popular culture has been made, sold, and often consumed in English. Moreover, the marketing tie-ins to which the products of American popular culture are linked, whether Mickey Mouse's ears or a *Star Wars* T-shirt, are often recognizably and obviously both American and in English. Accordingly, the use and consumption of American popular culture can also provoke concerns from people who believe that the very language in which movies, music, and television programs are being presented is systematically destroying their native culture. Language thus presents another dimension on which objections to American popular culture can be raised.

It is important to remember here that while each of the issues addressed above—gender, sexuality, violence, and the like—was discussed individually, they are experienced cumulatively. No film or video or song or program features only one of these controversial aspects; each inevitably contains several of, if not all, these concerns. Thus sexual violence can be used to dominate women and pressure them into accepting traditional gender roles that bring them access to great wealth and security, particularly against an alien, dangerous other—be he or she African American, Latino/a, poor, or any of a number of other fear-inducing persons or groups. Any or all of this can be and often is objectionable, offensive and norm challenging both in the United States and around the world. Much of this (potentially) offensive material is further embedded in cross-marketing tie-ins, meaning that violence, sexuality, diversity, gender, and other complex social phenomena can become associated with fast-food restaurants, cell phone ring tones, clothing choices and styles, or any other commodity that can be sold through a movie, a piece of music, a performer's endorsement, or a television program. Linked to the kinds of political values also embedded in American popular culture's products, American movies, music, and television programs provide endless ammunition and evidence for those who oppose both American values and the process of globalization. In such a circumstance, any expectation that globalization is either inevitable or unidirectional is, at best, misinformed. At worst, it betrays an ignorance of the way globalization is experienced in people's homes around the world.

Conclusion

American popular culture, particularly as manifested in movies, music, and television programs, has a relatively specific content. American television shows, movies, and music tend to emerge from the core variables of American civic culture. While the individual values evident in American public culture may be mixed in different proportions in different works and may even be used to paint a negative portrait of the values in some cases, these values substantially shape the message and meaning of particular television programs, music, and films. The products of American popular culture are further embedded in formulas and narrative conventions that further define their "American-ness." These factors combine to define American popular culture.

107

GLOBALIZATION, FRAGMEGRATION, AND AMERICAN POPULAR CULTURE

This chapter explores the legal context of international trade in popular culture—a trade that is tightly linked to global fears of the power of American popular culture to corrupt societies and overwhelm competitors. It then offers a series of case studies of the ways American popular culture has encouraged processes of fragmegration in diverse societies. To the degree that people link American values with globalization as such, they tend to resist and reject those forces that promote globalization worldwide. Thus, like the process of globalization itself, the relationship between American popular culture and its international audiences is a complex one. At the least, no simple line between the use of American popular culture and support for contemporary patterns of globalization can be drawn.

Global Law and American Popular Culture

As was addressed in chapter 1, globalization has not occurred independently of the nation-state and the system of international laws various countries have negotiated to facilitate the growth of open markets, the exchange of capital, and the internationalization of global economic, political, and cultural systems. Rather, globalization has been significantly shaped by state action. Notably, concerns that popular culture and other forms of mass communication may harm or destroy local cultures have been central to the history of modern globalization. In fact, other than enforcing restrictions on population migration and requiring their residents to register with the state, thus limiting the free movement of people as well as goods and services that a truly globalized world would allow, some of the most restrictive state actions regarding the liberalization of international trade have been focused on cultural issues. Such restrictions have been built into international trade treaties since the very first General Agreement on Tariffs and Trade was passed to promote freer trade in the Western world in 1947, suggesting the significance of cultural products as an element of contemporary globalization.

At the core of these trade disputes lies a deceptively simple question: is popular culture a commodity like rice or computers or automobiles, or is it an agent of socialization that shapes culture? If popular culture is a commodity, the logic of the free market concludes that few, if any, restrictions ought to be placed on its global exchange. If people like American popular culture products, and those products can be created in the United States more cheaply than they can be produced anywhere else, then people ought to be allowed to enjoy as many American popular culture products as they like without regulation. Anything less will guarantee that people will have access to fewer movies, at a higher price, with less enjoyment than they would have from those created and presented in an unrestricted market.

By contrast, if popular culture is a meaning-bearing entity, if its products both manifest and shape culture, then diverse states and communities have an interest in limiting the access and influence of an alien popular culture to their own. That is, if American popular culture is, in fact, American, and it does, in fact, produce changed values and attitudes in its consumers, then local communities have reason to fear American popular movies, music, and television programs. This is all the more the case given the multiple ways in which American popular culture is expressed in movies, music, and television programs—product tie-ins, clothing, virtual communities, sponsored tours, and the like. Such products are, in these circumstances, a potential tool of cultural imperialism—the harbingers and agents of the replacement of local values and norms with American globalized ones.

Unsurprisingly, the United States has been at the forefront of efforts to reduce barriers to the trade in cultural products since the beginning of the era of contemporary globalization in the 1940s. The U.S. position has been and remains that popular culture products are no different from any other commodity and so no special rules or exemptions ought to govern their trade worldwide. Speaking of efforts to liberalize the trade in movies in the late 1980s and early 1990s, for example, Peter Morici, who served as director of the U.S. International Trade Commission during the period, noted,

"When we're talking about cinema, I think it's largely a commercial issue and not a cultural issue. Globally there's a preference for what Hollywood puts out. We have a very competitive industry, and that is certainly evidenced by the amount of film we sell worldwide." Similarly, a spokesman for the California Trade and Commerce Agency, Mike Marando, insisted: "Making movies is a market-driven product. We don't see it as cultural imperialism. We see it as a marketplace issue."[1]

Resistance to the American position has often been centered in France, although many other nations have participated in efforts to curb the international trade in cultural artifacts. Notably, many of these countries have agreed to other trade rules that have materially harmed their citizens in terms of jobs, tax policies, and environmental regulations; these people have generally agreed to accept the negative consequences of free trade in most aspects of international economic life in exchange for the economic benefits it brings. The major exception is cultural affairs.

The countries generally insisting on exceptions for culture in free trade agreements make a series of linked arguments that, cumulatively, expose their collective fears that American popular culture products may lead to cultural corruption, cultural imperialism, and/or cultural homogenization. Each may have a distinct basis for opposing trade in cultural artifacts, but they combine in alliances that seek to limit cultural globalization's potentially negative effects. In 1993, for example, French president François Mitterand revealed his fears of American cultural imperialism when he claimed that "creations of the spirit are not just commodities; the elements of culture are not pure business. What is at stake is the cultural identity of all our nations—it is the freedom to create and choose our own images. A society which abandons the means of depicting itself would soon be an enslaved society."[2] Similarly, in 2002 a Canadian government group, the Cultural Industries Sectoral Advisory Group on International Trade, opposed free trade in cultural products on grounds that such trade would tend to create cultural homogeneity:

> The underlying principle and overall objective of the instrument is to ensure that cultural diversity is preserved in the face of the challenge posed by globalization, trade liberalization and rapid technological changes. Although new information technologies, globalization and evolving multilateral trade policies offer indisputable possibilities for the expression of cultural diversity, they may also be detrimental to ensuring cultural diversity. This is particularly the case when, for example, domestic cultural content is not accorded reasonable shelf space in its own domestic market, when the over-concentration of production and distribution of cultural content contributes to the standardization of cultural expression, or when

111

developing countries, because of lack of resources, run the risk of being excluded from the international cultural space as it is currently being constructed with new information and communications technologies. There is an urgent need to address these new developments to ensure that cultural diversity, as a factor of social cohesion and economic development, is preserved and enhanced.[3]

Likewise, in commenting on a proposed free trade agreement between the United States and Australia, the Music Council of Australia, in a report to the Australian government's Department of Foreign Affairs and Trade's Office of Trade Negotiations, insisted: "The larger context for this discussion is the need to maintain and foster cultural diversity. The rationale for trade liberalization depends upon the doctrine of comparative advantage which, in the cultural sphere, leads to cultural homogeneity. The two objectives are basically opposed. But in the cultural sphere, cultural diversity is more important than economic efficiency."[4] Culture is thus considered by many groups and nations to be different and thus in need of protection from normal free trading business practices.

The first General Agreement on Tariffs and Trade, adopted in 1947, created a special exemption for cultural artifacts. Article 4 of that original GATT addressed European fears of American cultural imperialism in that it allowed European countries still recovering from the devastation of World War II to impose quotas on the number of foreign films—usually American—that could be distributed and shown in their countries. This was intended to give the European film industry time to rebuild itself with the revenues generated from domestic audiences without competition from American movies. In addition, the 1947 GATT allowed the European countries to provide subsidies to their film industries. These subsidies served to supplement the costs associated with producing and distributing movies, meaning that the filmmakers did not need to generate enough money to produce movies from ticket sales in theaters. (Such subsidies, regardless of industry, are generally held to be unfair constraints on free trade by free trade advocates, since they mask the real cost of producing a given product and violate the logic of comparative advantage that is understood to make free trade work as a practice.) Finally, Article 20 of the first GATT allowed nations to protect their "national treasures," however defined.[5] Thus concerns about the protection of cultural products and culture-producing industries were enshrined in international law even as the era of modern globalization began. Culture was seen as different.

European nations—the countries originally tied to the United States in the early period of modern globalization—maintained their right to protect their culture industries through quotas and subsidies across the ensuing decades. Additionally, in an effort to avoid cultural homogenization, they also often declared their domestic movie, music, and television production companies and facilities to be national treasures not subject to purchase by international corporations. The United States was generally opposed to this position and insisted, during what was called the Uruguay Round of GATT talks in 1986, that cultural industries needed to be brought into the arena of free trade. The ensuing talks led to a new trade agreement more focused on service and entertainment enterprises, rather than the traditional heavy industries (steel, automobiles, and the like) that were the major focus of GATT. In the General Agreement on Trade in Service (GATS), negotiated during the Uruguay Round, signatories agreed to develop schedules in which their service and telecommunication industries were to be integrated into a global economy. As had happened in 1947, however, France continued to insist that audiovisual industries—movies, music, and television—be exempt from free trade rules. This demand was a central sticking point in what turned out to be seven years of negotiations during the Uruguay Round and very nearly led to the collapse of the GATT negotiations as their December 15, 1993, deadline approached. In the end, the United States relented and agreed to pursue the question at a later date. Culture, again, was treated separately from other forms of trade as fears of American imperial or homogenizing culture became front and center in the talks.[6]

While cultural issues served as a point of contention in the Uruguay Round, they also stimulated new areas of international agreement. First, rules on international copyright were strengthened and linked to free trade. Thus intellectual property—ideas, creative works (including television programs, movies, and music) and so on—was protected in order to guarantee a legal environment in which people could share the products of their intellect across national boundaries safely and profitably. This is a necessary first step to creating a truly global marketplace of ideas—without copyright protections, individuals and organizations have no incentive to publish their ideas for the world to use, develop, and implement. Second, rules governing the ownership of telecommunications companies—previously viewed as national treasures untouchable by international competition—were liberalized.[7] This set the legal conditions in which it became possible for telecommunications companies to become transnational corporations. It was thus a key step in encouraging the kinds of corporate centralization of the entertainment industry that was described in chapter 1.

Even as the United States pursued neoliberal policies on trade in culture at a global scale, it promoted similar policies in various regional agreements. It faced similar results. Most notable among these regional agreements is NAFTA, the North American Free Trade Agreement signed by the United States, Canada, and Mexico in 1993. NAFTA serves as an interesting case study for the role cultural products play in globalization because it links three countries noted for the production of popular culture—both Canada and Mexico have substantial popular culture industries separate from that centered in the United States—that nonetheless stand in very different competitive positions when it comes to trade in their products. The United States, as has been made clear throughout this book, is the world's leading provider of popular culture products. However, the vast majority of these products are presented in English, and while they might be dubbed into Spanish, they lack the kind of cultural transparency they might have if sold to an English-speaking country. Accordingly, Mexico produces—and Mexicans enjoy—a substantial amount of domestically produced programming, particularly in the areas of television and music. This is true even in the case of Spanish-speaking people living in the United States; they are far more likely to watch Mexican-produced programming in Spanish than Mexicans are to watch American programming in English. American products are less competitive across this cultural gap. In contrast, while the Canadian popular culture industry is well developed, it is predominantly an English-speaking enterprise. Moreover, the vast majority of Canadians live within one hundred miles of the U.S. border, making cross-border transmission and reception of programming easy and attractive. As a practical matter, the Canadian popular culture industry is far more vulnerable to American products than is Mexico's.

This difference in power and vulnerability is reflected in NAFTA. The regulations protecting Canadian cultural artifacts are far more extensive than are those affecting Mexican-U.S. trade. Annex 2106 of NAFTA exempts Canadian audiovisual industries from the free trade requirements embedded in the treaty. It also empowers the Canadian government to review and limit any U.S. investments in what the annex calls Canada's "cultural heritage or national identity"—clauses that, as was noted above, generally refer to television stations, film production facilities, and the like. By contrast, Mexican negotiators generally accepted the logic of free trade in their cultural exchanges with the United States. The major exceptions were that foreign ownership of Mexican audiovisual production companies was limited to 49 percent, and a quota of 30 percent was established for Mexican movies on theater screens. (This quota was never enforced. The percentage of Mexican movies shown in Mexican theaters decreased to 10 percent by 1997.) However, the increasing size of the Hispanic market in the United States has opened new markets for Mexican programming, markets made available only because of the free trade rules negotiated in NAFTA.[8]

Notably, the Mexican case may ultimately undermine Canadian resistance to free cultural trade as regulated in NAFTA. American popular culture providers continue to pressure the U.S. government to reject protectionist clauses in trade treaties, even for cultural products. Among other threats, the major American popular culture corporations have urged the U.S. government to place import tariffs on other Canadian products, such as lumber, to force the Canadian government to eliminate barriers to the free exchange of cultural artifacts. Mexican authorities, too, have recognized a large and growing market of Latino/as in Canada for whom Mexican-produced television programs and music might be particularly attractive. Thus Mexican negotiators are also pushing Canada to reduce its trade restrictions on popular culture products.[9] The likely outcome of these pressures is not immediately clear; however, the desire to protect culture and culture-producing enterprises from alien values and norms is clearly central to contemporary globalization—as is the desire to eliminate such barriers in favor of a truly free market.

The diverse issues, concerns, and rules governing international trade in popular culture have continued to drive international talks and law in the years since NAFTA was formed. In 2001, for example, the United Nations Educational, Scientific, and Cultural Organization, UNESCO, passed a Universal Declaration on Cultural Diversity. In that document the United Nations and the declaration's signatories insisted that cultural diversity is a "common heritage of humanity." It then called for the development of a treaty to promote and protect cultural diversity on a global scale.[10]

The delegates to the 2001 conference then followed with a draft treaty in 2005. Passed on October 20, 2005, the treaty was intended to empower states to protect their interests in their cultural industries. This treaty clearly illustrates the tension between the integrating and fragmenting forces of globalization as it relates to fears of American popular culture corruption, imperialism, and homogenization. As the specific language states, the objectives of the Convention on the Protection and Promotion of the Diversity of Cultural Expressions are

(a) to protect and promote the diversity of cultural expressions;
(b) to create the conditions for cultures to flourish and to freely interact in a mutually beneficial manner;
(c) to encourage dialogue among cultures with a view to ensuring wider and balanced cultural exchanges in the world in favour of intercultural respect and a culture of peace;
(d) to foster interculturality in order to develop cultural interaction in the spirit of building bridges among peoples;

Table 4.1 Global Restrictions on Trade in Popular Culture

Nation/Group	*Rules Limiting Free Trade in Popular Culture*
European Union	Requires that a majority of programming be of European origins, when practical
Italy	Requires that multiscreen movie complexes with more than 1,300 seats reserve 25–30 percent of their seats for audiences of European Union-produced films
Spain	Requires that one day of European films be shown for every three days during which non-European films are shown; requires dubbing of movies into Catalan and imposes quotas for the showing of Spanish-language (Catalan) films
Canada	Requires the 35 percent of radio broadcasts be certifiably Canadian, as determined by a formula created by the Canadian government; bars foreign ownership of Canadian film production studios
Malaysia	Requires that 80 percent of television programming and 60 percent of radio programming be of local origin, although these standards are poorly enforced; requires that video rental stores stock 30 percent locally produced movies at all times
Hungary	Requires public television to show 70 percent European-produced programming (with exceptions for advertisements, news, and similar shows), at least 51 percent of which must be Hungarian in origin; requires private television stations to show at least 15 percent Hungarian programming
South Korea	Requires domestic movies to be shown in each cinema for at least 146 days per year, barring special exemptions; has agreed to reduce this requirement only if Korean-produced films capture 40 percent of market share

Source: Adapted from Shapiro, "The Culture Thief."

(e) to promote respect for the diversity of cultural expressions and raise awareness of its value at the local, national, and international levels;

(f) to reaffirm the importance of the link between culture and development for all countries, particularly for developing countries and to support actions undertaken nationally and internationally to secure recognition of the true value of this link;

(g) to give recognition to the distinctive nature of cultural activities, goods, and services as vehicles of identity, values, and meaning;

(h) to reaffirm the sovereign rights of States to maintain, adopt, and implement policies and measures that they deem appropriate for the protection and promotion of the diversity of cultural expressions on their territory;

(i) to strengthen international cooperation and solidarity in a spirit of partnership with a view, in particular, to enhancing the capacities of developing countries in order to protect and promote the diversity of cultural expressions.

These goals, in turn, were to be met according to the following principles:

2. Principle of sovereignty
States have, in accordance with the Charter of the United Nations and the principles of international law, the sovereign right to adopt measures and policies to protect and promote the diversity of cultural expressions within their territory.

3. Principle of equal dignity of and respect for all cultures
The protection and promotion of the diversity of cultural expressions presuppose the recognition of equal dignity of and respect for all cultures, including the cultures of persons belonging to minorities and indigenous peoples.

4. Principle of international solidarity and cooperation
International cooperation and solidarity should be aimed at enabling countries, especially developing countries, to create and strengthen their means of cultural expression, including their cultural industries, whether nascent or established, at the local, national, and international levels.

5. Principle of the complementarity of economic and cultural aspects of development
Since culture is one of the mainsprings of development, the cultural aspects of development are as important as its economic aspects, which individuals and peoples have the fundamental right to participate in and enjoy.

6. Principle of sustainable development
Cultural diversity is a rich asset for individuals and societies. The protection, promotion, and maintenance of cultural diversity are an essential requirement for sustainable development for the benefit of present and future generations.[11]

Yet even as protectionism was to be allowed—and even promoted—in given communities, freedom in cultural exchanges was to be promoted:

7. Principle of equitable access
Equitable access to a rich and diversified range of cultural expressions from all over the world and access of cultures to the means of expressions

and dissemination constitute important elements for enhancing cultural diversity and encouraging mutual understanding.

8. Principle of openness and balance

   When States adopt measures to support the diversity of cultural expressions, they should seek to promote, in an appropriate manner, openness to other cultures of the world and to ensure that these measures are geared to the objectives pursued under the present Convention.[12]

Thus protection is to walk hand-in-hand with interaction. Notably, the vote on the convention was 148 for, 2 against, with 4 abstentions. Only the United States and Israel voted no. If 30 UN member states ratify the convention, it will go into effect three months later. Concerns about the meaning and significance of American popular culture thus remain at the heart of debates about contemporary globalization.

American Popular Culture and Fragmegration in Four Countries

The rest of this chapter offers analyses of the ways four countries—Iran, Venezuela, Hong Kong, and France—have reacted to at least some aspects of American popular culture. Notably, these four countries share little in common:

- France, like the United States, is an advanced industrial democracy. France and the United States have a long, deeply interconnected history: France helped the United States at its creation and was liberated by the United States and its allies in World War II, but it has maintained an uneasy alliance with the United States in the years since. Regardless of their policy differences, however, the two nations share a basic political and economic philosophy.
- Iran, by contrast, is a theocracy run by Islamic mullahs. Prior to 1979 Iran and the United States were close allies; however, after the Islamic Revolution of 1979, Iran's leaders declared the United States the "Great Satan" and became one of the United States' most active enemies—in cultural as well as political affairs.
- Hong Kong was, for most of the twentieth century, a colony of Great Britain, and so a haven for American ideas and people. It was also a center of production of the associated products of American political culture—movie and band T-shirts; the actual videotapes consumers purchased once a movie was released to cassette, and the like. In 1999, however, Hong Kong was returned to China's control, putting

one of the world's economic powerhouses under the control of the world's foremost—supposedly—Communist countries.

- Venezuela is a South American country that has had a mixed relationship with the United States throughout its history—Venezuelan-U.S. relations have been volatile as various American and Venezuelan leaders have tried to promote each nation's interests against the other. Venezuela is in a contested relationship with the United States as its president, Hugo Chávez, attempts to resist U.S. economic and political authority in the Western Hemisphere.

The lack of common politics, social and economic life, and history among these four nations is actually quite useful for this study. After all, it would not be all that surprising if groups and countries that share values and ideals reacted similarly to what might be seen as alien concepts or demands. However, to the degree that disparate systems react in similar ways, the influence of the independent force can be assessed. As will be seen, American popular culture is a source of controversy in each of the four countries examined here. In addition, its effects play along the three dimensions of globalization described in chapter 1: economic, political, and cultural. It can, accordingly, be seen as an agent of fragmegration in contemporary global politics.

Fragmegration and American Popular Culture in Iran

From the mid-1950s through the end of the 1970s Iran was one of the United States' closest allies in the Middle East. In 1953, the United States supported a political coup in Iran that led to the reinstallation of the nation's monarchial ruler, Mohammad Reza Shah Pahlavi. From 1953 to 1979 the shah linked Iranian and U.S. politics and tried to promote the benefits of Western capitalist consumerism by allowing large numbers of Iranians, including women, to get educations and build lifestyles similar to those in the West. (The major exception in lifestyle came in the areas of democracy and human rights; the shah and the Iranian secret police, SAVAK, were savage in repressing movements for political democracy and human rights in his authoritarian state.) In return, the United States offered Iran protection from the Soviet Union (with which Iran shared a border) and guaranteed a market for Iran's oil. The United States even sold Iran its most sophisticated fighter aircraft, the F-15, making Iran the first nation other than a NATO ally or Israel to whom the United States had sold this weapon. Iran was a central component of U.S. foreign policy in the Middle East for over twenty-five years.

Perhaps as a result of the close relationship between the United States and Iran, including the close relationships many Americans had with Iranian friends and colleagues, U.S. and other spy agencies largely missed an emerging cultural rebellion that was growing in Iran in the late 1970s: the rise of fundamentalist Islam. While the ideas and attitudes of people in the Islamic world are as varied as anywhere else, Islamic fundamentalism is characterized by the desire to return the social and political values and practices of Muslims to those that existed soon after the emergence of Islam as a religion in the seventh century. As a partial list, women were to be tightly controlled within the family, wearing long robes to cover their bodies and faces when they went out in public; men were to grow beards; and, most important, Islamic clerics were to have the final political authority—a form of government known as a theocracy.

The emergent Iranian Islamist movement centered on the teachings of an Iranian cleric exiled to Iraq—Ayatollah Ruholla Khomeini. Khomeini, with the assistance of the Iraqi government (long an enemy of Iran), built a movement grounded on resentment of the shah's repression of political liberty and human rights. In particular, the movement's members demanded the freedom to practice Islam as they desired. The movement was further grounded on anti-American, anti-Western principles. Since the United States and its allies supported the shah despite his repression of the human rights of his citizens (for the United States and others, the shah's support of their side in the context of Cold War negated expectations that his government should follow human rights norms), the United States and the West became the locus of evil—the masters who controlled the shah. This argument included a rejection of Western ideas of human rights: human rights clearly had no substance in the West since they were ignored in Iran. Accordingly, a movement for social change could not be built on Western, liberal principles. Instead, a counterforce grounded on the "true" principles of the nation—which Khomeini and his supporters saw as fundamentalist Islam—was needed to get rid of the shah and his hated regime.

Frustrations with the shah came to a head in 1978 when antigovernment riots broke out across the country. In January 1979 the shah fled Iran, first to the United States and later to Egypt, where he died in 1980. In February 1979 Khomeini returned to Iran and declared the nation to be a theocracy. As a final symbol of hatred of the United States and the West, a group of Iranian radical students occupied the U.S. embassy in Tehran starting in November 1979—technically an act of war. They and a series of government supporters held fifty Americans hostage for the next 444 days, releasing them only after Ronald Reagan was inaugurated president of the United States on January 20, 1981.

Since 1979 Iran has been a relative political pariah worldwide. The Islamic fundamentalist revolution that led to the overthrow of the shah brought with it limited contacts from the Western world, especially once Iran was identified as a state supporter of international terrorist organizations. In addition, the political leadership of post-revolution Iran worked hard to enforce traditional religious law across Iranian society. Similarly, the education system was altered to focus on religious teaching, and women were largely banned from public life. Finally, the political system was changed to ensure the dominance of the clerics: while elections might take place for city, regional, and even national governments, the list of possible candidates for a given office had to be cleared by the clerics. Efforts were made to purge Iran of its secular history in favor of the Islamist political agenda preferred by Khomeini (who died in 1989) and his supporters and successors.

An additional intent of many of Iran's laws was to prevent the seepage of Western American culture—especially popular culture—into Iranian culture and society. The nation passed laws limiting access to satellite dishes, Western music, and Western movies to limit the corrupting influence of American popular culture on what Iranian youths see, think, and want. It further established standards of dress that forbade women in particular from wearing Western clothing or makeup. Perhaps most famously, in 1988 Ayatollah Khomeini issued a fatwa, or religious order, that authorized any Muslim to kill the author of *The Satanic Verses,* an Indian-born ex-Muslim named Salman Rushdie. (The fatwa has been reauthorized since Khomeini's death.) In addition, as recently as October 2005 the president of Iran declared that no one should be allowed to watch Western movies or television programs, and in December of the same year he expanded his order to ban listening to Western music. In many ways, then, Iran can be seen to have attempted to isolate itself from the effects of Western ideas and experiences, including those associated with American popular culture.

Yet even as it attempted to segregate itself from corrupting foreign influences in the immediate aftermath of the 1979 revolution, Iran remained profoundly integrated into the world economy. Crude petroleum constituted 75 percent of Iran's exports in 2000–2001, while refined petroleum accounted for a further 8.8 percent. In the same year Iran had extensive import-export ties with Germany, the United Arab Emirates (UAE), Italy, Russia, Japan, and South Korea. In all, Iran imported over $15 billion worth of goods and services while it exported almost $28.5 billion.[13] Such extensive contacts with outside countries and forces has certainly limited Iran's attempted cultural isolationism.

Iran's cultural retreat from the world has been further limited because it has experienced a dramatic series of demographic shifts in its population in recent years. The generation that lived through and led the 1979 revolution has been substantially replaced by much younger people who, although they grew up in an Islamic state, lack the memories of life under the shah that legitimate Iran's social and political isolation in the minds of many of their elders. As of 2002 over 30 percent of its population was under age fifteen; an additional 34.1 percent was between fifteen and thirty.[14] Thus, almost two-thirds of Iran's population was born after the 1979 revolution—meaning that the majority of Iran's citizens have different social and political experiences from those held by the country's political leaders.

Iran has also undergone a political crisis in recent years. Former president Khatami initiated a series of political reforms intended to reduce the influence of religious leaders over Iranian political life as well as to reduce corruption within the political system. This led to increased access to Western goods and ideas—including popular culture—for ordinary Iranians, especially younger ones. In response, the religious leadership exercised its constitutional authority to strike the names of candidates it deemed unacceptable for election to the national assembly and a wide range of regional offices. Many reform leaders were excluded from elections both in 2004 and in 2005; as a consequence, a new, more conservative leadership came into power in Iran without the legitimacy of having won a truly representative election.

This combination of sought/enforced isolation, economic integration, demographic shifting, and electoral crisis has combined to make Iran a useful case for describing and analyzing the influence of American popular culture on contemporary globalization in both its fragmenting and integrating dimensions. A significant dimension of the current crisis has been the demands of Iran's younger voters for greater political, social, and cultural freedom. Younger women desire the right to wear something other than the *hijab* and have spent years slowly amending the published dress code to allow more hair and more skin to be exposed in what has been called the "pink revolution."[15] Others have insisted on the right to wear makeup and otherwise challenge public control of women's lives.[16]

More broadly, much of Iran's youth is demanding the liberalization and Westernization of Iranian culture. Many young people are teaching themselves English through the Internet as well as with imported Western music and satellite television; they are, at the same time, exposed and drawn to Western fashion and programming and social styles.[17] In addition, there are now resorts outside the major cities that cater to young people and provide a zone of freedom and a lifestyle similar to that of their Western counterparts.[18] Likewise, movies like *Titanic*, *Face/Off*, and *Air Force One* have been widely available through satellite services and bootleg videotapes for many years.[19] American popular culture has undoubtedly led many Iranians to desire closer contacts with the rest of the world—the integrating dimension of globalization.

Yet even as American popular culture has lured some Iranians, it has repelled others. More conservative members of Iranian society clearly link Westernization and Americanization as the forces they are fighting to resist. One, a woman named Khaki, notes: "You as a person should never forget your country. Iranian people prefer to go out of the country and show themselves as American." Similarly, she notes, "My uncle has been in the U.S. for 25 years. I can never accept his ideas. Too much democracy."[20] Other social conservatives have come to believe that encroaching American popular culture is a dangerous consequence of globalization, one that threatens the stability and cultural integrity of Iran. As Ayatollah Jannati recently put it, "The biggest vice facing us is the cultural offensive. . . . What are those seeking the opening of the way for the U.S. thinking about? Why are you betraying Islam?"[21] Exposure to the products of American culture can thus cause fragmentation even as they prompt others to call for integration.

It is not particularly surprising, of course, that social conservatives resist change—such resistance is a useful working definition of what it means to be a social conservative regardless of one's country or community. Likewise, it is not all that unexpected that young people attempting to establish their own identities resent and resist establish rules and norms. Notably, many nonconservatives have also expressed worry at the threat of an American cultural invasion in Iran. Even people who have largely accepted the goods and benefits associated with Western life and American culture—*Titanic* and Nike, Levis and rock and roll—are concerned that American popular culture "will destroy the culture."[22] As a particular example, Iranian filmmakers—even reform-oriented, progressive ones—have worried that the unleashing of restrictions on American movies will lead to American cultural imperialism and the destruction of the native film industry.[23] Concerns about globalization and American popular culture, then, are not just expressed by those who oppose American values. The fragmegration dynamic is embedded as a feature of the globalization-popular culture intersection regardless of simple ideological formulations.

123

Fragmegration and American Popular Culture in France

As was noted earlier, France was and remains one of the United States' closest allies in world affairs. While relations between the United States and France are often tense, theirs are the differences of family members—they dispute how best to achieve what are generally shared goals of democracy, human rights, and capitalism but share a broad agreement that such ends are the proper ones for society. Hence even as the U.S.-France relationship waxes and wanes from tight alliance (the American Revolution, World War I, and World War II) to skeptical and even wary distance (the Napoleonic years; France's post–World War II rejection of NATO membership), the relationship endures for social, political, economic, and ideological reasons.

France finds itself in a relatively difficult position today, especially in terms of its cultural identity. This has made it particularly sensitive to fears of American cultural imperialism. For most of the last one thousand years, France has stood as one of the great powers of Europe. It had substantial power, both militarily and economically, and used this power to build wealthy cities filled with great art and attractive to many of the world's most famous and important artists, thinkers, and scientists. Its borders at one time housed the capital of the Roman Catholic Church at Avignon, and it built a vast colonial empire that stretched across the Pacific, Southeast Asia, and a large part of Africa.

Yet even as France was powerful, it was also under threat. Its wealth and power made it a target for other regimes in Europe; many of the second millennium's most horrible wars were fought on French soil. Some, like the French Wars of Religion (1562–1598) were fought in the name of religion (this war saw a significant portion of France's population slaughtered over the question of whether or not people should be Catholic or Protestant), while others, like World War I, were intradynastic struggles to protect and acquire international empires.

Throughout this period France was faced by two external challengers for European supremacy in particular: Great Britain and Germany. Germany in its modern form is a creation of the latter part of the nineteenth century; however, various elements of modern Germany, particularly Prussia and neighboring regions, have attacked and invaded France across the centuries many times—only to have France reciprocate time and again. Great Britain, by contrast, used its position astride Europe's sea-going trade routes to dominate international trade and try to limit France's ability to develop and expand its colonial empire.

Just as it faced external challenges (like Britain's attempt to limit its sea-based trade), France also endured a great social upheaval: the French Revolution, which started in 1789. France's revolution took a very different course from the American one, largely because the French revolutionaries were fighting against the king and the king's allies (a combination of foreign forces who were sent to support Louis during the early period of the Revolution and the money and ideological power of the Catholic Church, whose clerics supported Louis against the revolutionaries) in France itself. The French Revolution was notable for its hostility to religion, particularly Catholicism, as a consequence of the church's support for the monarchy. The French Revolution was likewise notable for its violence as, in time, what came to be known as the Terror began and thousands of people lost their lives to the guillotine and other killing devices. This, in turn, was followed by the Napoleonic Wars as Napoleon Bonaparte took control of the revolutionary French army, drove back the foreign armies sent to restore Louis to the throne, declared himself emperor, and then set off to conquer Europe and, fatally, Russia. Indeed, by the time the French Revolution can be said to have ended, in 1815 after Napoleon had escaped from prison and been beaten after launching a second series of wars against the rest of Europe, the nation had endured some of the most dramatic changes any society had ever faced—all in the space of twenty-six years.

As would be expected from the discussion of culture in chapter 1, no society can survive such profound changes so quickly without facing major disruptions—and without establishing new ways to build loyalty and support for the new regime. Three means the French revolutionaries used to establish the legitimacy of their new system deserve discussion here, for they contextualize France's contemporary difficulties with globalization. These are secularism, language, and nationalism.

Secularism is a clear by-product of the French revolution. In response to the Catholic Church's support for the monarchy, the revolutionaries set out to purge organized religion in France. Churches and cathedrals were destroyed, and many priests and cardinals were killed or exiled. Marriage was stripped of its religious sacrament, and people who wished to get married could do so only in a secular civil ceremony. State documents and rituals were stripped of reference to God or a higher authority. To be French was to be secular; to be religious was to be *not French*. And while many of these restrictions were lifted or reduced in the ensuing centuries, the legacy of secularism remains a crucial component of contemporary French identity: the French are today, for the most part, the least religious, God-believing, church-attending people in Europe. (An exception to this pattern will be addressed later in this section.)

A second component of French identity insisted upon by the revolutionaries was the creation of universal literacy in formal French. This, too, countered the Catholic Church's monopoly on education through its restriction on who could or could not read the Bible, but more broadly it was intended as a way to link the disparate parts of France into a unified whole. (Like many European nations, modern France was created over time as a central kingdom—in France's case the one centered in Paris—slowly conquered and integrated other regional governments into a centralized whole.) French was seen as a way to guarantee that everyone everywhere could and would read the same material, converse in the same language, and maintain their shared identity as citizens of France. Speaking French became an essential component of being French.

Questions of secularism and language took on particular power during the French Revolution, when they were linked to the development of the first real nationalist movement in world history. The desire for secularism and the unity of the French language were used, for the first time in history, to mobilize enormous armies of conscripts, factory workers, and civilian adjuncts to fight and support France's wars during the Revolution. Where in the past a European army might have once consisted of thirty thousand trained troops, Napoleon's armies swelled into the hundreds of thousands. Supporting such an army meant that millions of others would have to sacrifice food and jobs and family members to the war machine. Much of this sacrifice was justified in terms of war necessity—the nation was under invasion—but much more of it was linked to a new ideology of French nationalism: that France was a great nation and needed to behave like one in order to achieve its destiny. Individual identities were thus linked to the destiny of the state: if France fell, so might one's sense of being French. The wars of the French Revolution can in this sense be said to be the first wars of national survival. To lose the war was to lose the state to which one's own identity was linked.

It is this troika of secularism, language, and nationalism that problematizes France's relation with globalization today. Secular values are perceived to be under assault as new populations, particularly Muslims from former French colonies in North Africa, immigrate to France in search of the nation's jobs and freedoms. These new immigrants may speak French, but they reject the secularism of French public culture out of hand. Instead, they insist on their right to wear religious and other culturally appropriate symbols in public life. This insistence has led to a significant confrontation between French school officials and the new immigrants: French schools are proactively secular, banning the display of religious garb or symbols outright (although many smaller-sized Christian crosses are worn by students in French classrooms). In one recent case French officials barred a young Muslim girl from wearing her headdress in school; in response, her parents refused to send her to public schools and kept her at home. Unlike the American public cultural definition of religious tolerance as "I'll leave you alone to do your thing if you'll leave me alone to do mine," the French insist that it is only in denying any connection between the religious and political that the rights of all their people can be assured.

Even as the French feel under assault from Muslim immigrants, they feel additionally challenged by the expansion of English as the language of worldwide daily discourse. English has become not just the language of popular culture but of business in general. Many Europeans learn English as a second language; fewer and fewer learn French for the same purpose. Moreover, as English-language movies, music, and television penetrate French popular culture, English is increasingly integrated into casual French. Terms like *le deal* and *le cash flow* substitute for more cumbersome, or perhaps nonexistent, French equivalents. English appears to spread everywhere it touches.

There is, of course, no reason why the spread of English is necessarily a bad thing; indeed, one can argue that the greater degree to which different people can communicate will likely improve, rather than undermine, world affairs. This argument falls on relatively deaf ears in France, however, because of the intimate connection between language, identity and what it means to be "French." As was noted above, to be French is to be secular and French speaking. To be *not French* is to not be secular and French speaking. Hence, religious French speakers (typically Muslims today, although U.S. evangelical churches are spreading across France) *and* secular English speakers are both *not French*.

To protect the linguistic and cultural status of French, France has since 1975 passed a series of laws governing the use of French. Prime among these has been a series of laws requiring the use of proper French in commercials, advertisements, and popular culture programming. Law 94-665, passed in August 1994, is typical. Article 1 notes the key position of the French language in the French constitution and goes on to state that French "shall be the language of instruction, work, trade and exchanges and of public services." Article 2 extends this requirement into the commercial sphere, requiring: "The use of French shall be mandatory for the designation, offer, presentation, instructions for use, and descriptions of the scope and conditions of a warranty of goods, products and services, as well as bills and receipts. The same provisions apply to any written, spoken, radio and television advertisement." The law does make exceptions for television and movie productions presented in their original language,

127

however, opening space for the distribution of American (and other foreign) films and TV shows to French audiences (Article 12).[24]

Enforcement of these rules has been spotty, and as was noted earlier, English continues to creep into everyday French. In response, French authorities have cited and fined companies, individuals, and Web sites for violating French law. For example, by 1998, just four years after the passage of Law 94-665, French language police had checked the advertisements of fifteen thousand companies and issued fines ranging from $150 to $1,000 for violations.[25] In 1997 French authorities threatened to fine the Georgia Institute of Technology $5,000 per visitor to a Web site on which it advertised the services of a branch campus it operates in Metz, in eastern France. All the course descriptions on the Web site were in English, which French officials insisted violated the 1994 law's requirement that advertisements be in French or that other descriptive material be accompanied by a French translation. As Marceau Dechamps of the Defense of the French Language Association explained, "We're starting with this case, but we're convinced there are others. We must . . . begin to regulate the Internet. There can be no 'outlaw' space."[26]

More broadly, France requires 60 percent European content on broadcast entertainment, 40 percent of which must be French. Forty percent of all songs on radio must be in French. It also imposes an 11 percent tax on movie tickets for admission to foreign-made movies. These taxes are used to subsidize the French film industry.[27] And, of course, as was discussed earlier in this chapter, France has taken a leadership role in limiting or rolling back every free trade agreement in those areas in which they touch the international ownership, production, and distribution of culture and cultural industries.

The success of these measures is hard, at best, to assess. English, for example, continues to expand its foothold in French daily linguistic practice, and increasing numbers of French people now seek to have their children become literate in English.[28] The language restrictions for radio play have certainly helped maintain a space for French popular culture acts, whether in pop music, rock and roll, or other genres.[29] Yet the genres themselves are American, suggesting that traditionally French music has been largely pushed aside. Subsidies to the French film industry, which in the early 1990s ran over $350 million per year, have allowed the nation to maintain an active role in movie production.[30] But as was shown in chapter 2, it is American movies that dominate French screens, while French-made movies have virtually no presence in American viewers' lives. Moreover, in light of French birth rates and the rate of African immigration into France, it seems hard to believe that any restrictions on popular culture will ensure the survival of French culture as the French think of it today. (This point will be addressed further in chapter 5.) However, the fact that it is on cultural restrictions in international trade that the French have affixed their attentions is itself indicative of the importance of culture to contemporary globalization: France's restrictions may be misaimed and ineffective, but they are passionately cared about, and modern globalization's course is altered as a consequence of that passion.

Fragmegration and American Popular Culture in Venezuela

Venezuela is the sixth-most populated country in South America and is an important producer of oil, much of which is exported to the United States. In addition, Venezuela was the first country in South America to win its freedom from Spain, in 1821. It did so under the leadership of Simón Bolívar; so important is Bolívar in the history of the nation that the full name of the country, as defined in the constitution of 1999, is the Bolivarian Republic of Venezuela. In contrast with many Latin and South American countries, Venezuela has been governed by civilians in relatively democratic ways since the late 1950s.

Venezuela's status as an oil-rich country on the northern edge of the South American continent has encouraged a close relationship with the United States across much of its history. Some of the closeness of this relationship has been based on the United States' assertion, in the Monroe Doctrine, of its right to intervene in the political affairs of any country in the Western Hemisphere in order to protect U.S. interests. For a nation with a tradition of proud independence like Venezuela, such claims have been viewed as arrogant and misguided. Yet the United States and Venezuela have engaged in a long history of cooperative relations as well; the United States is Venezuela's biggest trade partner, and Venezuela ranks fourth among foreign suppliers of oil to the United States. Venezuela is also the third-largest export market for U.S.-produced goods and services in Latin and South America. In addition, Venezuela shares a border with Colombia, and the United States provides substantial support to the government of Venezuela to assist the United States in interdicting illegal drugs being transported from Colombia for consumption in the United States.[31]

This description of the economic, political, and geographic position of Venezuela, as well as the historical relationship between the United States and Venezuela, suggests that U.S.-Venezuelan relations might offer an ideal-type example of how contemporary globalization can work: Venezuela produces oil; the United States provides needed goods and services in exchange. Two democracies work together toward mutually beneficial goals. However, contemporary patterns of globalization have exacerbated, rather than improved, U.S.-Venezuelan politics. Indeed, Venezuela's president, Hugo Chávez, has become an international hero to the anti-globalization movement worldwide for his efforts to extricate Venezuela from the globalization process shaping the world today.

At the core of Chávez's objections—along with those of his supporters, whether inside Venezuela or outside—to contemporary globalization are the inequities that emerge as free trade and other dimensions of globalization expand in various societies. As was noted in chapter 1, globalization is often accompanied by significant disruption in people's jobs and lives as new, often foreign, companies enter local markets and provide goods and services more cheaply than the community can. (Wal-Mart's "Always Low Prices" slogan serves as a useful example here—their prices are low because of high volumes of international sales and the corporation's concomitant ability to negotiate cheap prices from suppliers. Local stores lack such sales and negotiating power and so cannot offer the cheap prices available at Wal-Mart. Many therefore go out of business.) Moreover, these jobs are often replaced by lower-paying jobs (if they are replaced at all)—again, a job at Wal-Mart is likely to pay less, with fewer (or no) benefits than were available at the prior position. Many people find their lives devastated as a consequence.

Of course, investors, those who supply the new transnational companies with services and goods the companies cannot acquire elsewhere, and many others in society benefit from globalization—in some cases, they benefit by becoming extraordinarily wealthy. Others benefit as corruption often follows the infusion of large amounts of foreign currency. This, in turn, makes it easy for some to acquire good educations for their children, good homes for their families, and good health insurance for their loved ones, even as others struggle to feed themselves. Societies experiencing globalization often face growing inequities across a range of social and political arenas.

Advocates of globalization insist—as was also discussed in chapter 1—that such disruptions are only temporary as new ways of making a living emerge, as people get retrained for new jobs, and the like. In the long run, they insist, everyone will be better off if they simply put up with the pain for the short term. Everything will work out for the best in the end.

Unsurprisingly, many people are not persuaded by the globalizers' promises, and in any case people and their families have to eat in the short term in order to make it to the long. As a consequence, people often put pressure on their government to set policies and laws that lessen their immediate pain and suffering regardless of their (alleged) effects on the long-term promise of globalization. Hugo Chávez has become a populist hero, both in Venezuela and among anti-globalization groups worldwide, by leveraging Venezuela's status and wealth as a major oil exporter to limit the power of transnational corporations in favor of lessening inequities in Venezuelan society. (In so doing, of course, he made himself an enemy to those people and groups—including many inside Venezuela itself—who had benefited from globalization.) For example, in 2001 Chávez passed a new hydrocarbons law that limited foreign ownership of Venezuelan oil companies. It nationalized the production and distribution of oil, making profits earned from the sale of oil a part of the state's budget rather than a corporation's. It further limited the degree to which foreign companies could own other aspects of the oil production industry.[32]

Chávez has used the new revenue derived from oil production to increase social programs aimed at the poor and disadvantaged across Venezuela. The money has been used to build schools and health clinics across the country. Against the claims of the globalizers, then, Chávez has tried to show that the state can still play an important role in limiting the worst effects of globalization in his home country—at least when the nation in question controls a large amount of a significant resource like oil.

Chávez has gone further in his anti-globalization rhetoric and policies than simply redistributing revenue within Venezuela. He has regularly opposed U.S. efforts to push for lower oil prices and has established close ties to Fidel Castro's Cuban government—perhaps the United States' most hated government since it is explicitly anti–United States, a former close ally of the Soviet Union, is at least nominally Communist, and only ninety miles from Florida. He has opposed U.S. policy in Iraq and Haiti and is the region's leading opponent of establishing a free trade agreement among the United States and all the countries of Latin and South America. In November 2005 he successfully opposed the creation of CAFTA, the Central America Free Trade Agreement, at a conference of hemispheric leaders in Argentina. Chávez has subsequently become a symbol of the rejection of Western-style American globalization in favor of more regionally and culturally based political and economic coalitions. As such, he has become a major thorn in the side of the administration of President George W. Bush. Indeed, one of Bush's supporters, the Christian evangelical leader Pat Robertson, once used his television religious/news show, *The 700 Club*, to call for Chávez's assassination by U.S. special forces.

Notably, there has been a popular culture component to Chavez's anti-globalization challenge. In the summer of 2005, in an effort to oppose the threat of American cultural imperialism and to guarantee the diversity of Venezuelan music against American cultural homogenization, Venezuela

passed a law requiring that 50 percent of all music played on its radio stations had to be Venezuelan in origin. The effect of the law, in turn, was
to challenge the globalizers' assertions that American popular culture was
providing a market for the products it truly wanted to enjoy: in the aftermath of the law's passage, sales of traditional Venezuelan music skyrock-
eted, while sales of American acts declined. One record store manager in
Caracas put it: "We've always had traditional Venezuelan records in stock,
but before a few months ago we never sold any—not one. It was all Britney
Spears, Backstreet Boys and that sort of thing. But now I'd say one-third of
our business comes from Venezuelan artists, which is absolutely incredi-
ble." Similarly, a nineteen-year-old Venezuelan music fan noted, "It's kind
of fashion now to listen to traditional music. It has just taken off in three
months."[33]

In Venezuela, then, popular culture is only a small component of the
nation's challenge to the integrationist forces at the core of the globalization process. However, it plays an important role in generating national
pride and identity. Given the hostility of the United States to the Chávez
regime, this reservoir of nationalism may prove to be an important resource as Venezuela attempts to chart a course of trade with, but not domi-
nation by, the United States, economically, politically, and culturally.

Fragmegration and American Popular Culture in Hong Kong

The case of Hong Kong offers another, but very different, example of
the way American popular culture shapes contemporary globalization.
Hong Kong had, through much of the twentieth century, one of the world's
most powerful capitalist economies. Its status as a British colony with a
unique combination of a large population of well-educated people, one of
the world's most accessible and strategic ports, and very loose regulations
on business encouraged many companies to set up operations in Hong
Kong to produce goods and services for worldwide consumption. So successful was this combination of forces that Hong Kong, in the latter half of
the twentieth century, became one of the so-called Asian Tigers, the Asian
economic superpowers like Japan, South Korea, and Singapore (another
small island nation with a global economic presence far larger than its geographic position would predict). Hong Kong was a central hub in the
emerging globalist capitalist order from at least the 1950s on.

Given Hong Kong's status as a British colony, English became the common language. The colony also enjoyed relative political and social freedoms, including access to and widespread enjoyment of an array of
popular culture entertainments from the United States, Thailand, Korea,

Japan, and traditional Chinese musical forms.[34] As a consequence, Hong Kong's citizens were broadly integrated into the West's economic, political, and cultural systems throughout the 1900s.

This integration was challenged in 1997 when Hong Kong reverted to Chinese rule. This transfer was complicated by the fact that China's government had come under Communist control in 1949. Accordingly, the reversion of Hong Kong to Chinese rule meant that one of the most productive, integrated capitalist economies in the world was to be administered by a nation whose formal political doctrine was anti-capitalist. Moreover, China does not legally recognize other Western legal and political principles, such as democracy and human rights. Many people wondered how—or whether—Hong Kong could survive the transition.

At one level, the concerns of those who doubted China could effectively manage a capitalist Hong Kong were misbegotten. China had, by 1997, begun a large-scale process of turning significant areas of its countryside into havens for capitalist production and development. Shanghai, in particular, has grown into an enormous city and region in which capitalist business practices are encouraged both for international corporations wishing to trade with or manufacture products in China, and for Chinese citizens who wish to engage in entrepreneurial capitalist business ventures themselves. Accordingly, China promised to allow Hong Kong to continue to play its central role in international capitalist trade and has largely done so in the years since it assumed political management of the former British colony.

At another level, however, concerns about Chinese rule seem appropriate and inevitable. To return to the arguments described in chapter 1 for a moment, it is worth remembering that many advocates of globalization insisted that capitalism and democracy were inextricably intertwined; in order to have true economic flexibility, nations would have to allow their people to be as creative and innovative as possible. This, in turn, would require democracy and other forms of respect for human rights. Chinese policy, by contrast, is grounded on the assertion that capitalist economic growth can be separated from democracy and demands for human rights: Shanghai remains under strong control of the state, for example, and individual rights are not protected there. When China took over administration of Hong Kong it assumed control of an area that had not only been capitalist for a long time, but that had been relatively integrated into Western norms of democracy and human rights as well. While China promised to promote democracy in Hong Kong, it has not, in fact, done so. It also has to effectively manage and control whatever limited democracy exists in Hong Kong in the first place—most importantly by not letting democratic

133

ideals and practices escape Hong Kong for the mainland. This is a profound challenge.

Given the linkages among capitalism, globalization, and American popular culture, there is inevitably a connection between American popular culture and the way China manages Hong Kong. For example, large numbers of the actual consumer goods people enjoy that are based on popular American movies, music, and television programs (e.g., action figurines, CDs, DVDs, clothes, T-shirts, bags, dolls, and everything in between) are manufactured in Hong Kong. Hong Kong is one of the world's largest producers of illegal bootleg copies of American popular culture products. Many of these are consumed in Hong Kong. If American popular culture tends to corrupt or replace indigenous values, as adherents of mass society theory or cultural imperialism suggest, this will be a problem for authorities who want their citizens to produce the products and participate in a capitalist system but avoid the political and social effects of such production and participation. Put another way, American popular culture is still widely used and consumed in Hong Kong, and Chinese authorities act as if they are afraid the messages embedded in American popular culture will corrupt their people.

One example of Chinese concerns with the social and political effects of American popular culture in Hong Kong can be seen in the relationship the Chinese government has established with the Walt Disney Company's newest theme park, Disneyland Hong Kong. The Hong Kong government invested almost 80 percent of the costs to build the park and owns 57 percent control of it. As a consequence, the government can control what does or does not go into the park. More broadly, the Chinese government has resisted Disney's offer to develop another theme park on mainland China, in already well-developed Shanghai, precisely because Disney insisted that it would need to broadcast the Disney Channel in China to introduce its characters to the nation's population. China is reluctant to allow such broadcasts, despite the fact that the face value content of Disney programming—Bambi, for example, or even the Mighty Ducks (discussed in chapter 2)—is fairly unobjectionable on moral grounds. This bland content still manifests American political and cultural values, however, and so remains a concern for the Chinese government.[35]

The Internet has provided another arena in which the Chinese government has acted to limit the effects of Western ideas or entertainments in Chinese life. Yahoo!, the Internet search and content firm, has been strongly criticized for giving the government the name of a Chinese dissident journalist who had posted information embarrassing to the Chinese government on a Yahoo! site in Hong Kong. Notably, this provision of information occurred without a court order—as Hong Kong law requires. (The dissident journalist was sentenced to ten years in jail.) Similarly, Microsoft has empowered China's desire to limit Western cultural and political effects by embedding banned-words filters in the Internet-search software it sells in Hong Kong. Google likewise blocks content from certain Chinese news sites from its searches if the request for information or content comes from mainland China.[36]

In the case of Hong Kong and China, then, American popular culture is a source of concern and resistance for political and cultural reasons, not economic ones. It is the potential messages, rather than a desire to protect native industries, that encourage barriers. That said, both governments are willing to make significant decisions, ranging from the jailing of dissidents to the limiting of economic development, to support their cultural and political visions against the threat they believe is posed by American popular culture.

Conclusion

Whether in individual cases or as a matter of international law, then, American popular culture has been and remains one of the most divisive, most limiting forces in the process of globalization. Fears of cultural imperialism; values distortion; or simple, idiotic mimicry of the acts, ideas, values, norms, and practices embedded in American movies are central to international efforts to restrain the effects of American popular culture in the lives of people around the world. In addition, restraints on trade in cultural items can be a component in national plans for economic, social, and political development. In effect, American pressures to make the trade in cultural artifacts mere commodities of exchange as part of the larger process of globalization may well be encouraging the fragmentation that globalization seems inevitably to stimulate. As Rosenau's fragmegration concept predicts, the dynamics of globalization are varied and variable. At the least, there is no single path to the condition Steger defines as globality.

AMERICAN POPULAR CULTURE AND THE FUTURE OF GLOBALIZATION

As has been seen throughout this book, there is something different about the products of American popular culture. The early transnational corporations that produced movies, music, and television programs took advantage of permissive laws, an open culture, and ideal filmmaking weather to build global empires of audiovisual entertainment—empires that largely excluded new producers, whether in the United States or elsewhere, from successfully competing for the mass international entertainment audience. As a consequence, American movies, music, and television programming, whether produced in the United States or derived from forms of entertainment created by Americans, largely dominate world trade in popular culture. The civic values expressed in American popular culture and the formulas in which American popular culture presents itself (violence, sexuality, individualism, and so on) are both transparent and attractive to worldwide audiences *and* repellent to governments, communities, and individuals worried that the very attractiveness of American movies, music, and television programs will serve to corrupt, destroy, or homogenize local cultures. American movies, music, and television programming are, in effect, seen to have a greater power to transform other societies than virtually any other form of trade or relations ever developed in human history. Such fears have in turn led to the substantial exemption of the trade in popular culture from the core trade agreements by which globalization has been advanced for the last fifty years. Indeed, the recently proposed UNESCO

137

treaty on global diversity seeks to make the exemption of trade in cultural artifacts permanent, thereby protecting world culture from the apparently corrupting, imperial, and homogenizing effects of American popular culture.

Now that I have described the history and present state of American popular culture's role in globalization, it is the task of this chapter to assess its likely future as an agent of globalization—and fragmegration. It argues that the fears and reactions to the global trade in American popular culture has improperly reified and sanctified current cultural orders into eternal "cultures" that need protection from the prevarications of an "other." This chapter challenges this reified, frozen vision of cultures in conflict through the use of two concepts introduced in chapter 1, hybridity and glocalization. Neither the programming being produced in the United States (or in genres created in the United States) nor the rest of the world to which it is being exported is made up of rigid, fixed values that bring cultures into inevitable conflict. Accordingly, while fears of corruption, imperialism, and homogenization will likely continue so long as human beings seek to train their children to share their values and to live in communities of like-minded people—in other words, forever—the nature and terms of the debate will shift over time as both the products of American popular culture and the audiences that enjoy them change. This change will subsequently alter the way American popular culture affects globalization as a process toward globality. While it is likely that true globality will never be achieved, it is also the case that American popular culture cannot and will not utterly corrupt, overwhelm, or wash away all diversity in cultures across the globe.

Cultural Responses to Change

Consider the following facts:

- Salsa generates the most revenues of any condiment sold in the United States.[1]
- The long-running American television hit *The Simpsons* has been adapted and is now being shown in the Arab world as *Al Shamsoon*. Homer's name has been changed to "Omar," while Bart is "Badr."[2]
- Telemundo, a Spanish-language American television network owned by NBC Universal (itself a subsidiary of GE) has 10 million subscribers in the United States.[3]
- The most popular form of television programming in Latin and South America, the *telenovela*, or soap opera, has gone global; one,

Los Ricos Tambien Lloran (The Rich Also Cry) became the single most popular television show in Russia, with ratings of 70 percent (more than 100 million viewers). Some 2 billion people worldwide regularly watch *telenovelas.*[4]

- There is now a thriving industry in Japanese rap, and indeed rap music has spread worldwide, with local performers singing in indigenous languages.
- The last Mexican state without a McDonald's, Zacatecas, opened one in 2004.[5]
- The Colombian pop singer Shakira has sold some 31 million albums worldwide, including almost 7 million in the United States, despite the fact that most of her albums are in Spanish.[6]
- The martial arts movie *Crouching Tiger, Hidden Dragon* was a breakaway hit in the United States despite the fact that it is in Chinese, stars Chinese actors, and is in the style of traditional Chinese martial arts films, not an established American genre.

The analysis of American popular culture's role in contemporary globalization offered in the preceding chapters of this book—and suggested in the foregoing list—reveals a dimension of the issue that has been underrecognized both by those who see nothing but corruption, imperialism, and homogenization in the effects of American movies, music, and television programming and by those who imagine a world of liberal democracy at the end of the free trade rainbow: the fact that culture is dynamic, not static. As was discussed in chapter 1, cultures tend to be stable, but they do change over time. Culture is not an all-or-nothing concept in which everyone believes the same thing and behaves the same way. Instead, culture is a set of general principles and norms around which social action is formed and from which social meanings are derived, but even among peoples sharing a recognizable culture, there are variations in attitudes, beliefs, and behaviors. Thus an analysis of the cultural impact of anything, whether popular culture or steel or anything else, that assumes the product will interact with a fixed set of values and norms is simply wrong. Neither the culture importing the product nor the culture exporting it is identical with some former, earlier version of itself, and neither will be in the future exactly as it is today—regardless of whether the import-export transaction ever takes place. Likewise, intracultural variations mean that particular products and ideas will be responded to in different ways by diverse groups and individuals. Fixing this misperception is key to understanding the likely future of globalization and American popular culture.

At least three types of cultural change can be expected over time. Two of these—pattern-maintaining change and change toward flexibility—generally reinforce existing cultural patterns, beliefs, institutions, and behaviors. The third—cultural disruption—tends to undermine established structures.

Pattern-maintaining change describes those circumstances in which new technologies, ideas, attitudes, norms, and values enter a culture and are integrated into it in ways that usually strengthen established forms of social organization. An obvious example is the way that the automobile was adopted by Americans. The car transformed America in numerous ways—it moved people off farms and out of cities into suburbs, for example, even as it sped up the pace of American life by making trade and travel across large distances convenient for most people. Such changes might have disrupted society utterly (as it certainly did for blacksmiths and cart salesmen), but if anything the automobile instead expanded American predispositions toward individualism, personal freedom, and consumerism. Thus a technological development that transformed American economic and social structures was nonetheless integrated into American culture in a way that served to strengthen American cultural norms. The car reinforced American culture rather than shattering it.

Change toward flexibility occurs as societies grow more complex, or what sociologists refer to as differentiated. Agrarian societies, for example, are relatively non-differentiated and non-hierarchical; most everyone in a given community grows their own food, with the intent of feeding their own family, and while political, religious, military, or other leaderships usually exist, their sizes are typically constrained by the necessity for all able-bodied people to grow food for the community's survival. The culture of such societies can likewise be simple; roles can be well defined, taboos made clear, and social practices highly rule bound. As society differentiates, however, its culture has to grow more flexible. For example, if some people are to be trained and supported as full-time health-care workers (whether MDs or medicine people), the society needs to have a role and a place for such "professionals" to have an identity and a place. A similar process of cultural adaptation needs to occur if an Industrial Revolution takes place, science expands the realm of the known, or previously repressed groups (like women) are integrated into the workforce. The more functions, ideas, institutions, and values a society admits, the more flexible it can be said to be.

Culturally disruptive change occurs when the existing institutions, values, norms, and practices of a society are overwhelmed in the face of some challenge. An obvious example would be the changes that may follow when a society is conquered in a war. The winning group has the opportunity, if it wishes, to try to remake the culture of the loser by reorganizing schools, retraining teachers, barring local religions, and numerous other acts. Similarly, mass disease or a severe environmental crisis may make it impossible for a society to maintain its beliefs and practices. In such conditions, ordinary life cannot sustain itself, and unanticipated cultural consequences are likely to follow.

A crucial component of the process of cultural disruption is the speed with which the changes affect a given culture. Both pattern-maintaining change and change toward flexibility require that the culture experiencing the change has time to integrate, accommodate, and at some level embrace the new roles, ideas, experiences, or technologies that are causing the changes. Cultural disruption occurs, by contrast, when changes come too quickly to be assimilated effectively. Change is thus likely to be both painful and destructive.

It is important to recognize that all three kinds of change are likely ongoing in any given culture at the same time. Pressures to integrate new ideas, technologies, and institutions (pattern-maintaining change) tend to make societies more complex (change toward flexibility) at the cost of undermining various members' livelihoods, ideals, and cultural identities (cultural disruption). To return to earlier examples, the automobile may have reinforced cultural attitudes, but it did so at the cost of entire industries—and the jobs of all the harness makers, ox breeders, and blacksmiths who sustained the pre-automobile economy. It would be quite a surprise if such people had embraced the car—and indeed, as cars were introduced, protest movements against motorized vehicles emerged, some of which led to laws restricting their use. What was pattern-maintaining change for some was cultural disruption for others. Similarly, the integration of women in the American workforce has provided remarkable opportunities for growth and development for millions of American women and their families, but these changes challenge the values and norms of those Americans who believe women have a traditional responsibility to raise children inside the home. Accordingly, the change toward cultural flexibility that lies at the heart of women's entry into the workplace is disruptive at least for some cultural traditionalists who wish to maintain an established way of life. Accordingly, the dynamics of any society—especially ones facing the economic, political, and cultural pressures associated with contemporary globalization—are likely to be diverse and range from excited acceptance to angry rejection.

As has been shown throughout this book, American popular culture has had precisely this fragmegrationist effect as it goes out to the world. Many people have embraced American movies, music, and television programming; otherwise, these enterprises would not be as pervasive and profitable as they are. In contrast, others fear that American popular culture will corrupt their children, destroy their values, and install a homogenized alternative culture in its place. They push for laws and rules to restrict the impact of American popular culture across the globe. American popular culture is, at the least, believed to be a central component in promoting cultural change.

Hybridity, Cultural Change, and American Popular Culture

The question of how the products of American popular culture might cause cultural changes around the world is an important one. One crucial explanation for how American movies, music, and television programs can influence various cultures lies in the concept of cultural hybridity. In the discussion of the concept of hybridity in chapter 1, hybridity was roughly defined as "mixing," or "the ways in which forms become separated from existing practices and recombine with new forms and new practices."[7] It is a consequence of such mixing that many cultural changes ensue.

From the point of view of cultural hybridization, the intermixing of cultural values and practices has been and remains a central feature of human life. Moreover, cultural communication and hybridization are a two-way process—Western societies are as likely to be influenced by non-Western ones as non-Western communities are to be influenced by the West. As a brief example, it is worth noting that the English in which this book is being written is an evolved combination of Anglo-Saxon and Norman French that began developing well over a thousand years ago and has continued to evolve with considerable influence and loaned words from classical Latin and Greek, as well as modern French, Italian, Spanish, Arabic, Turkish, Persian, and numerous other language groups. In other words, one of the core components of American culture—English as a language system—is a hybrid of former forms.

Why does cultural mixing occur? At least part of the answer lies in the historical pattern of population migrations that have led the world's peoples to be distributed across the planet as they are. A central feature of human history is that human populations have regularly migrated in search of resources, safety, and opportunity. As people move, they bring their cultures with them, making cultural contact, and perhaps mixing, inevitable.

Contemporary population migrations are generally from what is termed, awkwardly, the Global South toward what is called, again somewhat awkwardly, the Global North. While this hemispheric labeling misses the fact that there are many underdeveloped areas in the North and, likewise, that there are developed areas in the South (e.g., Australia and Singapore), it does capture the essence of the contemporary flow: from less developed, less safe, less politically free areas toward safer, more developed, and more democratic regions. Thus while it is obvious that in coming to the United States, Latin and South Americans are moving north, and it is likewise apparent that people emigrating from Africa to Europe are coming from the South, it is important to recognize that people from Central Europe struggling to enter the countries in the European Union are also moving from the Global South to the Global North despite the fact that they are actually traveling west, and in some cases south. Alternatively, such shifts can also occur within countries, as is happening in China; while China has a population living in its largest cities that exceeds the population of the United States (the world's largest economy), China still has nearly a billion peasants living in rural areas, many of whom earn less than a dollar a day. As these rural populations move to China's major cities—as they are doing at rates of millions per year—they, too, are effectively moving from the Global South to the integrated, globalized North, even if they never leave their home nation. Finally, such shifts can occur both within and across nations, as is happening in India. India has the world's largest population of English-speaking, technically sophisticated workers on the planet. These people seek employment and opportunities in India's globalized cities *and* through mass emigration around the world, leaving behind a rapidly increasing, rural, and desperately poor home population in the Global South. Regardless of the direction of travel, then, these movements are toward globally integrated regions and away from rural, underconnected ones.

Notably, it is at such points of contact that, as was discussed in chapter 1, Samuel Huntington and Benjamin Barber see conflict of one form or another inevitably emerging. Thus, since Indians (or Hispanics or Asians or any other ethnicity) may come to America with different religions, different moral and social codes, and different dietary and social practices than are common in the United States today, authors like Huntington and Barber predict cultural war will result as one group tries to impose its worldview on the other, while the latter resists.

Yet, empirically, culture wars, cultural corruption, imperialism, or homogenization does not necessarily follow such mixing. They can and have but need not. For example, no American cultural or political leaders are currently engaged in a campaign to stamp out salsa eating as dangerous to American national pride or cultural integrity, even though salsa now outsells ketchup in America's grocery stores. Likewise, when reporter Jake Silverstein asked his Mexican contacts if going to McDonald's instead of making their own lunch over a fire was not likely to undermine or corrupt Zacatecan culture, he noted that "without exception . . . [they] seemed to think I was insane to suggest that it might be preferable to build a small wood fire and reheat a taco when there was a possibility of visiting McDonald's for a burger and fries. . . . After all, a man could still build a fire and reheat his wife's cooking if he wanted to."[8] Cultural contact does not automatically breed culture wars.

When we assess the impact of any cultural form on globalization, then, it is important to assess whether (and how) the particular ideas, images, values, and norms embedded in the cultural artifact are perceived and responded to by the societies and groups experiencing the "other" culture. The interaction of the "other" and the known *might* lead to cultural conflict, but such contacts can also bring adaptation, learning, shading, and subtlety rather than brute force and the thoughtless imposition of another's values on a hapless, innocent population.

Take, again, the rise of salsa as a condiment in the United States. Increased use of salsa has been associated with a series of social and cultural changes in America. Large and increasing populations of people from Latin and South America have been legally and illegally immigrating to the United States in the last several decades. This, in turn, has been linked to an expansion of Hispanic political influence in the United States. In the 1970s the Frito-Lay company, for example, was forced to eliminate the "Frito Bandito" character (discussed in chapter 3) by Hispanic economic and social action at about the same time César Chávez was able to unionize itinerant Hispanic farm laborers under the auspices of the United Farm Workers. Subsequent political activism has brought one Latino politician, New Mexico governor Bill Richardson, to the position of an apparent front-runner for the 2008 Democratic Party presidential nomination; in both the 2000 and 2004 presidential elections, every major-party candidate went out of his way to speak Spanish at several points in the campaign. This political presence has been mirrored by an increasing Hispanic presence in American social and cultural consciousness. Many Americans now enjoy Cinco de Mayo, Mexican Independence Day, as an informal holiday, and Spanish is now among the most sought-after language skills among employers and job seekers in the United States. Salsa did not cause these changes, of course, nor have all these changes occurred smoothly and without resistance. They have, however, largely occurred without the kind of violence and cultural warfare expected by pessimists about cultural globalization.

Nothing about the changes being integrated into contemporary American society as a response to Hispanic immigration is new. Similar changes have followed previous periods of mass immigration. Alcohol, for example, was not commonly used by most Americans throughout the day until large numbers of Germans moved to the central United States in the latter half of the nineteenth century and established, among other breweries, what became the Anheuser-Busch in St. Louis, Missouri. Likewise, it took the immigration of large numbers of Irish Catholics into the major cities of the American northeast to change the anti-Catholic bias of traditional American culture in the late 1800s; where American cultural traditionalists once formed political organizations like the "Know-Nothing" Party to stop Irish (and other) immigration, cities like Boston, which had long been controlled by a Protestant aristocracy, eventually were transformed into Catholic Irish-run cities. What appears to be *the* culture of the United States today is in fact the result of these, and many other, changes over time. Few people born in 1825 America would recognize the way Americans live today.

Such contacts need not occur only through population shifts. Notably, as people move, they take their entertainments with them. As was noted earlier, Telemundo has 10 million subscribers in the United States. Similarly, one American soldier deployed to Kuwait as part of Operation Iraqi Freedom in 2003–2004 reported that the large number of Asian, Indian, and Arab workers hired by American contractors to load trucks, staff military bases, and perform manual labor for American units sent to war came together regularly to watch Bollywood movies; some American soldiers and contractors would watch as well.[9] In return, American popular cultural products have stimulated the growth of forms like the emergence of localized rap music scenes surrounding native performers using indigenous languages ranging from Japanese to Sri Lankan Sinhala. The U.S. success of movies like *Crouching Tiger, Hidden Dragon*, as well as its Westernized variants like *The Matrix* trilogy and the two parts of *Kill Bill*, provides additional evidence for the ways American popular culture can shape local cultures even as it is shaped by others. Such cross-cultural contacts have borne fruit in the music industry as well. Both the American singer-songwriter Paul Simon and the English singer-songwriter Peter Gabriel used and introduced the music of Ladysmith Black Mambazo, a group that performs traditional South African music, in different projects. The infusion of Caribbean reggae and Cuban forms enshrined in movies like *The Buena Vista Social Club* into American popular culture likewise illustrates the flexibility, rather than the rigidity, of culture.

Pieterse has referred to the mixing of cultures as tending toward mélange—a system in which many hybridized cultures interact in a constantly evolving process. While certain cultural forms may have predominance—Western values may supersede local ones because of their market advantages or the preponderance of American military power, for example—there is nonetheless variation within "Western" culture, and non-Western cultures have and continue to influence one another. Likewise, cultural values from the Global South can infiltrate and shape the cultures of the Global North. The final product of these interactions is neither corruption, imperialism, nor homogenization but is instead something entirely new.[10]

Glocalization, Cultural Change, and American Popular Culture

Another mechanism for cultural mixing lies in what Roland Robertson has termed "glocalization."[11] As I discussed briefly in chapter 1, Robertson pays particular attention to questions of identity—how individuals and groups define their values, ideals, and communities. He describes glocalization as a "massive, twofold process involving *the interpenetration of the universalization of particularism and the particularization of universalism.*"[12] Glocalization describes the process by which established cultures both shape and are challenged as a new cosmopolitan culture, the values and ideals of which are to a large degree determined by the demands of globalization.[13]

The idea that American popular culture might play a role in creating a world culture by "glocalizing" diverse populations may be surprising to some, even to those who admit that American popular culture might promote hybridity. After all, it is one thing to argue that populations (and entertainments) mix, perhaps constructively; it is another thing to argue, as Robertson does, that the elements being mixed have a direction of movement, a tendency to promote some values over another. Yet as chapter 3 showed, American popular culture is American in both form and content. It expresses American values and American assumptions about the world at large. While mixing exists (e.g., Paul Simon and Ladysmith Black Mombazo), the preponderance of the trade is from the United States to the rest of the world. Thus, while the end result need not be the establishment of "American" culture everywhere, it seems likely that other societies will move further than will the United States.

The cultural dimensions of glocalization can be illustrated through a return to the discussion of Latino/as in America. Careful readers of this book may have noticed that throughout it there has been an apparent inconsistency in the way in which people originally from Latin and South America but now living in the United States have been referred to: sometimes they are called Hispanics, while at others they are called Latino/as. This inconsistency has, in fact, been deliberate because it points directly to the ways global concerns can interact with local politics to shape and re-shape cultural identities worldwide.

For much of U.S. history, the people living in the United States but whose national and cultural heritage came from "south of the border" were referred to as "Mexicans," regardless of their national heritage. A subsequent label—Chicano—was adopted as Hispanic activism grew in the United States in the 1970s, but it was particularly associated with people of Mexican heritage already living in the United States. Accordingly, the term left out or diminished the cultural and national heritages of a vast array of people living in Latin, South, and Caribbean American countries and communities. The U.S. Census Bureau adopted the term "Hispanic" as an attempt to overcome the limitations of Mexican-specific labels to describe a diverse continent of people. However, Hispanic is problematic as well; it refers back to Hispaniola, the European isthmus containing both Spain and Portugal. It thus implies that everyone in Latin, South, and Caribbean America is of Spanish or Portuguese heritage. Yet Latin and South America have large numbers of indigenous tribes as well as substantial African and Asian populations. Likewise, a significant number of the residents of the islands of the Caribbean are African in origin and were brought to the islands as part of the international slave trade in the seventeenth, eighteenth, and nineteenth centuries. Thus the label "Hispanic" is improperly limited. This problem, in turn, has led some scholars and activists to offer a new concept, Latinos (males) and Latinas (females), as an all-inclusive label through which to describe the identity of those people formerly known as "Mexican." This label is understood to avoid the ethnic and social assumptions embedded in prior concepts and so to more properly reflect the heritage of Latinos and Latinas in the United States. In adopting the Latino/a terminology, then, American culture is accounting for the diversity of Latin, South, and Caribbean American nations and cultures—glocalization.

Another way to conceptualize how glocalization influences culture is to ask a question that follows from the history of the development of the concept of Latino/a: are there any Latino/as in Latin, South, and Caribbean America? This may seem to be a surprising question since, as a practical matter, it seems obvious that in order to be a Latino/a in the United States, one ought to be a Latino/a in Latin, South, or Caribbean America. The assumption that there must be Latino/as outside the United States has been wrong, however, at least historically. For most people who live in Latin, South, or Caribbean America, nationality and ethnicity have been far more important as sources of identity than has the pan-regional label Latino/a. One is Peruvian, not Chilean, for example, or one is white, not Indian. It was only in coming to the United States and entering a society that was ignorant of and indifferent to the complexities of life outside American borders that a pan-regional identity like Latino/a could be formed.

Yet the process of establishing a Latino/a identity in the United States may serve to expand the concept across the hemisphere and even the globe. It is possible, for example, that people who have considered themselves Latino/as in the United States will return to their birth nations for work or family reasons. While many may return to their old identities and beliefs, others may teach their friends, families, co-workers, and communities about their experiences in the United States. This may, in turn, trigger new social movements across the region as people consider their shared fates in relation to the United States instead of as members of individual nations or communities. Indeed, something like this appears to be emerging as millions of people across Latin, South, and Caribbean America (as well as within the United States itself) respond to Venezuelan president Hugo Chávez's anti-globalist, pro-regional development message, described in chapter 4. Moreover, as returned Latino/as maintain the networks of professional and social contacts they establish in the United States—and around the world—they will also retain emotional and economic links to their American friends and partners. As a consequence, many Latino/as may well enjoy closer relationships with their compatriots in the United States and elsewhere than they do with their fellow countrymen and women—especially those living in rural, disconnected areas. The resultant hybridity of cares and interests can only serve to further link local concerns with global society.

Technology and popular culture are obvious agents of glocalization. This is particularly the case for television and other mechanisms of instantaneous communication such as the Internet. Events that occur anywhere in the world can be broadcast globally. This can stimulate international attention to issues and create bonds of knowledge and concern where none previously existed. Notably, American popular culture has been at the forefront of such international moments. In 1971, for example, Beatles member George Harrison sponsored a rock concert to raise money and awareness for the suffering of Bangladesh, which was at the time engaged in a civil war for independence from Pakistan. Similarly, in 1985 American pop singers came together to perform "We Are the World" to raise funds and gather international attention for the victims of famine in Africa. Such fund-raising efforts have become routinized in popular culture in the ensuing years. Country music superstar Willie Nelson, among others, created

"Farm Aid" to help struggling farmers; musician Bob Geldof created "Live Aid" to support African famine victims; and diverse performers came together after Hurricane Katrina to raise money for the victims of that Gulf Coast storm. Indeed, these kinds of efforts are so ubiquitous today they arise spontaneously even at the grassroots level. Shortly after the December 26, 2004, tsunami devastated large areas of Thailand, Indonesia, and other Indian Ocean countries, the author witnessed an Indian bagpipe group—in full Scottish regalia—performing for donations in London, England's Leicester Square. Whereas once most of the world's people would likely never have known about even a horrible natural disaster like the December 26, 2004, tsunami, today the mechanisms of popular culture provide both an awareness of the local-global interchange and an opportunity to take action in response.

This glocalist dynamic is not inevitably painless, however. Indeed, as with all questions of culture and identity, there is often resistance, discomfort, and challenge as "foreign" ideas/products/values/people cross intellectual, economic, and social boundaries.[14] Likewise, as the concept of fragmegration suggests, hybridization is likely to bring challenge and resistance, particularly in cultural matters since culture tends toward stability. This, in turn, may lead to surprising alliances emerging in opposition to the globalization of American popular culture—as, for example, is the case in Iran as cultural conservatives share a common desire but for different reasons with domestic film producers to exclude American movies from the country. Contemporary globalization will be influenced by such dynamics for the foreseeable future.

The Future of American Popular Culture and Globalization

As has been seen throughout this book, many people, groups, institutions, and communities oppose and challenge the products of American popular culture on an array of grounds. Cultural traditionalists fear corruption, imperialism, and heterogeneity. Economic groups and industries worry about being replaced by transnational corporations peddling American cultural forms. Political leaders feel pressure to respond to these concerns and also sense opportunities to build political coalitions around the cultural and economic concerns shared among the communities they head. There is, as a consequence, an active and potentially global movement to counter the spread of American popular culture, and since popular culture remains America's biggest export, to limit the impact of globalization worldwide.

Yet there are powerful forces driving the globalization of American popular culture. Some, like the marketing, distributional, and technological advantages of scale, finances, and talent that the major producers of popular culture leveraged to take control of the global entertainment market (chapter 2), are asymmetrical; they constitute structural advantages that could allow the transnational corporations that produce American popular culture to impose their products on the rest of the world through free trade competition or the ruthless undercutting of locally produced movies, music, and television programming. Others, however, such as the natural evolutionary flexibility of culture and the transparent appeal of American values and products (as filtered through the formulas and conventions of American popular culture) are social advantages that are shaped by time and context and may be advanced without recourse to social or cultural violence and shock.

Given the various forces competing against or supporting the globalization of American popular culture, it is appropriate to ask: how will American movies, music, and television programs shape globalization in the future? While no complete answer to this question can be offered, several developments seem likely to emerge over time. The following section takes each in turn as it seeks to frame a final answer to the question of how American popular culture will affect globalization for years to come.

- *American popular culture will continue to be a major force in global trade and entertainment well into the future.* As a consequence of both its established position and the increasing spread of satellites, VCRs, DVD players, and streaming Internet content, American movies, music, and television programming can be expected to retain their position as the most watched, most used, and most traded types of popular culture around the world. Indeed, the decline in numbers of restrictive authoritarian regimes that accompanied the end of the Cold War, combined with the movement of people from the under-connected, underdeveloped Global South to the connected Global North, suggests that the market for American audiovisual entertainment products is likely to expand at an escalating rate as new markets are identified and developed. Whereas the Global North has been largely saturated with American programming for nearly a century (at least in the case of films), the Global South and its billions of people are a relatively untouched market. As a consequence of their established production, financial, distribution, and marketing capacities, the transnational corporations that control American popular culture are well-positioned to take advantage of these new markets as they open. American movies, music, and television programming can therefore be expected to increase in global influence in the coming decades.

150

- *American movies, music, and television programming will continue to be linked to fast-food restaurants, soft drink companies, product tie-ins, virtual communities, and other forms of popular culture, thereby serving as vehicles by which many aspects of American life are carried around the world.* As a practical matter, the kinds of marketing tie-ins that have been described throughout this book are far too profitable for movie, music, and television program producers and the makers of other products to ignore. Movie audiences are essentially captive, and once an audience member buys a DVD of the film, he or she willingly watches the advertiser's product time and again in the comfort of his or her own home. The same is true for music videos, songs that promote particular products like cars and television programs. The existence of virtual communities, whether created by producers (like *Dawson's Creek*'s Capeside) or built by fans (as has happened for generations of *Star Trek* followers), creates a dynamic in which active participants in the program's culture are likely to spend substantial amounts of money on associated products— thereby expanding the program's profits that much more. Notably, such product tie-ins provide another level of insight into American life and culture, and in so doing, provide another set of reasons why some people exposed to American popular culture can be attracted to what they see (integration) or horrified by it (fragmentation). The many levels on which American popular culture is experienced as it is used worldwide can thus be expected to encourage fragmegration as a central characteristic of globalization well into the future.

- *Attempts to limit access to American popular culture, whether by state action or social rules, are likely to prove ineffective in the long run.* While numerous nations and social groups are attempting to limit the influence and power of American popular culture in their communities, three factors appear likely to limit the effectiveness of these efforts in the long run: 1) the spread of the technology through which American movies, music, and television programs can be accessed; 2) the global appeal of American programming; and 3) global population movements. The first of these was addressed above in this chapter, as well as in chapter 2. As a practical matter, satellites and the Internet make access to American popular culture relatively easy. Almost all national efforts to ban satellite dishes have failed for lack of enforcement, even in what are perceived to be fairly restrictive regimes like Iran and China. North Korea may be the world's only exception, and even it is now facing the problem of smuggled Internet content that both exposes the regime's practices and allows its citizens access to the wider world. The global transparency of American popular cultural programming was addressed in chapter 3: the products created within American popular culture are desirable and sought after worldwide. This does not mean that local forms need disappear, as the experience of Venezuela suggests (chapter 4), but it does suggest that efforts to ban appealing programming wholesale are unlikely to succeed—especially given easy technological access to them. Finally, the contemporary worldwide population migration from the Global South to the Global North (however conceived) means that there will be increasing numbers of people in areas and communities in which American popular culture is already present and pervasive. Under such conditions, plans or hopes to ban American movies, music, and television programs are doomed to failure.

- *Increased awareness of and exposure to American popular culture will encourage the integration of these forms into local cultures.* As was addressed earlier in this chapter, exposure to the ideas, forms of entertainment, values, and social practices of one culture does not necessarily breed resentment, anger, and rejection. Rather, people can learn from each other. This has certainly happened with American music; the band that many people consider the greatest rock group of all time, the Beatles, was British, after all, and rap music has become local in many cultures around the world. Similarly, many stars of American country music today are from Australia. Television programs, too, can sponsor copycat products, as happened in the case of *Wheel of Fortune* in Russia. Similarly, as is evidenced by the morphing of *The Simpsons* into *Al Shamshoon*, it is possible to adapt almost any American product—regardless of its inherent offensiveness, and *The Simpsons* is noteworthy for the number of theocratic, social, and cultural norms it flouts—to an international market. It is only in the arena of blockbuster action-adventure movies that local alternatives to American products are unlikely to emerge. The extraordinary cost and technological sophistication of the special effects in such films makes it doubtful that these kinds of movies can be created outside the system created and controlled by the audiovisual corporate empires.
- *Just as other cultures can adopt and integrate American programming, American culture can adapt and integrate entertainment forms originated elsewhere.* As the example of Americans' acceptance of salsa suggests, Americans are no more likely to automatically reject everything from "somewhere else" as "alien" and "other" than are people around the world. Moreover, as the concept of glocalization

suggests, the megacorporations that produce American popular culture have an economic interest in surveying world markets in search of programming that might be popular in the United States. In fact, reality shows like *Big Brother, American Idol,* and *Whose Line Is It Anyway?* originated in Great Britain before coming to America. Humiliation TV—such as *Fear Factor* and similar American programs in which people engage in dangerous stunts or subject themselves to "gross-out" eating or endurance contests in pursuit of various prizes—was pioneered in Japan. As more pleasant examples, the success of the Colombian pop singer Shakira has occurred across language boundaries, and it is worth noting that many subscribers to Telemundo are not native Spanish speakers. Likewise, Spanish-language channels are available as part of many subscriptions for cable and satellite users. Such cultural learning constitutes a two-way street, with each side enriching—and perhaps debasing—the other.

- *Pop cultural interchanges can create economic and cultural bonds among people that may not be represented by political institutions.* Whether as producers or consumers or as participants in shared entertainments that develop subcultures, it is likely that diverse people around the world will develop relationships of mutual interest around the products of American popular culture. An obvious example of such linkages has been the worldwide spread of fan clubs of the *Star Trek* series; *Star Trek* is literally a global phenomenon, and millions of people worldwide collect paraphernalia, attend conferences, and assert the IDIC (infinite diversity in infinite combinations) creed at home and abroad. Likewise, golfers can recognize each other globally by what they wear and what they carry; similar subcultures exist around the world covering "sk8ters," rappers, and coffee aficionados. In one striking example, there is now a small but growing contingent of American basketball players under contract to professional basketball teams in Iran—a country the Bush administration has termed part of the "axis of evil" sponsoring world terrorism. Such common bonds may not be expressed in the political system, however, for a variety of reasons ranging from the rules of the system being written to advantage cultural conservatives (Iran) to sheer democratic inertia—sk8ters and American basketball players in Iran lack either (or both) the numbers or the desire to challenge American policy toward specific countries. When we analyze the effects of American popular culture on globalization, then, it is important to look beyond the public statements of political leaders.
- *The hybridization and glocalization processes in American popular*

153

culture and local cultures may facilitate the emergence of a global culture, at least to a limited extent. As American popular culture reaches larger and larger audiences, as local cultures adapt and integrate American forms, and as American culture itself adapts to the ideas, norms, and values of other cultures for a variety of economic and pragmatic reasons (e.g., population movement), it is likely that relatively shared vocabularies, concepts, and frames of reference will emerge to serve to the global structure of American movies, music, and television programming. The fact that most of American popular culture's products are presented in English, which is also the international language of global commerce, will only facilitate the rise of a some kind of a common global culture. Moreover, the fact that American popular culture is substantially "American" (chapter 3) suggests that the general form and character of any emergent global culture is likely to be based on principles of choice, freedom, and consumption, at least in commercial affairs. It is easy to image Internet slang as a nearly universal linguistic, for example: new vocabulary such as "btw," "u," "r," and other contractions can be deployed by people with only limited understanding of English spelling and no understanding of English grammar to get their meaning across. Likewise, common cultural moments now exist across the world. "Okay" is perhaps the first truly global word, while phrases like "I'll be back" (*The Terminator*) or "Whassup?" (Budweiser commercial) spread around the world. In these circumstances it seems that at least some version of a consumer-driven, product choice-filled culture is likely to emerge, at least among the worldwide users and marketers of American popular culture.

* *Increased contact and adaptations among cultures are likely to promote increased competition against the products of American popular culture, especially in television and music.* The international popularity of the *telenovela* suggests that those countries and communities with indigenous popular culture production capacity can also use the technologies of satellites, VCRs, DVDs, and the Internet to push their products worldwide. Similarly, the relatively inexpensive cost and diffused technology for producing and marketing music (e-studios, the Internet, radio, and the like) guarantee a space for the creation and dissemination of music produced outside the "American" system to find a niche. Indeed, the development and profusion of digital cameras have opened new opportunities for filmmakers to create small, inexpensive movies that may rise to popularity outside the Hollywood system, whether in Bollywood or elsewhere. However,

the ultraexpensive blockbuster is likely to remain a Hollywood product for the foreseeable future.

- *Cultural integration is more likely within and among components of the Global North than it is within and among the Global South, thereby deepen the gap between north and south.* The sharing of popular culture products is, by definition, more likely in areas that have markets—the interest in and capacity to consume a given product. Put another way, it makes little economic sense for Disney or any other transnational corporation to market a global blockbuster in rural India or rural China since a ticket might cost eight dollars, and many of the people there make less than a dollar a day. Thus global exchanges of dollars, ideas, experiences, values, images, and technologies are likely to be concentrated in the globalized parts of the world. This, in turn, can be expected to encourage global migration from north to south as the gap between how one *is* living and how one *might* live widens. Indeed, the popular appeal of American movies, music, and television programs should add energy to this migration as people literally move "off the farm" in order to experience the world of possibilities manifested in the products of American popular culture—including the wealth, freedom, and lifestyles embedded in American culture. Accordingly, concerns of nations in the Global North about immigration, cultural cohesion, and the identity of the nation's people can be expected to grow more intense for the foreseeable future.
- *Challenges to American movies, music, and television programs will arise for a variety of economic, political, and cultural reasons, leading to new alliances seeking to limit the effects of American popular culture within their communities.* As products in the marketplace, American movies, music, and television programs generate enormous profits worldwide and by extension limit the number of dollars any community can spend on locally produced culture. This provides economic incentives for states and competitor companies to try to limit the local scope of American popular culture. In addition, as culture-bearing and -generating artifacts, American movies, music, and television programs—and the production facilities in which they are created—have cultural value to society. Thus, as has been the primary focus of this book, many people seek to limit the apparently corrupting, imperial, and/or homogenizing influence of "American" popular culture either through regulating how much of it may be consumed locally or through limiting the degree to which indigenous production facilities can be integrated into or owned by the

155

transnational audiovisual entertainment empires—or both. As a consequence, whether as a result of economic or cultural pressures, or for their own interests, political leaders around the world have made limiting popular culture a central platform of their national and international agendas. New political alliances, such as the one between Iranian mullahs and filmmaking progressives against American films or the one between Christian evangelicals and some American feminists in the United States against pornography, have formed across political, cultural, and economic lines. Similar combinations can be expected to form as more and more places and people experience the political, economic, and cultural effects of American popular culture programming. The globalizing of American popular culture is thus a factor in creating resistance to it.

- *American popular culture will continue to be a major source of controversy in global trade agreements.* Given the economic, political, and cultural dimensions of the globalization of American popular culture, it is likely that while the United States will continue to push for free trade in cultural artifacts, most of the rest of the nations of the world will resist—whether for economic, political, or cultural reasons (or all three combined). Any prediction that total globalization is inevitable, then, is likely to fail due to the significance that culture is understood to hold within and across nations and communities. Instead, continued resistance to the globalization of culture is likely whether or not the proposed UNESCO treaty on cultural diversity is adopted. The importance of culture is challenged by the pervasiveness of American popular culture and thus is likely to generate continuing controversy even in the technical realm of free trade agreements.

- *The continuing domestic and international controversies surrounding the content of and trade in American popular culture may lead to the emergence of new transnational anti-globalization social movements.* As domestic groups struggle to oppose the apparent political, economic, and cultural effects of American popular culture, and as these concerns take root and find expression in free trade agreements, it is likely that new international alliances may form among groups and people across the globe who share common concerns about American movies, music, and television programs. Indeed, the same technologies that promote the spread of American popular culture (the Internet, satellites, etc.) can facilitate the emergence of such organizations. Such associations might be connected to the already-developed network of groups and leaders acting to limit globaliza-

156

tion's negative effects (chapter 1) or might emerge independently. This, in turn, would have the ironic effect of globalizing a diverse set of groups and persons in terms of their opposition to the global force of American popular culture—further altering the course of contemporary globalization.

- *Nothing is inevitable in the process of globalization and American popular culture.* Among other things, the analysis of the ways in which American popular culture has affected the process of globalization offered in this book ought to, at the least, provide an empirically based challenge to those scholars and pundits who insist that globalization is inevitable. As chapter 4 made clear, states still actively work to limit what are believed to be the pernicious economic, political, and cultural effects of American popular culture for their communities. Whatever the advocates of total globalization say about how people ought to behave in the marketplace, many peoples and governments, seeking maximum value for minimum cost, are quite happy to accept less American programming, however enjoyable or inexpensive it might be, in favor of higher-priced, tax-subsidized local products. Nothing about globalization can be inevitable in such a world.

Resistance need not lead to culture war, however. As was addressed earlier in this chapter, cultures learn, change, and adapt. It is possible for cultures to integrate new ideas and experiences without necessarily experiencing corruption, imperialism, or homogenization. Accordingly, the interchange of American popular culture and cultures around the globe may encourage the emergence of new hybrid forms that accommodate new identities and opportunities for literally billions of people around the world. While this process will inevitably displace or distort some ideas and practices, the cumulative effect may be seen as beneficial rather than harmful. To the degree such change occurs, the world's movement toward globality will be enhanced.

Conclusion

This book began by addressing the role American popular culture played in the Cold War. It has concluded with a consideration of how American movies, music, and television programs may influence the future of globalization. The evidence offered here shows that as one of the central components of contemporary global trade, American popular culture both encourages integration and promotes fragmentation as it shapes the way contemporary globalization is unfolding. Thus nothing about globalization is inevitable: neither universal free trade (and, as some advocates insist, global democracy) nor eternal culture war need follow from the way American popular culture interacts with existing institutions, values, norms, and behaviors around the world. Instead, the long-term course of globalization is, as Manfred Steger has suggested, likely to be toward globality without ever actually achieving it.[15] American popular culture is one important component of this dynamic, and is likely to remain so for a long time to come. Accordingly, as chapter 1 argued, popular culture has and will continue to play a key role in international affairs. It is through popular culture that the rest of the world learns what "American" means, and any attempt to understand globalization without attention to the central role played by global interest in and fear of American popular culture is consequently doomed to fail. To the degree globalization is linked to American interests and American values, it is through American popular culture that the rest of the world may decide whether to fear or favor the promise of a globalized planet.

NOTES

Chapter 1: American Popular Culture and Globalization

1. Paul Farhi and Megan Rosenfeld, "American Pop Penetrates Worldwide," *Washington Post*, October 25, 1998.

2. Quoted in National Center for Policy Analysis, "Idea House," 1997, www.ncpa.org/pd/trade/pdtrade/oct98c.html (accessed October 17, 2005).

3. David Steigerwald, *Culture's Vanities: The Paradox of Cultural Diversity in a Globalized World* (Lanham, MD: Rowman & Littlefield, 2004), 29.

4. Steigerwald, *Culture's Vanities*, 29–33.

5. Todd Gitlin, "Television Screens: Hegemony in Transition," in *Cultural and Economic Reproduction in Education*, ed. M. Apple (London: Routledge and Kegan Paul, 1981), 202, quoted in Robert Burnett, *Global Jukebox: The International Music Industry* (New York: Routledge, 1996), 33.

6. Quoted in Steigerwald, *Culture's Vanities*, 38.

7. Cf. Herbert Gans, *Popular Culture and High Culture: An Analysis and Evaluation of Taste* (New York: Basic Books, 1974); Mary Douglas and Baron Isherwood, *The World of Goods* (New York: Basic Books, 1979).

8. Steigerwald, *Culture's Vanities*, 40.

9. Thomas Friedman, *The Lexus and the Olive Tree* (New York: Farrar, Straus and Giroux, 1999), 248.

10. Marc Howard Ross, "Culture and Identity in Comparative Political Analysis," in *Comparative Politics: Rationality, Culture, and Structure*, ed. Mark I. Lichbach and Alan S. Zuckerman (New York: Cambridge University Press, 1997), 42–80.

11. The following discussion rests on a number of works. See, for fuller discussion, John Kenneth White, *The Values Divide: American Politics and Culture in Transition* (New York: Chatham House, 2003); John W. Kingdon, *America the Unusual* (New York: Worth, 1999); Daniel Judah Elazar, *American Federalism: A View from the States*, 3rd ed. (New York: Harper & Row, 1984); Daniel Judah Elazar, *The*

American Mosaic: The Impact of Space, Time, and Culture on American Politics (Boulder: Westview, 1994); Richard Ellis, *American Political Cultures* (New York: Oxford University Press, 1993); Louis Hartz, *The Liberal Tradition in America* (New York: Harcourt, Brace, 1955); Richard Hofstadter, *The American Political Tradition and the Men Who Made It* (New York: Vintage, 1974); Samuel P. Huntington, *American Politics: The Promise of Disharmony* (Cambridge, MA: Belknap, 1981); Seymour Martin Lipset, "American Exceptionalism Reaffirmed," in *Is America Different? A New Look at American Exceptionalism*, ed. B. Shafer (Oxford: Oxford University Press, 1991), 1–45; Frederick Jackson Turner, *The Frontier in American History* (New York: Holt, Rinehart and Winston, 1962); Aaron Wildavsky, *The Rise of Radical Egalitarianism* (Washington, DC: American University Press, 1991). See also David Boorstin, *The Genius of American Politics* (Chicago: University of Chicago Press, 1953); James Davison Hunter, *Culture Wars: The Struggle to Define America* (New York: Basic Books, 1991); Seymour Martin Lipset, *American Exceptionalism: A Double-Edged Sword* (New York: Norton, 1996); Charles Lockhart, *The Roots of American Exceptionalism: Institutions, Culture and Politics* (New York: Palgrave MacMillan, 2003); Deborah L. Madsen, *American Exceptionalism* (Jackson: University of Mississippi Press, 1998); and Trevor B. McCrisken, *American Exceptionalism and the Legacy of Vietnam: U.S. Foreign Policy since 1974* (New York: Palgrave MacMillan, 2003).

12. Isaiah Berlin, *Two Concepts of Liberty* (Oxford: Clarendon Press, 1958).

13. Cf. Sidney E. Mead, *The Nation with the Soul of a Church* (New York: Harper & Row, 1975); Sacvan Bercovitch, *The American Jeremiad* (Madison: University of Wisconsin Press, 1978); Sacvan Bercovitch, *The Puritan Origins of the American Self* (New Haven, CT: Yale University Press, 1975); Robert N. Bellah et al., *The Good Society* (New York: Knopf, 1991); Robert N. Bellah et al., *Habits of the Heart: Individualism and Commitment in American Life* (Berkeley and Los Angeles: University of California Press, 1985).

14. Manfred Steger, *Globalization: A Very Short Introduction* (New York: Oxford University Press, 2003), 7–12.

15. James N. Rosenau, *Distant Proximities: Dynamics Beyond Globalization* (Princeton, NJ: Princeton University Press, 2003).

16. See Manfred Steger, *Globalism: Market Ideology Meets Terrorism*, 2nd ed. (Lanham, MD: Rowman & Littlefield, 2005) for a full discussion of this argument.

17. For more expanded explorations of this summary, see: Robert Kuttner, *Everything for Sale: The Virtues and Limits of the Market* (New York: Knopf, 1997); Harvey Cox, "The Market as God: Living in the New Dispensation," *Atlantic Monthly*, March 1999, 18–23; Edward Luttwak, *Turbo-Capitalism: Winners and Losers in the Global Economy* (New York: Harper & Row, 1999); Robert Reich, *The Work of Nations* (New York: Vintage, 1992); Robert O. Keohane, *After Hegemony* (Princeton, NJ: Princeton University Press, 1984).

18. Steger, *Globalization*, 37–55; Steger *Globalism*, 24–28. See also Robert J. Holton, *Globalization and the Nation-State* (New York: St. Martin's, 1988); James H. Mittelman, *Globalization: Critical Reflections* (Boulder, CO: Lynne Rienner, 1996);

Roland Robertson, *Globalization: Social Theory and Global Culture* (London: Sage, 1992).

19. Cf. Lowell Bryan and Diana Farrell, *Market Unbound: Unleashing Global Capitalism* (New York: Wiley, 1996); Kenichi Ohmae, *The End of the Nation-State: The Rise of Regional Economies* (New York: Free Press, 1995); Kenichi Ohmae, *The Borderless World: Power and Strategy in the Interlinked World Economy* (New York: HarperBusiness, 1990); Lester Thurow, *The Future of Capitalism: How Today's Economic Forces Shape Tomorrow's World* (New York: William Morrow, 1996).

20. Jan Nederveen Pieterse, *Globalization and Culture: Global Mélange* (Lanham, MD: Rowman & Littlefield, 2004), 12–13.

21. Steger, *Globalization*, 67.

22. Nigel Harris, *National Liberation* (London: I. B. Tauris, 1990); Francis Adams, Satya Dev Gupta, and Kidane Mengisteab, eds., *Globalization and the Dilemmas of the State in the South* (London: St. Martin's, 1999); Philip G. Cerny, *The Changing Architecture of Politics: Structure, Agency and the Future of the State* (London: Sage, 1990); Michael Connors, *The Race to the Intelligent State: Charting the Global Information Economy in the 21st Century* (Oxford: Capstone, 1997); Liah Greenfield, *Nationalism: Five Roads to Modernity* (Cambridge, MA: Harvard University Press, 1992).

23. For fuller discussion of each of these points, see: Warren Agee, Phillip Ault, and Edwin Emery, *Introduction to Mass Communication*, 10th ed. (New York: HarperCollins, 1991); John R. Bittner, *Mass Communication: An Introduction*, 4th ed. (Englewood Cliffs, NJ: Prentice Hall, 1986); Stanley J. Baran and Dennis K. Davis, *Mass Communication Theory: Foundations, Ferment and Future* (Belmont, CA: Wadsworth, 1995); Ronald T. Farrar, *Mass Communication: An Introduction to the Field* (St. Paul, MN: West, 1988).

24. Donald K. Emmerson, "Singapore and the 'Asian Values' Debate," *Journal of Democracy* 6 (4): 95–105.

25. Samuel Huntington, *The Clash of Civilizations and the Remaking of World Order* (New York: Simon & Schuster, 1996).

26. Benjamin Barber, *Jihad vs. McWorld: How Globalism and Tribalism Are Reshaping the World* (New York: Ballantine Books, 1996), 9.

27. George Ritzer, *The McDonaldization of Society: An Investigation into the Changing Character of Contemporary Social Life* (London: Sage, 1993).

28. Arjun Appadurai, *Modernity at Large: Cultural Dimensions of Globalization* (Minneapolis: University of Minnesota Press, 1996); Ulf Hannerz, *Cultural Complexity: Studies in the Social Organization of Meaning* (New York: Columbia University Press, 1992); Ulf Hannerz, *Transnational Connections: Cultures, People, Places* (London: Routledge, 1996); Pieterse, *Globalization and Culture*, 52–55.

29. William Rowe and Vivian Schelling, *Memory and Modernity: Popular Culture in Latin America* (London: Verso, 1991), 231.

30. James L. Watson, ed., *Golden Arches East: McDonald's in East Asia* (Stanford, CA: Stanford University Press, 1997).

31. Daniel Miller, *Worlds Apart: Modernity through the Prism of the Local* (London: Routledge, 1995).

32. See Pieterse, *Globalization and Culture*, for a full discussion of this point.

33. Marwan M. Kraidy, *Hybridity, or the Cultural Logic of Globalization* (Philadelphia: Temple University Press, 2005).

34. Robertson, *Globalization*, 100 (emphasis in original).

35. Robertson, *Globalization*, 100–2.

Chapter 2: The Global Scope of American Popular Culture

1. Columbia Journalism Review, "Who Owns What: Bertelsmann AG," www .cjr.org/tools/owners/bertelsmann.asp (accessed January 20, 2006).

2. Columbia Journalism Review, "Who Owns What: Sony Corporation," www .cjr.org/tools/owners/sony.asp (accessed January 20, 2006).

3. PBS, "The Merchants of Cool: Sony," 1995–2006, www.pbs.org/wgbh/ pages/frontline/shows/cool/giants/sony.html (accessed January 25, 2005).

4. Columbia Journalism Review, "Who Owns What: Sony Corporation."

5. Columbia Journalism Review, "Who Owns What: Time Warner," www.cjr .org/tools/owners/timewarner.asp (accessed January 20, 2006).

6. PBS, "The Merchants of Cool: Walt Disney Co.," 1995–2006, www.pbs.org/ wgbh/pages/frontline/shows/cool/giants/disney.html (accessed January 25, 2005).

7. Columbia Journalism Review, "Who Owns What: The Walt Disney Company," www.cjr.org/tools/owners/disney.asp (accessed January 20, 2006).

8. Columbia Journalism Review, "Who Owns What: Viacom," www.cjr.org/ tools/owners/viacom.asp (accessed January 20, 2006).

9. Matt Russell, "A Short History of *Start Trek*," www.trekdoc.com/database/ fanfeed/43.htm (accessed April 7, 2005).

10. Geraldine Fabrikant, "Viacom Board Agrees to Split of Company," *New York Times*, June 15, 2005, www.nytimes.com/2005/06/15/business/media/15viacom .html (accessed June 15, 2005).

11. Columbia Journalism Review, "Who Owns What: News Corporation," www.cjr.org/tools/owners/newscorp.asp (accessed January 20, 2006).

12. Columbia Journalism Review, "Who Owns What: Vivendi Universal S. A.," www.cjr.org/tools/owners/vivendi.asp (accessed January 20, 2006).

13. General Electric Company, "GE 2004 Annual Report," 2004, www.ge.com/ ar2004/cfs_e.jsp (accessed April 6, 2005).

14. Columbia Journalism Review, "Who Owns What: General Electric," www .cjr.org/tools/owners/ge.asp (accessed January 20, 2006).

15. General Electric Company, "GE 2004 Annual Report."

16. Paul Starr, *The Creation of the Media: Political Origins of Modern Communications* (New York: Basic Books, 2004), 23–46.

17. Starr, *Creation*, 47–86.

18. Starr, *Creation*, 267–402; see also Robert C. Toll, *The Entertainment Machine: American Show Business in the Twentieth Century* (New York: Oxford University Press, 1982).

19. Toll, *Entertainment Machine*, 19–30; see also Starr, *Creation*, 295–326.

20. Richard Maltby, *Hollywood Cinema* (Cambridge, MA: Blackwell, 2003), 126.

21. Maltby, *Hollywood*, 29–30.

22. Maltby, *Hollywood*, 128–29.

23. Maltby, *Hollywood*, 159–76.

24. All these quotes are from Stanley J. Baran and Dennis K. Davis, *Mass Communication Theory: Foundations, Ferment, and Future* (Belmont, CA: Wadsworth, 1995), 42.

25. Maltby, *Hollywood*, 60–63, 593–97; Starr, *Creation*, 318; Richard Maltby, *Harmless Entertainment: Hollywood and the Ideology of Consensus* (Metuchen, NJ: Scarecrow Press, 1983), 97–102; Robert Sklar, *Film: An International History of the Medium* (New York: Harry N. Abrams, 1993), 96–125.

26. Maltby, *Hollywood*, 177–79.

27. Toll, *Entertainment Machine*, 46–47.

28. Toll, *Entertainment Machine*, 48.

29. Toll, *Entertainment Machine*, 48–59.

30. Toll, *Entertainment Machine*, 70–74.

31. Toll, *Entertainment Machine*, 59.

32. Toll, *Entertainment Machine*, 72.

33. M. William Krasilovsky and Sidney Shemel, *This Business of Music*, rev. and enl. 7th ed. (New York: Billboard Books, 1995), xxxii–xxxvii.

34. Krasilovsky and Shemel, *Business of Music*, 73. See also Michael Fink, *Inside the Music Business: Music in Contemporary Life* (New York: Schirmer Books, 1989), 1–89; Cecil I. Hale, *The Music Industry: A Guidebook* (Dubuque, IA: Kendall/Hunt, 1990); Jeffrey Brabee and Todd Brabee, *Music, Money, and Success: The Insider's Guide to the Music Industry* (New York: Schirmer Books, 1994).

35. Starr, *Creation*, 368.

36. Answers.com, "Parents Music Resource Center," www.answers.com/topic/parents-music-resource-center (accessed March 30, 2005); Derek Lee, "Parental Advisory Warning Labels Steeped in Controversy," www.hushyourmouth.com/parental_advisory_labels.htm (accessed March 30, 2005).

37. Toll, *Entertainment Machine*, 60–61.

38. Toll, *Entertainment Machine*.

39. Toll, *Entertainment Machine*, 61–65.

40. Starr, *Creation*, 381.

41. Starr, *Creation*, 381.

42. Toll, *Entertainment Machine*, 66.

43. Toll, *Entertainment Machine*, 66–67.

44. Toll, *Entertainment Machine*, 195.

45. Both quotes are from Baran and Davis, *Mass Communication Theory*, 42–43.

46. SunFyre, "Justin Timberlake Exposing Janet Jackson's Breast during the Super Bowl Half-Time Show," www.sunfyre.com/janetjackson.htm (accessed April 4, 2005).

47. Corey Deitz, "FCC Fines Howard Stern, Two or More Clear Channels Stations, Revises Bono Ruling," March 19, 2004, http://radio.about.com/cs/latestradio news/a/aa031904a.htm (accessed April 4, 2005).

48. IMDB, "All-Time USA Box Office," www.imdb.com/boxoffice/alltime gross?/region = world-wide (accessed April 27, 2005, and January 27, 2006). See also "Top Ten Movies of All Time," http://showcase.netins.net/web/ssinc/movies .html (accessed April 27, 2005).

49. Benjamin Barber, *Jihad vs. McWorld* (New York: Ballantine Books, 1996), 92–93.

50. Barber, *Jihad vs. McWorld*, 93–94, 307.

51. "DVD Continues Spinning Success," *USA Today,* January 6, 2005, www.usa today.com/life/movies/news/2005-01-05-dvd-sales-inside_x.htm (accessed April 27, 2005).

52. "Top Selling DVDs of All Time in Australia," *Sydney Morning Herald,* June 30, 2005, www.smh.com/au/news/Film/Top-selling-DVDs-of-all-time-in-Australia/ 2004/06/30/1080544533352.html (accessed April 27, 2005).

53. Scott R. Olson, "The Globalization of Hollywood," *International Journal on World Peace* 17 (December 2000): 3–18; Franco Moretti, "Planet Hollywood," *New Left Review* 9 (May–June): 90–101.

54. Moretti, "Planet Hollywood," 90–101.

55. IMDB, "All-Time USA Box Office." See also "Top Ten Movies of All Time."

56. Neosoul, "Top Artists," www.neosoul.com/riaa/artists (accessed April 27, 2005). Note: All sales certified by the RIAA, the Recording Industry Association of America. All sales figures cited in this chapter are RIAA certified.

57. Fact Monster, "The Recording Industry Association of America's Top-Selling Albums of All Time," www.factmonster.com/ipka/A0151020.html (accessed April 27, 2005).

58. Corinna Sturmer, "MTV's Europe: An Imaginary Continent," in *Channels of Resistance: Global Television and Local Empowerment*, ed. Tony Dowmunt (London: BFI Publishing, 1993), 51–52.

59. Barber, *Jihad vs. McWorld*, 105–7.

60. Kerry Seagrave, *American Television Abroad: Hollywood's Attempt to Dominate World Television* (Jefferson, NC: McFarland, 1998), 1.

61. Julian Petley and Gabriella Romano, "After the Deluge: Public Service Television in Western Europe," in *Channels of Resistance*, 31.

62. Petley and Romano, "After the Deluge," 31–32.

63. Petley and Romano, "After the Deluge," 50–95.

64. Star, "About Us," www.startv.com/eng/aboutus.cfm (accessed June 15, 2005).

65. Talk Satellite, "Eutelsat Announces Headline Results of Its Two-Yearly Survey of Cable/Satellite Homes for 2005," www.talksatellite.com/EMEAedd111.htm (accessed June 15, 2005).

66. Star, "About Us."

67. Sky Corporate, "Factsheet," http://media.corporate-ir.net/media_files.lse/ bsy.uk/factsheet.pdf (accessed June 15, 2005).

Chapter 3: "American" Popular Culture

1. Ernest Gellner, "From Kinship to Ethnicity," in *Encounters with Nationalism* (Cambridge, MA: Blackwell, 1994), 39.

2. Gellner, *Encounters*, 40–41.

3. Gellner, *Encounters*, 42.

4. Allen McBride and Robert K. Toburen, "Deep Structures: Polpop Culture on Primetime Television," *Journal of Popular Culture* 29 (4): 181–200. All subsequent references to this research are from this source.

5. Conrad Phillip Kottak, *Prime-Time Society: An Anthropological Analysis of Television and Culture* (Belmont, CA: Wadsworth, 1990). All subsequent references are from this source.

6. Kottak, *Prime-Time*, 53–57.

7. Timothy Havens, "The Biggest Show in the World: Race and the Global Popularity of *The Cosby Show*," in *The Television Studies Reader,* ed. Robert C. Allen and Annette Hill (New York: Routledge, 2004), 442–56.

8. Scott Robert Olson, "Hollywood Planet: Global Media and the Competitive Advantage of Narrative Transparency," in *The Television Studies Reader*, 114.

9. Havens, "Biggest Show," 451–52.

10. For a fuller discussion of this point, see Neal Gabler, *An Empire of Their Own: How the Jews Invented Hollywood* (New York: Crown, 1998).

11. Will Brooker, "Living on *Dawson's Creek*: Teen Viewers, Cultural Convergence, and Television Overflow," in *The Television Studies Reader*, 569–80.

12. Net Glimpse, "Britney Spears: Biography," www.netglimpse.com/celebs/bio/britney_spears.shtml (accessed July 5, 2005). See also VH1.com, "Britney Spears: Biography," www.vh1.com/artists/az/spears_britney/bio.jhtml (accessed July 5, 2005).

13. VH1.com, "Britney Spears."

14. VH1.com, "Britney Spears."

15. Britney Spears: The Official Site, "About Britney, Biography," www.britney spears.com/about-biography.php/f = print& (accessed July 5, 2005).

16. Quoted in "Britney Spears: Toxic? Indeed!" *Hilary,* www.hilary.com/features/britney-spears.html (accessed July 6, 2005).

17. Wikipedia, "Britney Spears," http://en.wikipedia.org/wiki/Britney_Spears (accessed January 31, 2006).

18. Answers.com, "Garth Brooks," www.answers.com/topic/garth-brooks (accessed July 5, 2005).

19. See, for fuller discussion, Answers.com, "Garth Brooks"; Country Music Television, "Garth Brooks," www.cmt.com/artists/az/brooks_garth/bio.jhtml (accessed July 5, 2005); SBC Yahoo! Music, "Garth Brooks Biography," http://music .yahoo.com/ar-288490-bio-Garth-Brooks (accessed July 5, 2005).

20. Quoted at Cowboy Lyrics.com, "Lyrics for American Honky-Tonk Bar," www.cowboylyrics.com/lyrics/brooks-garth/american-honky-tonk-bar-association-4986.html (accessed January 31, 2006).

21. Answers.com, "Tupac Shakur," www.answers.com/topic/tupac-shakur (accessed July 5, 2005).

22. Answers.com, "Tupac Shakur."

23. Answers.com, "Tupac Shakur."

24. Answers.com, "Tupac Shakur." See also Celebrity Wonder.com, "Tupac Sha-

kur," www.celebritywonder.com/html/tupacshakur_bio.html (accessed July 5, 2005).

25. Answers.com, "Tupac Shakur." See also Hot Shots Digital, "Tupac Shakur Biography," www.hotshotdigital.com/WellAlwaysRemember/TupacShakurBio.html (accessed July 5, 2005).

26. Answers.com, "Tupac Shakur."

27. Answers.com, "Tupac Shakur."

28. University of Michigan Health System, "What Do I Need to Know about Children and Television?" www.med.umich.edu/1libr/yourchild/tv.htm (accessed September 28, 2005).

29. Sarah Boseley, "Sex, Lies and Celluloid: Doctors Hit Out at Hollywood," *Guardian*, October 3, 2005, http://film.guardian.co.uk/News_Story/Guardian/0,4029,1583577,00.html (accessed October 3, 2005).

30. Dan Malachowski, "TV Dads: Real-Life Salaries Nearly $200,000," www.salary.com/careers/layoutscripts/crel_display.asp?tab = cre&cat = nocat&ser = Ser 372&part = Par546 (accessed October 4, 2005).

Chapter 4: Globalization, Fragmegration, and American Popular Culture

1. Quoted in Simona Fuma Shapiro, "The Culture Thief," *New Rules*, Fall 2000, www.newrules.org/journal/nrfall00culture.html (accessed October 19, 2005).

2. Quoted in Shapiro, "Culture Thief."

3. Cultural Industries Sectoral Advisory Group on International Trade, "An International Agreement on Cultural Diversity: A Model for Discussion," September 2002, www.dfait-maeci.gc.ca/tna-nac/documents/sagit_eg.pdf (accessed October 19, 2005).

4. Music Council of Australia, "Submission to the Department of Foreign Affairs and Trade's Office of Trade Negotiations," January 28, 2003, www.mca.org.au/pdf/mcadfat31jan03.pdf (accessed October 19, 2005).

5. Hernan Galperin, "Cultural Industries in the Age of Free-Trade Agreements," *Canadian Journal of Communications* 24 (1): 49–77, http://info.wlu.ca/~wwwpress/jrls/cjc/BackIssues/24.1/galperin.pap.html (accessed October 19, 2005).

6. Galperin, "Cultural Industries."

7. Galperin, "Cultural Industries."

8. Galperin, "Cultural Industries."

9. Galperin, "Cultural Industries."

10. United Nations Educational, Scientific, and Cultural Organization, "Preliminary Report by the Director-General Setting out the Situation to Be Regulated and the Possible Scope of the Regulating Action Proposed," August 4, 2005, http://portal.unesco.org/culture/en/file_download.php/2962532f35a06baebb199d30ce52956233C23_Eng.pdf (accessed October 27, 2005).

11. UNESCO, "Preliminary Report."

12. UNESCO, "Preliminary Report."

13. *Encyclopedia Britannica Almanac 2005* (Chicago: Encyclopedia Britannica, 2004), 435.

14. *Encyclopedia Britannica*, 435.

15. Barbara Slavin, "New Attitudes Color Iranian Society, Culture," *USA Today*, February 28, 2005, www.usatoday.com/news/world/2005-02-28-iran-pink_x.htm (accessed July 11, 2005).

16. Kaveh Basmenji, "Childhood's End," June 17, 2005, www.openDemocracy .net (accessed July 11, 2005).

17. "Iranian Youth Divided on Future," *Toronto Star Newspapers*, June 8, 2003, www.iranexpert.com/2003/iranianyouthdivided8june.htm (accessed July 11, 2005); "Iran: America as Forbidden Fruit," *Persian Journal,* September 5, 2004, www .iranian.ws/cgi-bin/iran_news/exec/view.cgi/2/3639 (accessed July 11, 2005).

18. Basmenji, "Childhood's End."

19. John Lancaster, "Barbie, 'Titanic' Show Good Side of U.S.," *Washington Post*, October 27, 1998, www.washingtonpost.com/wp-srv/inatl/longterm/mia/part3.htm (accessed July 15, 2005).

20. "Iranian Youth Divided on Future."

21. Lancaster, "Barbie."

22. Lancaster, "Barbie."

23. Lancaster, "Barbie."

24. Le ministère de la culture et de la communication, "Law No. 94-665 of 4 August 1994 relative to the use of the French language," www.culture.gouv.fr/ culture/dglf/lois/loi-gb.htm (accessed September 14, 2005).

25. Marilyn August, "English Creeps into French Culture," *AP Online*, September 7, 1998, www.discoverfrance.net/France/News/English_invasion.shtml (accessed October 10, 2005).

26. Gail Russell Chaddock, "English Web Sites in France Flamed by Language Police," *Christian Science Monitor*, January 10, 1997, http://faculty.ed.umuc .edu/~jmatthhew/articles/frenchflame.html (accessed October 10, 2005).

27. Adapted from Shapiro, "Culture Thief."

28. August, "English Creeps into French Culture."

29. Cf. Claire Allfree, "Vive le Rock 'n' Roll," *Independent Online Edition*, September 14, 2005, http://enjoyment.independent.co.uk/music/features/article14813 .ece (accessed September 14, 2005); Michael Kessler, "Vive le Dag," *The Age*, January 8, 2005, www.smh.com.au/news/Music/Vive-le-dag/2005/01/07/1104832290965 .html (September 14, 2005).

30. Barber, *Jihad vs. McWorld: How Globalism and Tribalism Are Reshaping the World* (New York: Ballantine Books, 1996), 92.

31. U.S. Department of State, "Background Note: Venezuela," www.state.gov/r/ pa/ei/bgn/35766.htm (accessed October 6, 2005).

32. U.S. Department of State, "Background Note."

33. SFGate.com, "Venezuela Imposes National Music Quotas, Law Limits Air-

play for Foreign Tunes," July 19, 2005, www.sfgate.com/cgi-bin/article.cgi?file
=/c/a/2005/07/19/MNG5FDQ2NI1.DTL&type=printable (accessed August 26, 2005).

34. For a fuller discussion, see Wai-chung Ho, "A Cross-Cultural Study of Preferences for Popular Music Among Hong Kong and Thailand Youths," *Journal of Intercultural Communication* 7.

35. Keith Bradsher, "Disney Takes Exception to China's Media Rules," *New York Times,* September 12, 2005.

36. BBC News, "Yahoo 'Helped Jail China Writer,'" September 7, 2005, http://news.bbc.co.uk/go/pr/fr/-/2/hi/asia-pacific/4221538.stm (accessed September 28, 2005).

Chapter 5: American Popular Culture and the Future of Globalization

1. Karla Carlsen, Ernesto Duran, John Landa, and Dennis A. Ferris, "A New Tomato-Based Salsa," Center for Food Science and Nutrition Research Publication 970901, May 1997, http://cati.csufresno.edu/cfsnr/rese/97/970901 (accessed November 15, 2005).

2. Genevieve Roberts, "Homer Becomes Omar for Arab Makeover of Simpsons," *Independent Online Edition,* October 20, 2005, http://news.independent.co.uk/media/article320877.ece (accessed October 20, 2005).

3. Telemundo Corporate Information, www.telemundo.com/telemundo/2449824/detail.html (accessed November 15, 2005).

4. Ibsen Martinez, "Romancing the Globe," *Foreign Policy,* November–December 2005.

5. Jake Silverstein, "Grand Opening: Ronald McDonald Conquers New Spain," *Harper's,* January 2005, 67–74.

6. Mara Technology, "Shakira," www.maratechnology.com/shakira.htm (accessed November 15, 2005).

7. William Rowe and Vivian Schelling, *Memory and Modernity: Popular Culture in Latin America* (London: Verso, 1991), 231.

8. Silverstein, "Grand Opening," 72.

9. Sgt. Tammy Johnson, 1244th Transportation Company, deployed to Kuwait and Iraq April 2003–August 2004, personal communication.

10. Jan Nederveen Pieterse, *Globalization and Culture: Global Mélange* (Lanham, MD: Rowman & Littlefield, 2004), 69–71.

11. Roland Robertson, *Globalization: Social Theory and Global Culture* (London: Sage, 1992), 174.

12. Robertson, *Globalization,* 100 (emphasis in original).

13. Robertson, *Globalization,* 102.

14. Robertson, *Globalization,* 104.

15. Manfred Steger, *Globalization: A Very Short Introduction* (New York: Oxford, 2003), 8.

RECOMMENDED READINGS

Allen, Robert C., and Annette Hill, eds. *The Television Studies Reader*. New York: Routledge, 2004.

Almond, Gabriel. *A Discipline Divided: Schools and Sects in Political Science*. Newbury Park, CA: Sage, 1990.

Almond, Gabriel, and Sidney Verba, eds. *The Civic Culture*. Princeton, NJ: Princeton University Press, 1963.

Appadurai, Arjun, ed. *Globalization*. Durham, NC: Duke University Press, 2001.

———. *Modernity at Large: Cultural Dimensions of Globalization*. Minneapolis: University of Minnesota Press, 1996.

Axford, Barrie. *The Global System: Economics, Politics and Culture*. Cambridge: Polity, 1995.

Banfield, Edward C. *The Moral Basis of a Backward Society*. New York: Free Press, 1958.

Baran, Stanley J., and Dennis K. Davis. *Mass Communication Theory: Foundations, Ferment, and Future*. Belmont, CA: Wadsworth, 1995.

Barber, Benjamin R. *Jihad vs. McWorld: How Globalism and Tribalism Are Reshaping the World*. New York: Ballantine Books, 1996.

Barker, Chris. *Global Television: An Introduction*. Malden, MA: Blackwell, 1997.

Beck, Ulrich. *What Is Globalization?* Oxford: Blackwell, 2000.

Benedict, Ruth. *Patterns of Culture*. Boston: Houghton Mifflin, 1934.

Bercovitch, Sacvan. *The American Jeremiad*. Madison: University of Wisconsin Press, 1978.

———. *The Puritan Origins of the American Self*. New Haven, CT: Yale University Press, 1975.

Berger, Peter L., and Samuel P. Huntington, eds. *Many Globalizations: Cultural Diversity in the Contemporary World*. New York: Oxford University Press, 2002.

Berlin, Isaiah. *Two Concepts of Liberty*. Oxford: Clarendon Press, 1958.

Bittner, John R. *Mass Communication: An Introduction*. 4th ed. Englewood Cliffs, NJ: Prentice Hall, 1986.

Boorstin, David. *The Genius of American Politics*. Chicago: University of Chicago Press, 1953.

Bordo, Susan. *Unbearable Weight: Feminism, Western Culture, and the Body*. Berkeley and Los Angeles: University of California Press, 1993

Brabee, Jeffrey, and Todd Brabee. *Music, Money, and Success: The Insider's Guide to the Music Industry*. New York: Schirmer Books, 1994.

Bryan, Lowell, and Diana Farrell. *Market Unbound: Unleashing Global Capitalism*. New York: Wiley, 1996.

Burnett, Robert. *The Global Jukebox: The International Music Industry*. New York: Routledge, 1996.

Carter, Erica, James Donald, and Judith Squires, eds. *Cultural Remix: Theories of Politics and the Popular*. London: Lawrence and Wishart, 1995.

Cerny, Philip G. *The Changing Architecture of Politics: Structure, Agency and the Future of the State*. London: Sage, 1990.

Chalaby, Jean K. *Transnational Television Worldwide: Towards a New Media Order*. New York: I. B. Tauris, 2005.

Collins, Patricia Hill. *Black Sexual Politics*. New York: Routledge, 2004.

Combs, J. *Polpop: Politics and Culture in America*. Bowling Green, KY: Bowling Green State University Press, 1984.

Connolly, William E. *Identity/Difference: Democratic Negotiations of Political Paradox*. Ithaca, NY: Cornell University Press, 1991.

Cornell, Grant H., and Eve Walsh Stoddard, eds. *Global Multiculturalism*. Lanham, MD: Rowman & Littlefield, 2001.

Cox, Harvey. "The Market as God." *Atlantic Monthly*, March 1999, 18–23.

Crothers, Lane. *Rage on the Right: The American Militia Movement from Ruby Ridge to Homeland Security*. Lanham, MD: Rowman & Littlefield, 2003.

Crothers, Lane, and Charles Lockhart, eds. *Culture and Politics: A Reader*. New York: St Martin's, 2001.

Dallmayr, Fred. *Achieving Our World: Toward a Global and Plural Democracy*. Lanham, MD: Rowman & Littlefield, 2001.

Devine, Donald. *The Political Culture of the United States*. Boston: Little, Brown, 1972.

Diamond, Jared. *Guns, Germs, and Steel: The Fates of Human Societies*. New York: Norton, 1999.

Douglas, Mary, and Baron Isherwood. *The World of Goods*. New York: Basic Books, 1979.

Dowmunt, Tony, ed. *Channels of Resistance: Global Television and Local Empowerment*. London: BFI Publishing, 1993.

Easton, David. *The Political System: An Inquiry into the State of Political Science*. 2nd ed. Chicago: University of Chicago Press, 1981.

Eckstein, Harry. "A Culturalist Theory of Political Change." *American Political Science Review* 82 (3): 789–804.

Edelman, Murray. *The Symbolic Uses of Politics*. Urbana: University of Illinois Press, 1964.

Eisenstadt, S. N. "Cultural Traditions and Political Dynamics: The Origins and Modes of Ideological Politics." *British Journal of Sociology* 32:155–81.

Elazar, Daniel Judah. *American Federalism: A View from the States*. 3rd ed. New York: Harper & Row, 1984.

———. *The American Mosaic: The Impact of Space, Time, and Culture on American Politics*. Boulder, CO: Westview, 1994.

Ellis, Richard. *American Political Cultures*. New York: Oxford University Press, 1993.

Ellis, Richard, and Michael Thompson, eds. *Culture Matters: Essays in Honor of Aaron Wildavsky*. Boulder, CO: Westview, 1997.

Emmerson, Donald K. "Singapore and the 'Asian Values' Debate." *Journal of Democracy* 6 (4): 95–105.

Enloe, Cynthia. *Bananas and Bases: Making Feminist Sense of International Politics*. Berkeley and Los Angeles: University of California Press, 1989.

Fanon, Franz. *The Wretched of the Earth*. Harmondsworth, UK: Penguin, 1967.

Farrar, Ronald T. *Mass Communication: An Introduction to the Field*. St. Paul, MN: West, 1988.

Featherstone, Mike, ed. *Global Culture: Nationalism, Globalization and Modernity*. London: Sage, 1995.

Fink, Michael. *Inside the Music Business: Music in Contemporary Life*. New York: Schirmer Books, 1989.

Fischer, David Hackett. *Albion's Seed: Four British Folkways in America*. New York: Oxford University Press, 1984.

Frank, Andre Gunder. *Re-orient: Global Economy in the Asian Age*. Berkeley and Los Angeles: University of California Press, 1998.

Freedman, Estelle B. *No Turning Back: The History of Feminism and the Future of Women*. New York: Random House, 2002.

Friedman, Jonathan. *Cultural Identity and Global Process*. London: Sage, 1994.

Fukuyama, Francis. *The End of History and the Last Man*. New York: Free Press, 1992.

Gabler, Neal. *An Empire of Their Own: How the Jews Invented Hollywood*. New York: Crown, 1988.

Galperin, Hernan. "Cultural Industries in the Age of Free Trade Agreements." *Canadian Journal of Communications* 24 (1): 49–77, http://info.wlu.ca/~www press/jrls/cjc/BackIssues/24.1/galperin.pap.html (accessed October 19, 2005).

Gamson, William. *Talking Politics*. Cambridge: Cambridge University Press, 1992.

Gans, Herbert. *Popular Culture and High Culture: An Analysis and Evaluation of Taste*. New York: Basic Books, 1974.

Gaventa, John. *Power and Powerlessness: Quiescence and Rebellion in an Appalachian Valley*. Urbana: University of Illinois Press, 1980.

Geertz, Clifford. *The Interpretation of Cultures*. New York: Basic Books, 1973.

Gellner, Ernest. "From Kinship to Ethnicity." In *Encounters with Nationalism*. Cambridge, MA: Blackwell, 1994.

———. *Nations and Nationalism*. Ithaca, NY: Cornell University Press, 1983.

Giddens, Anthony. *The Consequences of Modernity.* Stanford, CA: Stanford University Press, 1990.

Greenfield, Liah. *Nationalism: Five Roads to Modernity.* Cambridge, MA: Harvard University Press, 1992.

Gusfield, Joseph. *Symbolic Crusade: Status Politics and the American Temperance Movement.* Urbana: University of Illinois Press, 1966.

Hale, Cecil I. *The Music Industry: A Guidebook.* Dubuque, IA: Kendall/Hunt, 1990.

Hannerz, Ulf. *Cultural Complexity: Studies in the Social Organization of Meaning.* New York: Columbia University Press, 1992.

———. *Transnational Connections: Cultures, People, Places.* London: Routledge, 1996.

Harrison, Lawrence E., and Samuel P. Huntington, eds. *Culture Matters: How Values Shape Human Progress.* New York: Basic Books, 2000.

Hartz, Louis. *The Liberal Tradition in America.* New York: Harcourt, Brace, 1955.

Havens, Timothy. "The Biggest Show in the World: Race and the Global Popularity of *The Cosby Show.*" In *The Television Studies Reader,* ed. Robert C. Allen and Annette Hill. New York: Routledge, 2004.

Hayden, Patrick, and Chamsy el-Ojeili, eds. *Confronting Globalization: Humanity, Justice and the Renewal of Politics.* New York: Palgrave MacMillan, 2005.

Hebidge, D. *Subculture: The Meaning of Style.* London: Methuen, 1979.

Held, David, Anthony McGrew, David Goldblatt, and J. Perraton. *Global Transformations.* Cambridge: Polity, 1999.

Hines, Colin. *Localization: A Global Manifesto.* London: Earthscan, 2001.

Hirst, Paul Q., and Grahame Thompson. *Globalization in Question.* Cambridge: Polity, 1996.

Hofstadter, Richard. *The American Political Tradition and the Men Who Made It.* New York: Vintage, 1974.

———. *The Paranoid Style in American Politics, and Other Essays.* New York: Knopf, 1965.

Holton, Robert J. *Globalization and the Nation-State.* New York: St. Martin's, 1988.

Hunt, Linda. *Politics, Culture, and Class in the French Revolution.* Berkeley and Los Angeles: University of California Press, 1984.

Hunter, James Davison. *Culture Wars: The Struggle to Define America.* New York: Basic Books, 1990.

Huntington, Samuel P. *American Politics: The Promise of Disharmony.* Cambridge, MA: Belknap, 1981.

———. *The Clash of Civilizations and the Remaking of World Order.* New York: Simon & Schuster, 1996.

———. *The Third Wave: Democratization in the Late Twentieth Century.* Norman: University of Oklahoma Press, 1991.

———. *Who Are We? The Challenges to America's National Identity.* New York: Simon & Schuster, 2004.

Inglehart, Ronald. *Modernization and Postmodernization: Cultural, Economic and Political Change in 43 Societies.* Princeton, NJ: Princeton University Press, 1997.

————. *The Silent Revolution: Changing Values and Political Life among Western Publics*. Princeton, NJ: Princeton University Press, 1975.

Iriye, Akira. *Cultural Internationalism and World Order*. Baltimore: Johns Hopkins University Press, 1997.

Jameson, Frederick, and M. Miyoshi, eds. *The Cultures of Globalization*. Durham, NC: Duke University Press, 1998.

Johnson, Chalmers. *Blowback: The Costs and Consequences of American Empire*. New York: Henry Holt, 2000.

Katz, M. B. *The Undeserving Poor*. New York: Pantheon, 1989.

Keohane, Robert O. *After Hegemony*. Princeton, NJ: Princeton University Press, 1984.

King, Anthony D., ed. *Culture, Globalization and the World-System: Contemporary Conditions for the Representation of Identity*. Basingstoke, UK: Macmillan, 1991.

Kingdon, John W. *America the Unusual*. New York: Worth, 1999.

Kivisto, Peter. *Multiculturalism in a Global Society*. Malden, MA: Blackwell, 2002.

Klapp, Orrin. *Collective Search for Identity*. New York: Holt, Rinehart and Winston, 1969.

Kluckhohn, Clyde. *Culture and Behavior*. New York: Free Press, 1962.

Kottak, Conrad Phillip. *Prime-Time Society: An Anthropological Analysis of Television and Culture*. Belmont, CA: Wadsworth, 1990.

Kraidy, Marwan M. *Hybridity, or the Cultural Logic of Globalization*. Philadelphia: Temple University Press, 2005.

Krasilovsky, M. William, and Sidney Shemel. *This Business of Music*. Rev. and enl. 7th ed. New York: Billboard Books, 1995.

Kuttner, Robert. *Everything for Sale: The Virtues and Limits of the Market*. New York: Knopf, 1997.

Levine, Lawrence. *Highbrow/Lowbrow: The Emergence of Cultural Hierarchy in America*. Cambridge, MA: Harvard University Press, 1988.

Lewis, Bernard. *What Went Wrong? The Clash between Islam and Modernity in the Middle East*. New York: Oxford University Press, 2002.

Lipset, Seymour Martin. *American Exceptionalism: A Double-Edged Sword*. New York: Norton, 1996.

Lockhart, Charles. *The Roots of American Exceptionalism: Institutions, Culture and Politics*. New York: Palgrave MacMillan, 2003.

Lull, James. *China Turned On: Television, Reform, and Resistance*. New York: Routledge, 1991.

Luttwak, Edward. *Turbo-Capitalism: Winners and Losers in the Global Economy*. New York: Harper & Row, 1999.

McAdam, Doug, and D. Rucht. "The Cross-National Diffusion of Movement Ideas." *Annals of the American Academy of Political and Social Science* 527 (May): 56–74.

McBride, Allen, and Robert K. Toburen. "Deep Structures: Polpop Culture on Primetime Television." *Journal of Popular Culture* 29 (4): 181–200.

McCrisken, Trevor. *American Exceptionalism and the Legacy of Vietnam: U.S. Foreign Policy since 1974*. New York: Palgrave MacMillan, 2003.

Macedo, Stephen. *Liberal Virtues: Citizenship, Virtue and Community in Liberal Constitutionalism*. Oxford: Clarendon Press, 1990.

MacIntyre, Alastair. *After Virtue: A Study in Moral Theory*. Notre Dame, IN: University of Notre Dame Press, 1981.

Madsen, Deborah L. *American Exceptionalism*. Jackson: University of Mississippi Press, 1998.

Maltby, Richard. *Harmless Entertainment: Hollywood and the Ideology of Consensus*. Metuchen, NJ: Scarecrow Press, 1983.

———. *Hollywood Cinema*. 2nd ed. Malden, MA: Blackwell, 2003.

Mead, Sidney E. *The Nation with the Soul of a Church*. New York: Harper & Row, 1975.

Merelman, Richard. "On Culture and Politics in America: A Perspective from Structural Anthropology." *British Journal of Political Science* 19:465–93.

Miller, Daniel. *Worlds Apart: Modernity through the Prism of the Local*. London: Routledge, 1995.

Mittelman, James H. *Globalization: Critical Reflections*. Boulder, CO: Lynne Rienner, 1996.

Moretti, Franco. "Planet Hollywood." *New Left Review* 9 (May–June): 90–101.

Morris, Aldon. *The Origins of the Civil Rights Movement*. New York: Free Press, 1984.

Mukerji, Chandra, and Michael Schudson, eds. *Rethinking Popular Culture: Contemporary Perspectives in Cultural Studies*. Berkeley and Los Angeles: University of California Press, 1991.

Myrdal, Gunnar. *An American Dilemma*. New York: Harper & Row, 1944.

Neuhaus, Richard John. *The Naked Public Square: Religion and Democracy in America*. 2nd ed. Grand Rapids, MI: Eerdmans, 1984.

Ohmae, Kenichi. *The Borderless World: Power and Strategy in the Interlinked World Economy*. New York: HarperBusiness, 1990.

———. *The End of the Nation-State: The Rise of Regional Economies*. New York: Free Press, 1995.

Olson, Scott R. "The Globalization of Hollywood." *International Journal on World Peace* 17 (December 2000): 3–18.

———. "Hollywood Planet: Global Media and the Competitive Advantage of Narrative Transparency." In *The Television Studies Reader*, ed. Robert C. Allen and Annette Hill. New York: Routledge, 2004.

Page, David, and William Crawley. *Satellites over South Asia: Broadcasting Culture and the Public Interest*. Thousand Oaks, CA: Sage, 2001.

Pieterse, Jan Nederveen. *Globalization and Culture: Global Mélange*. Lanham, MD: Rowman & Littlefield, 2004.

Putnam, Robert. *Bowling Alone*. New York: Simon & Schuster, 2000.

Pye, Lucien W. *Asian Power and Politics: The Cultural Dimensions of Authority*. Cambridge, MA: Belknap, 1985.

Ranney, Austin. *Channels of Power*. New York: Basic Books, 1983.

Reich, Robert. *The Work of Nations*. New York: Vintage, 1992.

Reiss, Timothy, J. *Against Autonomy: Global Dialectics of Cultural Exchange.* Stanford, CA: Stanford University Press, 2002.

Riesman, David. *The Lonely Crowd.* New Haven, CT: Yale University Press, 1950.

Ritzer, George, ed. *McDonaldization: The Reader.* Thousand Oaks, CA: Pine Forge Press, 2002.

———. *The McDonaldization of Society: An Investigation into the Changing Character of Contemporary Social Life.* London: Sage, 1993.

Robertson, Roland. *Globalization: Social Theory and Global Culture.* London: Sage, 1992.

———. "Glocalization: Space, Time and Social Theory." *Journal of International Communication* 1 (1).

Rosenau, James N. *Distant Proximities: Dynamics Beyond Globalization.* Princeton, NJ: Princeton University Press, 2003.

Rupert, Mark, and M. Scott Solomon. *Globalization and International Political Economy: The Politics of Alternative Futures.* Lanham, MD: Rowman & Littlefield, 2006.

Said, Edward. *Culture and Imperialism.* New York: Knopf, 1993.

Sakr, Naomi. *Satellite Realms: Transnational Television, Globalization and the Middle East.* New York: I. B. Tauris, 2001.

Sassen, Saskia. *Globalization and Its Discontents.* New York: Free Press, 1998.

Schiller, Herbert I. *Culture, Inc: The Corporate Takeover of Public Expression.* New York: Oxford University Press, 1989.

Scholte, Jan Aart. *Globalization: A Critical Introduction.* London: Macmillan, 2000.

Seagrave, Kerry. *American Television Abroad: Hollywood's Attempt to Dominate World Television.* Jefferson, NC: McFarland, 1998.

Sklar, Robert. *Film: An International History of the Medium.* New York: Harry N. Abrams, 1993.

Skocpol, Theda. *State and Social Revolutions.* New York: Cambridge University Press, 1979.

Smart, Barry, ed. *Resisting McDonaldization.* London: Sage, 1999.

Smith, R. M. *Liberalism and American Constitutional Law.* Cambridge, MA: Harvard Univeristy Press, 1985.

Soros, George. *The Crisis of Global Capitalism.* New York: Public Affairs, 1998.

———. *On Globalization.* New York: Public Affairs, 2002.

Sowell, Thomas. *Migrations and Culture.* New York: Basic Books, 1996.

Starr, Paul. *The Creation of the Media: Political Origins of Modern Communications.* New York: Basic Books, 2004.

Steger, Manfred. *Globalism: Market Ideology Meets Terrorism.* 2nd ed. Lanham, MD: Rowman & Littlefield, 2005.

———. *Globalization: A Very Short Introduction.* New York: Oxford University Press, 2003.

———, ed. *Rethinking Globalism.* Lanham, MD: Rowman & Littlefield, 2004.

Steigerwald, David. *Culture's Vanities: The Paradox of Cultural Diversity in a Globalized World.* Lanham, MD: Rowman & Littlefield, 2004.

Strange, Susan. *The Retreat of the State*. Cambridge: Cambridge University Press, 1996.

Tapp, Robert B., ed. *Multiculturalism*. Amherst, NY: Prometheus Books, 2000.

Tarrow, Sidney. *Power in Movement: Social Movements, Collective Action, and Mass Politics in the Modern State*. New York: Cambridge University Press, 1994.

Thompson, Michael, Richard Ellis, and Aaron Wildavsky. *Cultural Theory*. Boulder, CO: Westview, 1990.

Thurow, Lester. *The Future of Capitalism: How Today's Economic Forces Shape Tomorrow's World*. New York: William Morrow, 1996.

Tilly, Charles. *From Mobilization to Revolution*. Reading, MA: Addison-Wesley, 1978.

Tocqueville, Alexis de. *Democracy in America*. New York: Knopf, 1945.

Toll, Robert C. *The Entertainment Machine: American Show Business in the Twentieth Century*. New York: Oxford University Press, 1982.

Tomlinson, John. *Cultural Imperialism*. Baltimore: Johns Hopkins University Press, 1991.

———. *Globalization and Culture*. Chicago: University of Chicago Press, 1999.

Turner, Frederick Jackson. *The Frontier in American History*. New York: Holt, Rinehart and Winston, 1962.

Wallerstein, Immanuel. *Geopolitics and Geoculture*. Cambridge: Cambridge University Press, 1991.

Waters, Malcolm. *Globalization*. London: Routledge, 1995.

Watson, James L., ed. *Golden Arches East: McDonald's in East Asia*. Stanford, CA: Stanford University Press, 1997.

Weiss, Linda. *The Myth of the Powerless State*. Ithaca, NY: Cornell University Press, 1998.

Whatmore, Sarah. *Hybrid Geographies: Natures, Cultures, Spaces*. London: Sage, 2002.

White, John Kenneth. *The Values Divide: American Politics and Culture in Transition*. New York: Chatham House, 2003.

Wildavsky, Aaron. "Choosing Preferences by Constructing Institutions: A Cultural Theory of Preference Formation." *American Political Science Review* 81 (1): 2–31.

Wolf, Naomi. *The Beauty Myth: How Images of Beauty Are Used against Women*. New York: William Morrow, 1991.

Wood, G. *The Creation of the American Republic*. New York: Norton, 1969.

Young, Robert C. *Colonial Desire: Hybridity in Theory, Culture, and Race*. London: Routledge, 1995.

INDEX

187

ABOUT THE AUTHOR

Lane Crothers is professor of politics and government at Illinois State University. He earned his Ph.D. in political science at Vanderbilt University and worked at both the University of Alabama in Huntsville and Eastern Washington University before coming to Illinois State University in 1994. His expertise is in the fields of political culture, political leadership, and U.S. foreign policy. He is author or co-author of four other books, including *Rage on the Right: The American Militia Movement from Ruby Ridge to Homeland Security* (with Rowman & Littlefield), *Street Level Leadership: Discretion and Legitimacy in Front-Line Public Service*, and *Culture and Politics: A Reader*, as well as several articles in the fields of political culture and political leadership.